Assaults on Convention

Essays on Lesbian Transgressors

Edited by Nicola Godwin,
Belinda Hollows and Sheridan Nye

CASSELL

Cassell
Wellington House, 125 Strand, London WC2R 0BB

215 Park Avenue South, New York, NY 10003

First published 1996

**British Library Cataloguing-in-Publication
Data**
A catalogue record for this book is available from
the British Library.

ISBN 0–304–32881–2 (hardback)
    0–304–32883–9 (paperback)

Typeset by York House Typographic Ltd, London
Printed and bound in Great Britain by Biddles Ltd,
Guildford and King's Lynn

A new series of books from Cassell's Sexual Politics list, Women on
Women *provides a forum for lesbian, bisexual and heterosexual
women to explore and debate contemporary issues and to develop
strategies for the advancement of feminist culture and politics into the
next century.*

COMMISSIONING:
Roz Hopkins
Liz Gibbs
Christina Ruse

contents

CHARLOTTE ASHTON

Charlotte Ashton has written for *City Limits, Time Out* and *Red Wedge*. She has also had fiction published in *Critical Quarterly*.

GERRY DOYLE

Gerry Doyle is an ex-journalist and an ex-separatist based in London. She now works in public relations.

NICOLA GODWIN

Nicola Godwin studied media and psychology in South Africa and London and worked for the BBC for three years before moving into print journalism and freelance radio production.

DAVID HARRISON

David Harrison (née Catherine Harrison) is a San Francisco-based playwright and performer. He is currently touring with his most recent work: FTM: A *Transsexual Journey from Female to Male*.

LISA HASKEL

Lisa Haskel is currently involved in a love–hate relationship with her lap-top. She is also a researcher and writer in the arts and new communication technology.

BELINDA HOLLOWS

Belinda Hollows works as a radio studio manager at BBC Westminster and was part of the team responsible for the first lesbian and gay magazine programme on BBC Radio 4.

JACKIE JAMES

Jackie James is twenty-eight and hails from Yorkshire. She studied journalism at the London College of Printing and has worked as a freelance writer since 1990.

VALERIE MASON-JOHN

Valerie Mason-John is co-author and editor of the first-ever books about black lesbians in Britain: *Making Black Waves* (Scarlet Press, 1993) and *Talking Black: Lesbians of African and Asian Descent Speak Out* (Cassell, 1995). She is a TV presenter, actor, writer and poet.

SHERIDAN NYE

Sheridan Nye is a journalist, freelance broadcasting engineer and trainer. In her spare time, she loiters in various London gymnasia.

JILL POSENER

Jill Posener was born in London in 1953. She is a photo-journalist and the author of two collections of billboard graffiti: *Spray It Loud* (Routledge and Kegan Paul, 1982) and *Louder Than Words* (Pandora Press, 1986). Her photographs have appeared in the anthologies *Stolen Glances* (Pandora Press, 1991), *Dagger: On Butch Women* (Cleis Press, 1994), and *Femalia* (Down There Press, 1993), and in publications from the *Village Voice* to the *New York Times*. She is co-editor with Susie Bright of a forthcoming book of lesbian erotic photography, *Nothing But the Girl*, to be published in 1995. She is the director of a San Francisco photographic publishing company, Picture This.

KARENA RAHALL

Karena Rahall recently completed an MA in Performance Studies at New York University. She has worked with the Split Britches theatre company on *Honey I'm Home: The Alcestis Project*, *Lesbians Who Kill* and *You're Just Like My Father*. An analysis of her direction and adaptation of Catherine Trotter's seventeenth-century play *Agnes de Castro* is featured in the book *Upstaging Big Daddy: Directing Theatre As If Race and Gender Matter*. She will be attending law school next autumn.

SHARON WHITTINGTON

Sharon Whittington works in housing policy and lives in central London with the statutory cat. She also writes crime fiction reviews for *A Shot in the Dark* magazine. She offers this article as a belated explanation to friends who think it's odd to pay someone to watch her lie on the floor and breathe.

photo credits

Chapter 1   kd lang. Reproduced by kind permission of Warner Music UK Ltd.

Chapter 2   Portrait of David Harrison, © 1995 Loren Cameron

Chapter 3   Portrait of Gina Guidi, © Jill Posener

Chapter 6   © Laurence Jaugey-Paget

Chapter 7   Wuornos Campaign, March on Washington, 25 April 1993, © Tanya Dewhurst

Chapter 8   Excerpt from 'The Women Who Hate Me' © 1991 Dorothy Allison, in *The Women Who Hate Me*, Firebrand Books, Ithaca, NY. Reprinted with permission of the publisher

Chapter 9   Posed by model, © Sophia Chauchard-Stuart

Chapter 10   © Sal Hodges

Chapter 11   © 1993 Diane DiMassa

Chapter 12   Portrait of Michele Saunders, © Tracy Woodford

introduction

Any society needs people who will push limits just to see how far they can go. In *Assaults on Convention*, we explore lesbian misbehaviour of various kinds: sleeping with men (Charlotte Ashton, 'Getting Hold of the Phallus'); murdering them (Karena Rahall, 'Roadkill: Aileen Wuornos's Last Resort'); wanting to be a man (David Harrison, 'Becoming a Man'); even violent behaviour towards other women (Belinda Hollows, 'Public Relations, Private Hell'). Other misdemeanours include buying and selling sex (Jackie James, 'Excuse Me Madam, Are You Looking for a Good Time?') and appreciating the spectacle of women fighters in the boxing ring (Jill Posener, 'Coming Out Fighting').

Disregard for conformity is sometimes quite deliberate, a challenge to generally accepted 'standards'. In some instances it is involuntary and hidden, part of a vicious cycle of impulsive action and denial that is ultimately harmful. We believe the common theme raised by all of the contributors is the need periodically to reassess and question our most fundamental values: are they still useful and appropriate? What beliefs are they based on? Whom do they benefit?

But who has the authority to say what is acceptable and unacceptable behaviour, anyway? Another theme that runs through this anthology is that there is no longer any single ideological framework with which all, or even most, lesbians feel an affinity. This lends a double edge to the attraction of the lesbian transgressor: on the one hand, one belligerent dyke's assault on convention can break down a whole layer of restrictive, outdated rules for the rest of us; at the same time, some standards of behaviour must be beyond question if a community is to have any stable sense of itself, or is to protect itself from misrepresentation and hostility. In 'Public Relations, Private Hell', perpetrators of lesbian domestic violence face condemnation from friends and professionals alike. The very idea that lesbians could exhibit the worst traits of male abusers is considered an abomination – if it is acknowledged at all. Hollows makes the case for facing the issue square on, putting the people most affected first, rather than being overprotective for the sake of our public relations image.

Denial and exclusion are powerful tools for uniting individuals behind a single, political objective. But as Gerry Doyle finds in 'No Man's Land', by failing to acknowledge the full diversity of lesbian experience, the lesbian separatist movement often led its followers to disappointment and disillusionment. Many of our contributors point to this period of lesbian history as the epitome of intolerance and didacticism, but such blanket criticism may be unfair. In her interviews with former and current lesbian separatists, Doyle shows how both theory and practice were continually under question. Even then, girls just wanted to have fun. As one former separatist recalls: 'I don't want to give the impression it was all holding hands under the sheets. We fucked a lot of women, we had fucking great parties and took a lot of drugs.'

Since separatism's influential heyday in the 1970s and early 1980s, more and more contradictions have surfaced, prising open the cracks in this and other identity-based theories. Where grand narratives have failed to provide all the answers, some lesbians have turned to more personal solutions. In 'Reclaim the Rite', Sharon Whittington describes how New Age spirituality helped her develop 'a practical philosophy for understanding what the events in my life were about'. And in Nicola Godwin's 'Whatever Gets You Through the Night', lesbian fans share their anguish and ecstasy, claiming their right to appropriate 'the gaze' of objectification through adoration of idols from kd lang to Maria Esposito.

With so many lifestyles and beliefs to choose between, familiar notions of 'lesbianness' are fast becoming unsustainable. In 'Getting Hold of the Phallus', Charlotte Ashton embraces a new plurality of lesbian identities. A fan of lesbian chic, Ashton argues for the validity of a heterosexual component to lesbian sexual behaviour, claiming lesbian culture is enjoying 'a new lease of life' by swapping 'dogma and dungarees' for 'fashion and femme'.

But the passing of old binary certainties and distinctions – heterosexual/homosexual, alternative/mainstream, even male/female – can be unsettling as well as liberating. Having to renegotiate identity on an almost day-to-day basis may leave us without a political voice. On a personal level this can be disorientating and isolating: with no clear allegiance to each other, our peer-group support is often nowhere to be found, even when it is most needed. In 'Keeping up Appearances', Valerie Mason-John blames 'a culture which emphasizes youth and beauty' for pressurizing women into dangerous eating habits such as anorexia, bulimia and compulsive eating. While acknowledging the influences of family life, sexuality and prejudice on women's self-esteem, she is nostalgic for a time when lesbians 'defied female stereotypes and dared to challenge society by allowing themselves to be fat'.

Inevitably, the body is a recurring theme in any discussion of identity. From a body-builder's heady combination of sexuality and power (Sheridan Nye, 'Better by Design'), to 'genderless' cyberdykes fucking via the 'light and magic' of the Internet (Lisa Haskel, 'Cyberdykes'), more lesbians are manipulating their physical presence as an expression of identity and its contradictions. For David – formerly Catherine – Harrison, these contradictions were overwhelming, and his means of resolution was to make the transition from female to male. In 'Becoming a Man', Harrison describes his internal battle with his gender and the final 'surrender' to change.

Transsexuality, like many of the subjects covered here, arouses strong feelings, striking as it does at our most fundamental beliefs about men and women. The case of Aileen Wuornos – on Death Row for the murder of seven men on the Interstate highways of Florida – provokes similar unease. In 'Aileen Wuornos's Last Resort', Karena Rahall looks at her treatment at the hands of the law, the media and other lesbians. The issue of whether Wuornos should be supported as a lesbian heroine or denied as a brutal maverick divided lesbian activists in the USA. Did she choose to become a killer to escape her role as victim, or was it forced on her by circumstance? Only Wuornos knows what happened to those men and why, and, chillingly, she claims: 'I did what anybody would have done.'

In *Assaults on Convention* our approach is journalistic rather than academic, and the opinions expressed are diverse and often contradictory. Transcripts of interviews form a significant part of most chapters because, firstly, we aimed to avoid the worst condescensions of the 'anthropological method', and, secondly, we wanted to make the subjects accessible. Many of the contributors are neither journalists nor scholars, but lesbians with a personal interest in the subjects they have chosen.

'whatever gets you through the night...'

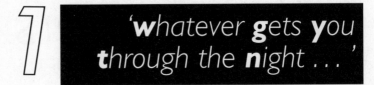

'whatever gets you through the night ...'

lesbians and the functions of fandom

nicola godwin

Tuesday 6 October 1992, Royal Albert Hall, London

Five and a half thousand groomed libidos swell, blister and burst in a frisson of fantasy. Five and a half thousand carnal incantations pupate, unfold and struggle – still blind and sticky – towards the stage. A cavernous hunger fills London's most stately concert venue: a giddy torrent stayed only by the tantalizing indifference of a crop-haired butch called kd lang.

The majority of people attending lang's opening night at the Albert Hall are 'women wearing sensible shoes' (the *Independent*'s euphemism of choice). Many are demure, intelligent, thirty-something professionals stricken by an adolescent dementia that testifies not only to the magnetism of 'the mob' but to an entire history of covert sexuality and subtle perversion: centuries of clandestine appetites thwarted by innocence and fear.

In the last decade of the twentieth century lesbians continue to wriggle from the tapered mendacity of heterodoxy, but whereas liberation was once 'wimmin's' work, it's now a job for the girls. The impassioned lesbian feminism of the 1970s – distilled through the alembic of Thatcher's Britain – has become the pierced and painted prurience of the 1990s; and a generation who regarded the systemization of women's image as a peculiarly male violation are suddenly indulging in a lang-playing, lustfest.

Alison – slim, distinguished, thirty-five – owns a two-bedroom house in the genteel riverside suburb of Richmond. She sits, poised and unpretentious, in her front room, exuding the ancient pain of unrequited love: 'I think to some extent she does owe us something,' Alison says of kd lang:

I think we do have . . . maybe 'right' is too strong a word, but it would be nice to have a little bit more. She stands up on stage, she engages in sexual teasing and innuendo with us, we get all wound up, we get all excited, we run round to the stage door and she gets her heavies to bundle her into the car and off she goes. It's not on, it's not fair. Why not sign a few autographs? Why not chat to us? I don't think it's too much to ask, to come and talk to lesbians and have a nice time for a while.

We're not saying 'we want to invade your life for ever, we want to know everything about you' – of course we do, but I think there's a limit and I don't think it's much to expect or to want her to do something for us.

I think she has a responsibility to acknowledge the effect she's having on lesbian experience. She has said she's a role model for women, but I haven't heard her say she's a role model for lesbians. She does have a responsibility just to be nice to us and not to say that we're some of her most disturbing fans.[1]

As she speaks, Alison's voice transforms into a quivering falsetto that belies her air of detached irony. Is she weird? Should we consider it freakish when a mature, level-headed woman trembles at the thought of a big-boned cowgal in rubber boots? Should we condemn a thirty-five-year-old sensibility swallowed by a teenage craving for an unobtainable pop star? Let's not mince words: is there any truth in the commonly held belief that people who develop profound attachments to celebrities lead otherwise empty and meaningless lives?

Images of young Beatles devotees – tortured teen faces buried in beseeching, snot-slick palms – are among our culture's favourites. They evoke amusement, amazement, embarrassment and, yes, disdain. There is, undoubtedly, a stigma of fandom, exacerbated by an insidious cultural extra who slinks through the pages of airport fiction and Sunday supplements: the stalker. He or she goes by many names – Mark Chapman, John Hinkley – but is catered for by a rather singular description – psychopath. However, the teen-boppers of the early 1960s, while sometimes construed as rebellious or juvenile, were never portrayed as violently psychotic. For them, fandom was not a response to emotional inadequacy, it was a deliciously *risqué* right of passage:

It was rebellious (especially for the very young fans) to lay claim to sexual feelings. It was even more rebellious to lay claim to the *active*, desiring side of sexual attraction: the Beatles were the objects; the girls were the pursuers. The Beatles were sexy; the girls were the ones who perceived them as sexy and acknowledged the force of an ungovernable, if somewhat disembodied, lust. To assert an active, powerful sexuality by the tens of thousands and to do so in a way calculated to attract maximum attention was more than rebellious. It was, in its own unformulated, dizzy way, revolutionary.[2]

But, where were the queeny-boppers? Several factors conspired (and continue to conspire) to keep them absent or disguised. The first – and most obvious – is the sheer lack of opportunity the adolescent has to safely express desire for a member of the same sex; the second – to a lesser extent – is an absence of publicly visible lesbian or gay idols. Also, while enthusiastically objectifying the Beatles may have been an empowering act for a generation of sexuality-free 'preppies' policed by stolidly raised eyebrows and double-bind, feminist orthodoxy dictated that the objectification of women was, quite frankly, unsisterly. This latter view is undoubtedly an empowering critique, but, as popularization carried feminists further from the Form of feminism, the principle became more indiscriminately applied, making it harder for lesbians to fancy the knickers off anyone. Number one kd lang fan, Alison, however, sees her adoration of lang as sexually liberating:

> I've been to concerts and I've been to concerts, but crikey, just whatever this women has got is having such an effect, such a collective effect on people at venues. I just found her, being sexual on stage, very sort of upfront dyke – as I was reading it – just so liberating, and coming from a feminist perspective, where you don't objectify women. My lesbian roots are around feminism rather than the straight lesbian scene. Here was this straight, butch dyke, being upfront and just liberating me and my sexual feelings about her, so in a sense that sort of turned upside down my feelings about lesbianism and feminism and all those things. I thought, 'It's not just me, it's been going on for such a long time: there are these women who just feel silly and crazy, and mad about her.' I wish I knew why … why kd lang is affecting women in their late thirties, why it's happening now and why she's being allowed to become mainstream.

It *is* empowering for lesbians openly to objectify celebrities, because the role of the subject has traditionally always been reserved for the patriarchally well-appointed male. Lesbian fandom digresses from its heterosexual counterpart, however, at the point of objectification. If a lesbian objectifies another lesbian, the latter must inevitably suffer the corresponding disempowerment of objectification. This is an unresolved predicament and one which may explain kd lang's reluctance to engage with her lesbian fans.

Postmodernists suggest we have entered an age of mythology, in which people and events are only as real as their endless reconstructions in the mass media. lang is open to objectification precisely because she has been cut loose from her corporeal moorings and exists only as a simulacrum: an effigy of lesbian talent, fame and sex.

What implications will the permission to objectify – granted at a cultural level – have within the personal relationships of lesbians? Is there a significant difference between the lesbian objectification of lang and the objectification of women by men? Parallels exist, but lesbian fandom digresses once more, this time at the site of identity. Cultural commentators of the 1960s used to say of Elvis Presley that his male fans wanted to be him, while his female fans wanted to sleep with him. More recently an article about lang in the *Guardian* observed that: 'fantasy flickers between the twin desires of having and being'.[3] In the lesbian experience of fandom, these two principles can reside discreetly in different individuals – particularly ones who ascribe to butch–femme role bifurcation – or merge within one. Through identification we can aspire to the laudable qualities we perceive in our idols, while at the same time casting them as fantastical lovers or partners.

Another reason for the pre-1990s absence of lesbian fandom is the well-documented desexualization of women, to which lesbians are doubly susceptible: as women and as participants in a sexuality that only recently learned to speak its name. Even once the latter was achieved, through the women's and gay liberation movements, lesbianism was popularly portrayed as a cosy affair, flush with fine sentiments and sensible fabrics. (I think it's significant that the majority of women I interviewed described their waking 'fan fantasies' as innocent or romantic – rambling walks across Primrose Hill, horse rides on the beach, lifelong relationships – but all admitted to fucking like bunny rabbits in their night-time dreams.)

Still besieged by patriarchal analyses, the query 'What do lesbians do in bed?' bore testiment to the belief that no female sexuality was complete without a phallic substitute of one sort or another – be it the infant of Freudian folklore or the phallic aestheticism of woman's (male-constructed) image in the popular media. The rise of the dildo as a peculiarly lesbian icon may have helped launch an era of conscious phallicism that has exorcized from the lesbian bedroom the ghost of the penis-laden male, and replaced it with upfront dick-dyke prowess.

The recent fevered flourish of mainstream lesbianism bears witness to how much things have changed. This new, middle-of-the-road Sapphistry is even permitted a public manifestation of adolescence – never mind that its proponents are in their mid-thirties; they were, out of necessity, straight-acting fourteen-year-olds. How long before 'real' thirteen- or fourteen-year-old lesbians act out the arcane rituals of adolescence, remains to be seen.

Bent, no chaser

Sara is – like Alison – composed, intelligent, thirty-something and a professional. She was not a kd lang enthusiast until one evening several years ago when she was gripped – firmly and perilously – by a fever that erased all reason:

> It happened when [kd lang] did a gig in Brighton – I met up with two friends [Lee and Jackie] outside The Dome. I really liked her music but I wasn't an obsessive fan at all. I'd been given a free ticket.
> The tickets were in the third row and it was brilliant. We were right up the front and it was a very, very good atmosphere; we were up dancing at the front – that was the first time I'd seen her live and she was very funny. Anyway, after the concert Lee and I went round the back of the building and we spotted this open window, and Lee said: 'Come on Sara, let's climb in here', and she scrambled through – I mean, I'm pretty short and this window was a good four or five feet off the ground, so she had to haul me through and we found ourselves in a tiny room by the back of the stage with musical gear in it.

Eventually, the two women found their way – with much innocent smiling at roadies and bouncers – to lang's dressing-room:

> There we were in her dressing-room; her suit was hanging up and all her stuff lying around. Lee picked up a pair of sunglasses and I picked up a little plastic percussion instrument and shoved it into my pocket. We were just walking out when one of the bouncers came in. He was very nice; we said to him, 'Oh, can we just go downstairs to the hospitality room, please?', but he said, 'No, I'm sorry. You've got to go.'

Sara and Lee managed to escape, however, and came frustratingly close to the hallowed ground of 'hospitality', before finally being rumbled by another, less amicable, bouncer. The two women were ejected via the backstage door to an admiring chorus from the group of vigilant lesbians waiting outside.

However, the trail was by no means dead. Jackie was waiting near the main entrance in her BMW urging Sara and Lee to join her on a high-speed tour-bus chase all the way up the M23:

> Eventually we came into London via Richmond. At one point [the lang tour-bus] suddenly swerved off at Hammersmith next to this roundabout and we nearly mounted the pavement trying to follow them, but we kept up and kept going. Then Jackie decides to put some lippie on – Lee and I are shouting: 'For God's sake girl, watch the road', but she was obviously thinking: 'If I'm going to meet kd lang, I've got to look my best.'
>
> We were heading towards Kensington when we suddenly noticed the bus had stopped and these two blokes – the driver and the road manager – got out and came walking towards us. They crouched down next to the passenger window and one of them had a knife and said, 'Look, you stupid, fucking women, we know you've been following us all the way from Brighton, now just lay off. We're going to slash your tyres unless you stop following us.' All the band were looking out of the window of the bus, and we were absolutely mortified, we just sat there saying, 'Oh, you know what it's like, we just got overexcited.' He was very angry; I can understand it in some ways when you think John Lennon was killed by a fan, but it was pretty obvious – three thirty-year-old women in a BMW were hardly likely to be out to murder kd lang. Anyway, they drove off and when they were about 200 yards down the road, I said, 'Come on let's go' and we carried on following them.

Only one of the three eventually met and spoke to kd, and she was rewarded for her trouble with 'an absolutely filthy look'. So why did they risk life, limb and steel-belted radials, chasing lang the length of southern England? Sara appears bemused by the question: 'It was just this mad feeling – an adrenalin rush, a totally crazy lust.'

Three mature, responsible women compelled by guileless ardour to career across country in the company car. Their ardour appears guileless because, like the Beatles in A Hard Day's Night, lang's stage sex is funny and ebullient – a cheery, eco-sexuality, calling dykes in from the far briny zone of sexual limbo and sanctioning them to have a good time. What's more, we're not obliged to abandon our sexuality when we pick up our concert tickets; we're allowed to take it *inside*.

If the dildo as lesbian artefact has smashed the enduring polarity of hetero-male sexuality and anti-phallic lesbianism, then lang has inadvertently raised the profile of this geriatric punch-up. Lesbians were once faced with two choices when it came to the worship of public figures: sit unobtrusively beneath the dinner table and hope to catch a crumb fallen from the weighted plates of heterosexual men, or eat at home. Now, lesbians can take their place at the table, smile sweetly at their fellow diners and order lang. Subtext − an inherently murky depth, intuitively plumbed − has become text.

Love match

It was the summer of 1981 and Chris Evert-Lloyd volleyed and sighed (but *never* grunted) her way to the final of Wimbledon and into the heart of a young Irish lesbian caught in the throes of sexual discovery. While kd lang acts as an enchanting coagulant − a spellbinding agent − clotting a collective lesbian love affair, Siobhan's experience of Evert-Lloyd was altogether more individual. Unlike the crinkly-boppers who follow lang, Siobhan was in her early teens when she became a fan of the All-American tennis ace who distinguished herself not just for her game but for her feminine bearing. The on-court syzygy of Evert-Lloyd and Navratilova took on sublime overtones: Evert-Lloyd was the keeper of public taste, the thin blonde line holding back the sleazy, locker-room lesbianism that threatened to ooze on court.

Ironically, it was adoration of Evert-Lloyd that helped Siobhan define her own sexuality:

> It started when I was fourteen, through my brother. He was two years older than me and he was watching Wimbledon and had a crush on Chris Evert-Lloyd. I wasn't really interested, but for some reason I started watching and I just thought: 'God, she's beautiful.'
>
> It grew from there really. I started talking about her to my friends. .... I suppose what came across was that I thought she was a really good tennis player, which I did; I loved the way she played the game, but it was more than that, it was everything about her. For me she was just perfect.
>
> I started to make videotapes of her off the TV. I remember, if there was no one in the house, I'd watch them over and over again. It really annoyed me if someone was in the room while I was watching her matches. I liked to watch them on my own ... my family were very accommodating. They never once

objected, they just went along with it. I'd pull down the blinds, pull the curtains closed and sit with the TV right in front of me in the dark, right up next to the TV, and I'd watch an hour and twenty minutes like that without budging, totally fixed on the telly.

I'd catch any interviews with her and I also started buying up all the tabloids for photos or stories, anything like that. My mother was doing this for me as well. She'd come home with five or six papers every day of Wimbledon. In my bedroom I had a huge wall and I started to put cuttings up. .... I stuck up everything about her I could find until eventually this whole wall was covered, corner to corner, with photos and newspaper clippings.

Siobhan says she never felt unfulfilled by her status as a fan. Within the context of her sexuality it was a positive and empowering role. Yet one of the most common portrayals of the obsessive fan is as the eminently exploitable consumer dupe. Those who spend thousands pursuing the object of their obsession ('one twenty-four-year-old has spent more than £37,000 on Michael Jackson's music and memorabilia, and on travelling to eighty-seven concerts all over the world'[4]) inevitably reinforce the image of fans as hapless stooges, stupefied by hype and ensnared by the celebrity system – a market-place ploy contrived to shift merchandise.

This idea builds on the work of cultural commentators such as Herbert Marcuse, Theodor Adorno and the philosophers of the Frankfurt School, who addressed the relationship between culture, politics and the economy. Put simply, mass culture was seen as an opiate used to dull and beguile the revolutionary classes and cunningly avert the triumph of Marxism in the West. Within this context, fans are construed as passive recipients buffeted by the appetites of those voracious 'lick-spittle, running dogs' (Mao Tse-Tung's term for capitalists):

> The fan is understood to be, at least implicitly, a result of celebrity – the fan is defined as a *response* to the star system. This means that passivity is ascribed to the fan – he or she is seen as being brought into (enthralled) existence by the modern celebrity system, via the mass media.[5]

More recently, in their book *Female Fetishism*, Lorraine Gamman and Merja Maleinen diagnosed the obsessive fan as suffering from the post-modern malaise of disavowal:

> In commodity fetishism, disavowal [the hyper-real dislocation of an object's function or intrinsic worth from its cultural meaning] occurs not only because

objects become separated from the meaning of the labour power that created them, but also because the intensity of the separation between the object and its meaning is exacerbated by marketing and advertising, which attributes qualities and auras that are not intrinsically part of the commodity.[6]

In 'the affective sensibility of fandom', Lawrence Grossberg counters this approach with the claim that by appropriating cultural texts and giving them new and original significance, audiences can rise above the rather inert status ascribed to them:

Audiences are constantly making their own cultural environment from the cultural resources that are available to them. Thus audiences are not made up of cultural dopes; people are often quite aware of their own implication in structures of power and domination, and of the ways in which cultural messages (can) manipulate them.[7]

Far from the troubling blight of post-modernity, Siobhan's experience of fandom served as a conduit, a bridge between the anticipation of heterosexuality that is heightened by adolescence and the realization of her lesbian identity:

When I was sixteen my best friend told me she'd met a girl who really liked Chris Evert-Lloyd, and that she'd told her about me and she wanted to meet me. I thought it would be really nice to meet someone to talk to about her, because even though my friends seemed to understand my interest, they weren't really interested themselves – I'd been boring the pants off them for ages.

I was introduced to this woman, who was quite sweet and about the same age as me. We only talked for about twenty minutes I think, it was quite a quick conversation because I felt really embarrassed. I think I was trying to suss her out . . . I was worried that, for me, it was becoming more than just the tennis. I had reached a point where I knew my interest in Chrissie was more than just tennis. I definitely thought: 'I fancy this woman.' I think I had started to watch who I talked to about it . . . I knew what was going on in my head and I was worried people would realize. I'd had a few minor encounters with women – the sort you have when you're very young – but this was different. This was when it all started; when I became totally obsessed with [Evert-Lloyd]. I was completely bogged down in her – all the time, living, breathing. If I wasn't talking about her, I was reading about her or looking at pictures of her.

Anyway, this woman – Debbie – actually sent me a note, on pink, scented paper, asking me to meet her again. I thought: 'Oh God, what am I getting myself into?', but I decided to meet her. This is what I had always wanted – to meet someone who was into the same thing as me.

Over the ensuing months, Siobhan and Debbie's relationship grew. They spent hours watching matches, exchanging cuttings and discussing Evert-Lloyd's game:

It was always about tennis, never anything more. It was all very innocent, but we did fancy each other and, in a way, the whole tennis thing was a sort of courtship. Then it all came to a head. It was during Wimbledon and we were both at my best friend's party, and Debbie became quite forward about things; and we ended up going upstairs to watch a match on video. We'd known each other nine or ten months and nothing had happened, then suddenly she kissed me.

The relationship, while maintaining a quality of innocence, *was* sexual and persisted, on and off, until Evert-Lloyd retired from tennis and the public eye: a stressful period for Siobhan:

I remember Chrissie's last Wimbledon. I watched the whole thing on my own, totally on my own … I don't think I talked to anyone. My mother kept saying: 'Oh, you mustn't be too disappointed if she loses, because she wants to have a family.' That was just about the worst thing she could have said.

I remember it was a really depressing two weeks because I never knew what was going to happen, every game could have been her last. It was a really bad way she went out in the end: she didn't go out in a blaze of glory, she went out on a double fault. I had wanted her to win so badly.

Afterwards, there was nothing for me any more. There was no point in reading the papers, I stopped getting the tennis magazines, I didn't even watch Wimbledon any more. I was totally gutted. I could barely keep things together. There was never anything else like it. I was totally in love with her and sometimes that was painful, but I never regret any of it; it was one of the best things in my life for quite a long time.

When asked what filled the emptiness created by Evert-Lloyd's departure, Siobhan replies:

I came to live in London and met lots of lesbians here, who had so much more opportunity to be themselves, because you couldn't do it in Ireland; you couldn't express feelings like that, for another woman. I would have been mortified if someone had said to me: 'You're perving after a woman' – I would have felt so guilty, because that's exactly what I was doing. It wasn't just the tennis, it was the woman: it was everything she was and everything she represented. It was sexual, but it was a sort of innocent sexual. This wasn't lust, it was love.

Truly, deeply, *madly*

Chris Evert-Lloyd served as a repository for the intense feelings of a young woman growing up in an intolerant environment: the experience of fandom, although painful at times, was ultimately a positive affirmation of identity. This is contrary to the notion of pathology that persistently attends the popular myth of the obsessive fan. In an article entitled 'Fandom as Pathology', Joli Jenson quotes a study by Horton and Wohl in which they characterize the media–audience relationship as a form of 'para-social interaction':

> when this para-social relationship becomes an autonomous social participation, when it proceeds in absolute defiance of objective reality, it can be regarded as pathological. These extreme forms of fandom are mostly characteristic of the socially isolated, the socially inept, the aged and invalid, the timid and rejected. For these and similarly deprived groups, para-social interaction is an attempt by the socially excluded (and thus psychologically needy) to compensate for the absence of authentic relationships in their lives.[8]

In their assessment, Horton and Wohl fail to acknowledge the simple fact that while a fan may feel socially isolated and rejected, these experiences are not necessarily an inherent part of the individual, but rather – as in Siobhan's case – reflect an instance of social intolerance. This process of pathologization (identifying a group/individual as deviant and then locating the cause of deviance within the individual) is, of course, common to most minorities in our society, including lesbians.

Jenson goes on to contextualize the image of the 'pathological fan' by pointing to issues of status and class that distinguish an *aficionado* (a Joyce scholar, for example) from a 'fan' (a Barry Manilow fiend):

> The obsession of a fan is deemed emotional (low class, uneducated), and therefore dangerous, while the obsession of the aficionado is rational (high

class, educated) and therefore benign, even worthy . . . The perjorative association of fandom with pathology is stunningly disrespectful, when it is applied to 'us' rather than 'them'.[9]

Although the 'otherness' critique is pertinent, most of the women I spoke to – irrespective of their status or class – were obsessed with so-called 'low' cultural icons. Some of them did in fact find their experience of fandom disturbing: especially when they thought their interest might proceed in 'absolute defiance of objective reality'. Once again, this disquiet could be interpreted as a response to anticipated intolerance rather than a pathological state in itself.

'It first started when I saw *Truly, Madly, Deeply*,' says Sarah, a lesbian in her mid-thirties who works in the medical profession:

> We're talking about the actress Juliet Stevenson here ... my passion, my crush, was very intense and possibly still exists if I'm honest. *Truly, Madly, Deeply* was a very moving film – the character she played was very attractive, not physically but spiritually. I hadn't seen her at the Royal Shakespeare Company, but I saw her in this film about eight times. Then I went to see *Death and the Maiden*, which clinched it for me rather – it has an extraordinary power. There was a sexual attraction; I think she's quite an ideal woman for lesbians to be sexually attracted to.
>
> When I saw *Death and the Maiden* I became completely smitten. I got very pissed one afternoon and I phoned her up – I phoned the theatre and just said: 'Hi, I'd like to speak to Juliet Stevenson please.' They were very nice, they said: 'Yes, you can talk to her.' As it happened, she was late that afternoon so I had to phone about twenty times – the level in the Bacardi bottle was sinking lower and lower and I was also very depressed at the time, for a number of reasons. So, by the time I got to speak to her I was almost completely incoherent. I said, 'I just wanted to hear your voice.' How embarrassing, but she was very nice. She said, 'I don't know what to say when you say that.' She was very straightforward and I started burbling on about how wonderful I thought she was. She was very acknowledging.

Encouraged by their initial contact, Sarah began writing to Stevenson and sending her gifts:

> Initially I sent this card saying how wonderful I thought her performance was in *Death and the Maiden*. Then I started writing more frequently. I'd re-draft these letters so they sounded as stimulating and as wonderful and witty as

they possibly could be. I used to show them to my girlfriend and she'd say, 'Oh, you're just trying to impress her.' That was a strange bit actually, my partner got a bit upset about it after a while . . . not surprisingly. Anyway, so I kept writing – she wrote back on a number of occasions; about three times she wrote back, and then I spent about £300 on her at Christmas. I just went into Heal's and bought all these wonderful things and put them in a beautiful box and took it down to her agent. I knew that would merit a long letter, which indeed it did, and I asked if I could meet her but she said she was going to America, so no.

Sarah is the first to admit that, as it developed, her attachment to Stevenson began to cause her distress. Ultimately she decided to address the problem through psychotherapy, which focused her attention on more fundamental issues in her life:

I've always been quite prone to this kind of obsession. I used to work in hospitals, and I'd have huge crushes on nurses and doctors. Even at school I had crushes on teachers and other girls. This thing with Juliet did engender me to go to psychotherapy, although I had been thinking about it for some time. It was making me so distraught and disrupting my life quite a lot. I thought about her all the time, fantasized about her all the time, I wanted to have sex with her all the time; it became very sexual. I think I was giving myself a very hard time about it. I stopped doing that when I went to my therapist, because she said: 'If you're going to do it, then enjoy it and if you're not going to enjoy it, don't do it.' But I did feel guilty about it. I thought it was weird and abnormal and objectifying her, and it had led to rather deranged behaviour. It was definitely the obsession that prompted me to go to a therapist and I think she construed it as the fact that I had other problems and this was just a catalyst, which clearly it was. I don't want to say Juliet Stevenson was just a thing, just a prop, because I had other problems, because I still have a feeling for her, but, objectively, I think she probably was.

Toni, a thirty-year-old living in south London, offers a similar analysis of her obsession with lesbian comic Maria Esposito:

Looking back, I obviously put her on a pedestal. I made her this thing that was untouchable. It was probably escapism . . . possibly from the other stuff that was going on in my life at the time. If I'd had a wonderful, loving relationship perhaps I wouldn't have sought to escape into it mentally. It was very safe – I wasn't going to get hurt because I was in control. It was like making movies in my head, but I was choosing what was on the screen. It was all about putting myself down ... making someone higher. It was all part of putting her on a pedestal and beating myself up for being beneath her: if I told myself I wasn't good enough, then I didn't have to make an effort because I had nothing to prove.

It was like having a massive crush. I first saw her in a cabaret at a local pub, and after about a month – after seeing her three or four times – I realized I was totally besotted by her. I thought about her all the time. It wasn't a sexual attraction, even though I fancied her; it seemed more than that. It seemed very powerful. I went to see her in everything she did ... I would go to any lengths to see her.

A friend of mine was in Tesco's one day on Stroud Green Road and saw Maria in there shopping. She knew how I felt about her, and she actually left the shop to phone me up. It was eight o'clock on a Saturday morning and she said, 'You've got to get to Tesco's now, because Maria's getting her shopping.' I staggered out of bed thinking: 'Got to get to Tesco's, got to get to Tesco's.' I pulled my jeans on over my pyjamas and jumped on my moped and belted up to Tesco's just to see her disappearing up the road. Even so, I thought, 'Well, that was worth it.'

Unlike Sarah, Toni describes her obsession as predominantly 'romantic' rather than sexual:

I used to think about things like ... my family have got a farm, and I used to think about how wonderful it would be to go away for the weekend, to go horse-riding and walk on the beach and chat ... I think the most physical my thoughts were was holding hands as the sun went down: very romantic, very meaningful. I was quite capable of running entire movies in my head because I'd seen her so often. I knew most of the clothes she had. I was able to imagine what she would wear in each season, what she'd say, what sort of expressions she'd use. I was able to imagine every detail.

I did have dreams that were sexual. I don't actually remember any of them, but they started ... it would be the nights I'd actually been to see her performing. I'd go home and I'd be thinking about her – again it would be going away and horse-riding thoughts and then, as I was drifting off to sleep, it would change from this nice sweetness into a sexual dream ... she was always the one who started it.

The dreams were very pleasant but they were a bit scary. The fantasies were safer: I wasn't going to get hurt, I wasn't going to be tortured, there wasn't going to be arguments; I could just go and see her perform, and it was like my mind stored all these little pictures and I had seven days to run them all back again however I wanted. And it was warm and safe and comfortable: she wasn't going to say 'fuck-off' because she couldn't, because it was my fantasy.

What happens, however, when that churlish upstart reality intrudes on our more accommodating fantasy life? Both Toni and Sarah experienced face-to-face encounters with their respective idols, but in decidedly every-day situations:

I was in town a couple of years ago [recalls Sarah], and my girlfriend wanted some jeans so we went into the Gap on Regent Street. She was trying on various pairs: she's very fussy and I was running backwards and forwards like a Gap assistant getting different pairs for her. Suddenly she was standing there in her knickers saying she'd heard Juliet Stevenson's voice in the cubicle next to her. I turned around and went 'bang', straight into Juliet. It was completely bizarre. I don't know what my blood pressure did.

In fact it was horrible; it was like physical pain. My heart was just … and I was shaking like a leaf and all I could say was: 'Oh my God', and she looked at me and then I said: 'Oh Juliet, it's me, Sarah Dempsy,' and she said: 'Oh, nice to meet you,' and she touched me – I didn't wash that shirt for ages, needless to say. She was really, really nice, and I think her response was quite genuine. It was brilliant because she was wearing exactly the same jeans and DMs as me and I thought: 'We have so much in common.' It was too marvellous.

I hadn't seen her perform for ages [says Toni], but I started seeing her around, in the street and things. Then I saw her quite recently at a party. Even though my life has changed a lot since I was at the height of my obsession with her, seeing her brought it all back. It all flashed in front of me and I got these embarrassed feelings and smiley feelings and warm feelings and the loving feelings, as well as the sexual feelings … everything just happened at once. It was like this volcanic eruption inside of me, from my feet to my head. But I still don't think I could talk to her. I actually stood behind her in the queue for the cash-till the other day and I thought: 'I could just talk to her, just say hello', but I couldn't.

Back to fandamentals

The title of this chapter is taken from a song by John Lennon. The effect of the song, when I first heard it in my teens, was emancipatory: it not only confirmed that even the outrageously rich and famous had bad days, but also that one was entitled to resort to any form of therapy in order to alleviate them. Now, however, I wonder if, when Mark Chapman gunned down the ex-Beatle in New York, he was exorcizing demons? Was he cathartically pumping his own anxiety and pain into Lennon's body? When I suggested to one of my interviewees that her obsession acted as a crutch during a difficult period in her life, she insisted I was trivializing the experience: to say it was simply an emotional prop is like calling a love affair utilitarian. Nevertheless, I believe that, as well as being both pleasurable and painful, the experience of fandom *is* functional: it's one of those things that gets us through the night.

Stalkers like Chapman are ironic figures: zealots who love to the point of destroying what they love. They're the bad-press end of fandom, but although the mass idolization of celebrities like lang by other women – perpetrators of 'the gaze', rather than its passive recipients – may be empowering, is there a pernicious element as well? I hope, and believe, that the objectification of lesbian icons does not translate into the acceptance of parallel, more sinister dynamics in the domain of personal relationships.

NOTES

1. *The Advocate*, June 1992.
2. B. Ehrenreich, E. Hess and G. Jacobs, 'Beatlemania: girls just want to have fun', in Lisa A. Lewis (ed.), *The Adoring Audience: Fan Culture and the Popular Media*. Routledge, London, 1992, p. 90.
3. *Guardian* August 1992.
4. 'Jackson is my passion', *Me*, 5 October 1994.
5. J. Jenson, 'Fandom as pathology – the consequences of characterization', in Lewis (ed.), *The Adoring Audience*, p. 10.
6. Lorraine Gamman and Merja Maleinen, 'Fetishism: the postmodern condition', in *Female Fetishism: A New Look*. Lawrence & Wishart, London, 1994.
7. Lawrence Grossberg, 'The affective sensibility of fandom', in Lewis (ed.), *The Adoring Audience*, p. 53.
8. Horton and Wohl (1956), quoted in Jenson, 'Fandom as pathology', p. 17.
9. *Ibid.*, pp. 21–23.

becoming a man

becoming a man

the transition from female to male

david harrison

I had just started school when the Beatles came out with 'All My Loving'. My parents gave me that record (it was my first) for my fifth birthday. Every night in bed I'd imagine I was Paul and George, and we would take turns doing sexual things to each other. It was also at about that age that I asked my mother if I could have a sex change. She said she knew about male into female but not the other way round. Still, I went to sleep every night wishing that I would magically wake up as a boy. Of course, part of me recognized that boys got to do things like play soccer, whereas girls at that time didn't. I've heard many women talk about wanting to be a boy so they would have more opportunities. What was different in my case was that I was distinctly aware of, and frustrated with, my body being the way it was. I felt a deep sadness at not being able to change that. Until puberty I'd more or less been able to pass as male, but then I started growing breasts. I couldn't run around without a top on any more, and as people started perceiving me as female, I became extremely uncomfortable, I gained a lot of weight. I felt so out of control of my life.

I did have friends, but I always thought I should be closer to them, that they should be people I could feel really connected to. Other children seemed to have that. It wasn't that I wanted to be isolated, it was just that I always felt different, and found it difficult to relate to others. So, I mostly played by myself – at home and at school. I created imaginary characters (all male) whom I'd draw and act out. I had a vivid imagination. Above all, it was a world where no one could interfere with my sense of myself.

When I was twelve, my family emigrated to Canada. It was what I'd been waiting for – the opportunity to reinvent myself. Saskatoon, Saskatchewan, was a whole different culture from north-west London. I didn't have to wear school uniform any more, and I could wear jeans as often as I wanted; at the same time, however, there was a social pressure to start behaving more like a girl. I was never really part of the clique, but I found ways to get along with most people, and it was at this time that I had my first crushes on girls. I was attracted to some boys, but the whole idea of being a girlfriend, and all the rituals that went with it, was so foreign – much as I tried to fit in. I went through the motions of going out on dates, but I never had a boyfriend. Nevertheless, I could pass pretty well as a girl, and developed an ability to let people think they knew me, while actually revealing very little about my true self. Not that I was conscious of doing it; my gender issues were pushed back so far, by this time. What was coming to the surface, however, was my attraction to women.

At nineteen, I came out as a lesbian. I felt sure this was linked to my early feelings, since I had heard other stories of growing up not unlike my own – usually from butch women. But I had never considered myself butch. Some women talked about life before coming out as a lesbian, how they'd wanted to be a boy so they could be with girls romantically and sexually. Now that they were out they realized there were more ways to be a woman than they had thought. For me, however, being a boy so I could be with girls had never crossed my mind; I always loved the woman-to-woman dynamic. I still chalked up my gender issues as just a part of being gay. And so I didn't think about it for many years.

When I first came out, I was totally into it. Young and wide-eyed, I moved to the San Francisco Bay area. There were so many women! And I just couldn't get enough of them. I was living in Berkeley and was a lesbian separatist for about six months. At that time I viewed men as a different species, figured they were the problem and assumed that they did not feel as deeply as women. I liked being around women, but I was aware that eventually I would have to deal with the fact that it's rather difficult to shut out half the world's population – some of whom I actually liked. Moreover, I have always been more comfortable in a room full of diverse people rather than one particular group. I wanted to be who I was, out there in the world, enjoying a sense of comfort and personal power irrespective of the people around me.

It was partly for this reason that I got involved with San Francisco Sex Information (SFSI), an information and referral hotline. At the time I took their training course, it was an overwhelming fifty-five hours spread over three weekends, covering every aspect of sexuality and lifestyle choice you can imagine. It was great! It totally changed my life. The aim of the training was to familiarize you with different sexual lifestyles so that when you'd had a caller on the phone, you could listen impartially – and without judgement. The training involved many different panels and presentations, and periodically we'd break up into small groups and discuss what came up for each of us. I had two big 'buttons'; SM was one of them, and the other was transsexuality. Transsexuality was the first to come up, but it was years before I really came to terms with it in my own life.

> One of the speakers was a beautiful woman in her late thirties. Almost shoulder-length curly brown hair, brilliant green eyes – and gorgeous! She sits there waiting patiently for the room to hush, and I wonder what she's going to talk about. Her story unfolds and she tells us that when she went through her gender change three years ago, she was reborn as Veronica. I'm stunned and confused. 'Oh God, I'm a lesbian and I'm attracted to a transsexual – what does this mean?' After I calm down, I actually listen to what she's saying. I'd always thought transsexuals hated themselves, and instead of mutilating their bodies, what they really needed was therapy. But then of course I hadn't met a real, live transsexual up till now. And here's Veronica, obviously so comfortable with who she is. Looking at her, it just seems so right.[1]

I didn't really know any female-to-males (FTMs). It was perhaps just as well because the subject was way too close to home, and even the thought made me really uncomfortable. But I found myself involved – as friends and sometimes as lovers – with male-to-female transsexuals (MTFs). Being around them was a relief. I could be myself in a way that I hadn't been able to before. I could talk about my own gender issues, and it was safe. They *weren't* going to tell me I was crazy. I even began to explore through them, and with them, the joys of 'being a girl'. This liberating experience coincided with a period in my life when I worked in the sex industry as a professional dominatrix. I was Mistress Marlene for over two years. I played the role of a femme top quite well and I enjoyed the costume. I was worshipped and adored by men on my terms, and I got a lot of validation for being attractive – something I had never really believed I was, as a woman. I'd stand there, dressed in corset, heels, stockings and make-up, with the client on his knees in front of me, and I'd be thinking: 'My God, he actually believes I'm a woman – I'm pulling this off!' Being an actor, I thought this was the ultimate acting exercise: I was in drag – clothes *and* flesh.

I also learned a lot about male sexuality, with hundreds of clients displaying hundreds of penises, body types and masturbation styles. Sometimes I felt I was collecting data for a science project. I also discovered that I liked most of my clients as people. I got to see men in a different light, and found that I was actually developing more compassion and understanding. The sex industry itself was a mixed bag. Some of it was a lot of fun, but most of the day-to-day experience wasn't. After I got out, it took me years to synthesize the experience. It was hard to explain to other people what it's really like. They'd react either with fear, or with exotic interest. Out of frustration, I was driven to write my first play, *Permission*.

A play for three actors, *Permission* is based very loosely on my experiences, and is constructed with a lot of short scenes and 'sessions' – some of which involve the audience. And it's done with a sense of humour. In the spring of 1992, we toured the eastern USA and Canada. Every night for six weeks I got up on stage and played a Mistress in her femme-top drag. I played it to the hilt, as a last-ditch effort. I was burning out. I couldn't keep up the façade any more. We were on the last leg of our tour, in Boston, when the dreams started:

> I used to have a few dreams about changing. It was like a leaky faucet – drip, drip, drip. But now the faucet is turned on all the way, and I can't turn it off. I wake up in the morning, rubbing my face – expecting to feel stubble – but I don't. There's an itch on my chest. I scratch it and I'm surprised when instead of finding hair, I find breasts. I go into the bathroom to wash my face. Taking some facial scrub, I smear it around the beard area, as if I'm about to shave. But then I realize I have no beard, no stubble. There's a man inside me trying to break through this shell. He will not let me rest. He is demanding I set him free.[2]

During the previous few years I had gone through what I call 'bouts' of gender anxiety. I would find myself looking in the mirror and being confused with the body I saw staring back at me. It was like looking at a stranger. And of course that's who people saw when they looked at me, not the person I felt I was inside. It's like wearing a mask.

After Boston the dreams continued. Within a three-month period I recorded about seventy-five dreams about the experience of a gender change – some very graphic, some more abstract:

> I am standing outside our house in London. There's a big earthquake. All the houses on the street are shaking. Some of them look like they're going to collapse. After it's over, the house most hit is ours. The insides are a total wreck. The only thing I am concerned about finding is my little green bag. It has all my money and my identification.

I am sitting on the sidelines watching a soccer game. I want to join in. I didn't get here in time. I couldn't find soccer cleats that fit. Now that I have a pair, I keep losing them. By the time I get them laced up, the game is over.

The morning sun is shining through my window. I look down at my chest, and see that my breasts are not there. I must have just had top-surgery. I am so relieved.

I am holding a half-gallon milk container full of testosterone. It's already been opened. I haven't had a shot yet. As I stand there, I realize I have to wait to see my endocrinologist first. I put the carton back in the fridge.

I'm in a public restroom, peeing with my cock. It's quite big, and I practise shaking it off when I'm done.[3]

I had been fighting this for so long, and all I could do now was surrender. It was much bigger than me. Sometimes I feel that I did not decide, but rather the decision was made for me. I made an appointment with a gender therapist. I told her I wanted to begin my transition. The dreams continued:

I am in downtown Berkeley walking around inside an empty building. It's being remodelled. I have make-up on. I'm in drag – wearing a skirt, heels, blouse and nylons. Suddenly I hear people around the corner. I don't want to be seen like this – hairy legs showing through my stockings. I can't find a bathroom or private place to change. I go out on to the street. They are tearing down a bunch of old buildings. It's totally changing the character of the town. I'm walking amid the rubble.

I am at a high-school reunion which is actually a lesbian and gay convention. I need to go to the bathroom first. I find it. The stall is too narrow. A man comes in. I'm not sure which bathroom I'm in. I go back into the main room where everyone is packing up. This guy – his name is Tru-man Capote – offers me a ride back to the city. I accept. I see my high-school friend Lela. The last time we saw each other – over fifteen years ago when I came out to her as a lesbian – she was crying. Now, she's sitting on a folding chair. I tell her I'm transsexual. I'm starting hormones in six months. She looks up, smiles, and says she thinks it'll suit me.

I am in a women's prison. It is just a matter of time before I get out. In the meantime I hang out with the other inmates. I see how they bend the rules. There are ways to get out for short periods of time without being caught. Then one must go back in and be accounted for.

I am filling out a huge questionnaire. It's like the one my therapist gave me so I can move forward with my gender change. I go through the long list of items and fulfil them one by one. It looks like a spreadsheet. I am balancing the column on the left. Then the column on the right. I am taking my time.[4]

Two weeks after I decided to go ahead with my gender change, I found a lump in my left breast. It was about as big as a golf ball. It seemed to have come out of nowhere. At the age of thirty-four, I was diagnosed with breast cancer. By this time, I had started telling people about my gender change. After hearing about my breast cancer, more than one person remarked: 'Maybe the breast cancer is related to your gender issues' implying that I must hate my breasts so much that I had created a cancerous lump. My lover – with a sense of humour – said: 'Maybe this is nature's way of telling you it's time for a gender change.' Whatever the reason, I was told that the tumour had probably been there for several years.

I decided on minimal surgery – a lumpectomy. The morning after the operation, I awoke, a bit nauseated but not in pain. I was feeling relieved and joyful. I was thinking about my gender change. The fear I had felt all those years dissolved overnight. It was as though I had just passed through a doorway, negotiated some rite of passage. A few days later, when I had returned home, my surgeon called to tell me that my results looked good. As far as they could tell, the cancer had not spread. I was cautiously relieved. A few months later I went through five and a half weeks of daily radiation treatment, and eventually, after another three weeks, I received my first shot of testosterone.

There are different routes for undergoing a gender change, depending on how much change you want. Some go the full distance, while others stop at places along the way. It is a very individual journey that takes into account personal comfort (and, of course, financial resources). Most people take it one step at a time. The *conventional* route is the one outlined in the Standards of Care guidelines produced by the Harry Benjamin International Gender Dysphoria Association. For FTMs this means that in order to go on hormones one must be undergoing counselling with a licensed psychotherapist (whose area of specialization is gender) for a minimum of three months. One must cross-live in the chosen gender for at least one year, and have two letters of recommendation (from therapist and doctor) before being approved for genital surgery. Because some individuals may need to have chest surgery in order to cross-live (having a D bra-cup size may make it difficult to bind), this is left to the individual and the surgeon. These are the basic guidelines for FTMs.

I am fortunate in having a therapist who is experienced, knowledgeable and very respectful. In my experience, she learns from her clients rather than projecting medical models onto them. I found counselling very helpful, not only because I got to relieve some of the pressure and talk, but also because it gave me time to prepare before starting the hormone treatment. It gave me the chance to discuss the emotional aspects of the process before embarking on the physical phase of my transition. After that initial period, in theory, the counsellor writes a letter of recommendation to the endocrinologist, and then an appointment is made with the doctor. The doctor conducts a physical, talks about possible health risks, about testosterone, gives the first shot, and then writes up a prescription. How long this process takes, of course, varies from doctor to doctor.

I was surprised when I got my first shot on my initial appointment with the endocrinologist. MTFs take oestrogen orally every day, but testosterone shouldn't be taken in pill form. It's too hard for the liver to process. Typically one injects a dose: 1 cc/200 ml of the hormone into the hip/buttocks muscle once every two weeks. I do it myself, but some people prefer to have others do it for them. At one time I hated the prospect of having to do this for the rest of my life and being dependent on the medical profession, but I've got used to it now. It's a small price to pay for a whole lot more comfort and peace of mind. I take extra good care of my liver, and I see an acupuncturist from time to time. I take supplements known to cleanse, detoxify and strengthen the liver: lecithin and herbs such as milk thistle and dandelion. But there are people I know who don't do any of this, and they are fine. I've been in fairly good health since I started hormones, but I also want to ensure that I stay that way – especially considering my medical history. Ironically, testosterone has been used as a drug to treat breast cancer.

The physical and emotional changes which occur once you're on hormones vary depending on your genetic make-up, and on your body chemistry. Certain things are common: deepening of the voice, putting on weight (water and muscle), more physical energy, increased sex drive, eventual loss of menstruation, to name a few. The first year on hormones is probably the most turbulent. Your body has been used to receiving a certain set of messages for so many years, and now suddenly it's confronted with a whole new set. There's an adjustment period: the body grows; shoulders get wider, the neck thickens, hair grows on your legs and stomach. And of course the clitoris grows – usually to an average of two inches when erect. It looks like a very small penis. While all these changes are wonderful, the physical shifts mean that social adjustments have to be made. There is a period of time when people out there just aren't sure what you are. It's incomfortable, and typically FTMs on hormones feel frustrated that the changes aren't happening fast enough. More comfort comes when one starts passing as male, but it doesn't end there.

There are as many different styles of chest and genital surgery as there are surgeons doing it, and it requires shopping around. The best way to find out is by talking to people about their surgeons and looking at the results. Although it is sometimes called a bilateral mastectomy, 'top' surgery is rather different from what you might imagine. Years ago I used to equate it with the gruesome appearance of the radical mastectomy my mother received when she had breast cancer. That seemed like mutilation. This is different. It's fine-art plastic surgery, and depending on one's breast size to begin with, and who the surgeon is, it can look pretty damn good.

What seems to be common is that to most FTMs top surgery is more important than 'bottom' surgery. Lower surgery is not yet very well developed. There are several different types: phalloplasty, which can involve the creation of a phallus through skin grafts and fashioning a flap of skin in front, sometimes incorporating muscle from the forearm. As far as I'm concerned, this would be completely unsatisfactory. What is more appealing, however, is genitoplasty, which frees up the already enlarged clitoris, moves it up onto the pubic mound, joins the labia together and inserts testicular implants into the new scrotum. It looks remarkably real, and sensation is maintained, but it is small, so if you want to practise penetration, you still have to whip out those trusty dildos! The penis and the clitoris are essentially the same organ, and I think someone needs to discover a way to make that thing grow. It is not inconceivable, considering the advances in biotechnology in the last few years. The physical changes involved in a gender change are tangible, and so they're easy to latch on to. What's more elusive, and perhaps even more profound, are the emotional, psychological and spiritual changes that go with it.

They say the first year of a gender change is the hardest. I prepared myself as much as I could, but there was just no way of knowing what was going to happen. For a start, as my body changed, would like what I saw in the mirror? Then there are the emotional changes that go with new hormones. And the reactions of everyone around me. However, when I received my first shot of testosterone, I immediately calmed down. How much was due to the hormones, and how much was just sheer relief, I don't know. I do know that I have a sunnier disposition, and that I'm more open with people, an experience that is also shared by many MTFs when taking oestrogen for the first time. It seems that hormones affect people differently depending on their physical and emotional make-up. For years I thought testosterone was the 'evil hormone' – responsible for a lot of the world's woes. While it certainly does affect one's behaviour, it acts differently depending on who the person is to begin with, how that individual is socialized and what society sanctions that person to do.

I enjoy the physical changes. They are most dramatic in the first year, but the masculinization process continues after that. It's male puberty. There was a time when I would have been horrified with the idea of hair on my tummy, but now I like it. My voice is a lot lower, and I have the sideburns I always wanted.

Although my family has had a hard time coming to terms with my change, they are at the same time very supportive. I am the eldest of four children. My sister is a lesbian, and she has gone through various stages from trying to be cool, to denial, to anger, to grief, to acceptance – and not necessarily in that order! Essentially she has been dealing with the death of her older sister. It *is* a death. I am the same inside – and I'm not. It's like being reincarnated into a new body while retaining all the memories from your previous life.

I was told to be prepared to give up everything, especially relationships. My friends over the last ten years or so have been accepting of transsexuals, largely because I wouldn't have it any other way. But it's quite another thing when you have known someone for a long time and she suddenly embarks on such a fundamental change. Some people who were initially great about it have gradually dropped out of my life, while others who I thought would have a hard time have been fabulous. And I've made many new friends. But loss is always sad on some level. I am fortunate to live in San Francisco, where we have an active transgender community. There's an organization called FTM International that publishes a quarterly newsletter and holds monthly support and informational meetings. The group is not only for self-identified transsexuals but also female-to-male cross-dressers, and anyone else who considers they have FTM gender issues.[5] These support meetings, in addition to my friends, have made my transition a lot easier than it might have been.

Then there is 'life' beyond being transsexual. I experienced something, seemingly unrelated to my gender change, but which curiously is not uncommon for transsexuals during the first year. A series of external events occurred, over which I had no control. Four months into my change I was evicted from my flat of seven years because the new landlord wanted to move in. At the same time, I was laid off from one of my jobs – my primary source of income. So my external life was also in upheaval. But eventually it all turned out for the best: I found a nice place to live with my lover, and started a whole new line of work. In the interim, I was very depressed:

> Sometimes I really don't want to have to think about my gender change. I'd rather be left alone and shut everyone out. See, every time I have contact with other people, I always have to deal with me. I always wonder how people are looking at me. Do they see a butch woman – or do they see me as a guy? Or do they just think I'm some freak? The other day I went to see a cabaret performance. A lot of lesbians were in the audience. A few smiled and checked me out in a way that made me uncomfortable. I was uncomfortable because they obviously saw me as a woman – which I'm not – and chances are, down the road a few months, they might not smile at me at all.[6]

Physically, I was right in-between. I wasn't yet being recognized as male. Strangers still called me 'Ma'am'. It was upsetting because it yanked me back to where I was coming *from*. I wanted to be able to pass as a man ... and yet I also wanted to experience this time of intense transition. I knew I would be in this twilight place only for a short time. Most transsexuals want to forget about this time because it's painful. But has anyone asked why it's painful? Has anyone noticed that when someone asks, 'Are you a boy, or are you a girl?', that it's meant as a put-down? In our culture, the ultimate degradation is to be neither, or somewhere in between. Are there really only two genders, and why is there such a pressure to belong to either one of them?

It took me seven months before I started to pass. And now, fifteen months after my first shot of hormones, most people don't believe me when I tell them I used to be a woman. Maybe it shouldn't matter so much, but it's really important to me to be referred to as 'he' or 'him'. Maybe gender *is* a social construct, but it feels good to me when I'm recognized as male. I've gone to great lengths to change the person I present to the world. But some people, who know I'm transsexual, continue to call me 'she' – regardless of my physical appearance. This is rude, and it hurts. It's like being a lesbian in a room full of straight people who keep insisting that it's only a phase you're going through. It represents a basic disrespect for your sexual orientation and your right to define yourself. Self-definition is important. Just as no one seems able to agree on what constitutes a 'real' lesbian, little consensus exists over the definition of a real man or a real woman. What personal investments lie behind our need to define other people, rather than allowing them to tell us who they are?

What I'm finding a challenge now is how to be a man. There are not many positive role models out there in the culture. I have the task of learning how to get along as a male, while integrating some of the values I grew up with as a female, and which I'd like to keep. Rather than trying to fit myself into some pre-defined idea of what a man is, I'm asking: what is a man? What *is* 'male' behaviour? If I am gentle, some people would say I'm not masculine enough. Gentleness is a human trait, but it is one that has been assigned to femininity. I noticed recently that behaviour I would have taken for granted eighteen months ago will be interpreted very differently now because of my perceived gender. For example, I find that I am much more aware of women's boundaries, and do not assume familiarity with women in a way that I could before. If I talk to small children, people might look at me a little more suspiciously now. If I walk too closely behind a woman on the street at night, I am considered a possible threat. While there may be a precedent for these cautions, my intentions are the same as they always were.

Yes, there is male privilege. I feel safer on the street at night. I don't get whistled at. People tend to listen to me and take what I say more seriously. In short, there is more respect. And while that's nice, it's also a double-edged phenomenon. It makes me *acutely* aware that this only happens because of my perceived gender, and how unfair that is for women. And while there is male privilege, it's not as black and white as I used to think. There is definitely a price. I'm still learning about that because, in effect, I'm an adolescent again. Give me a few more years and I will be able to tell you more.

I've appeared on a few talk shows and the first thing most producers ask is: 'Have you had the Sex-Change operation?', as if you go to sleep and suddenly wake up as another gender. As if it only has to do with genitals. They assume (as do most people) that everyone knows what a man is and what a woman is. But do we really? If you asked ten individuals what makes a man a man, I guarantee that all ten would say something different. One would say it's the presence of a penis, another might say it's all to do with hormones, whereas a third would assert that it's determined by chromosomes. But none of these examples is completely true. There are always exceptions. Being born with hermaphroditic genitalia is not uncommon: is it a very large clitoris or is it a penis? Some women have higher testosterone levels than many men. There are those who appear to be anatomically female who in fact have XY chromosomes, just as there are apparently anatomical males who have XX or XXY chromosomes. There are at least twenty-six different chromosomal configurations, so although you may think you're a genetic female, you don't really know for sure unless you've had your chromosomes tested.[7] Here's where the lines blur. Notice how, the more indistinct they become, the more people feel the need to uphold the demarcation between men and women. It's threatening. It shakes the foundation of our culture. What is at stake that makes people demand that the boundary remain so rigidly in place?

It's women who have asked me: 'Why do you want to be a man if you can't have a penis?' I used to feel the same way. I thought: 'What's the point?', and pushed the whole issue as far away from me as possible. It's was only when the penis ceased to be so important that I started to worry. That's when I knew my gender issues were more serious than I previously thought. It's to do with the 'whole body', how I relate to my own physical presence. Most people are dissatisfied with something about their body, and so I figure if I have most of what I want, I'm doing pretty well. Even though I haven't had top surgery yet, I'm still a lot more comfortable than I was.

A lot of people think they know what female-to-male transsexualism is about. It is assumed that a woman chooses to become a man because of the increased privilege and respect that comes with it. While I think there is often a grain of truth in myths, this one has been left unchallenged for a while. Certainly, there have always been women who have lived as men, and chances are that part of the motivation was socio-economic. Maybe some of those women would have considered themselves lesbians. However, many may have truly considered themselves *men*. It's complex and different for each individual. I used to think that FTMs were merely women who couldn't accept their lesbianism, but I had fifteen years of accepting my lesbianism, and I liked it. I enjoyed the female-to-female bonding. I don't need to be a man to get a better job, and I'm not doing it so I can be with women. I'm doing it for my physical, emotional and spiritual comfort. Besides, how do you explain FTMs who become gay men?

Is transsexual surgery mutilation of the body? Are face-lifts and breast enlargement forms of mutilation? What about getting rid of unwanted hair through electrolysis? Those are all changes designed to make a person more comfortable. Breast enlargement and reduction are socially accept-able, so long at the person is female, and she's doing it to be more comfortable with herself as female. But what about an MTF who has electrolysis or receives a breast implant? Different standards also apply when an FTM requests top surgery to create the appearance of a male chest. We have these operations in order to feel more comfortable with ourselves. Many of us have been through years of therapy, trying to make the inside match the outside. For us, making the physical change is because nothing else has worked. Do we say to a person who's getting a 'nip-and-tuck': 'Why do you want to mutilate your body? You should learn to accept yourself the way you are ... maybe you can work this out in therapy ... it's just not natural.' Is it natural that we live and work in overcrowded urban areas? Maybe we should go back to being hunters and gatherers. At what point do we decide what's natural and what isn't?

As I write this, it's been nearly fifteen months since I started the hormone treatment. My body has changed dramatically, and so has my life. I feel like a teenager. And this is only the beginning. What's ahead of me is full of possibilities. What I think is fixed now could all change tomorrow. I have to keep an open mind and an open heart. I am travelling uncharted territory, with only my instincts to help me navigate.

When I met my lover Kate, four and a half years ago, she fell in love with a woman. She's an MTF and someone who's out there on the front lines in her writing and performance – always searching, always asking questions. Being with her gave me the room to explore my gender issues in a safe environment. Kate saw my gender change coming long before I did. Knowing what to look for because she'd been through it, she'd ask, 'Are you sure you don't want to do this?' and I'd say, 'Oh, no. I have gender issues, but I know I'm *never* going to go through with it.' Not only did she see my change coming, but she was also afraid that if I went through with it I'd want to be with guys. Both of us were afraid that her attraction for me would diminish. Our fears came true.

I do find myself sexually attracted to other men these days, in a way that I wasn't before. I've discovered that I'm not alone in this: I know a number of other FTMs who were lesbians and are now gay-identified. Same-gender attraction and relationships have always resonated with me. I have never been comfortable with, or understood, the dynamic of the heterosexual relationship. And yet if Kate and I are lovers, what does it mean to be a transsexual man (which to me is another gender) in a relationship with a transsexual woman who considers herself *neither* man nor woman? What does that make her, and what does it make me? At this time we are in the process of separating. Love is not the issue here. We love each other a lot. We are both changing so much, and we each have to follow our hearts. Like everything else in my life I have no choice but to let this go and see what it turns into. Death is the great unknown. The only way to know what's on the other side is to go through it.

Being a woman was like wearing a party dress that someone else had picked out and forced me to wear. It wasn't a costume I chose to put on. I learned to live with it, forgot I was wearing it; but then I remembered, and began to see how I could have fun in it. When you dress up in black leather you're sending out a certain set of signals. People relate to you in large part through what you're wearing. Skin, muscle and hair are perhaps not quite as malleable as clothes – but they're still a costume. I eventually discarded that party dress in favour of a skin I feel more comfortable with and can move around in. It's what I wanted to wear all along. It's a lot more fun.

NOTES

1. From FTM: A *Transsexual Journey from Female to Male*, a full-length solo performance piece by David Harrison, 1994.
2. *Ibid.*
3. *Ibid.*
4. *Ibid.*
5. For information, write to FTM International, 5337 College Avenue, #142, Oakland CA 94618, USA.
6. FTM.
7. For a more in-depth discussion of this topic, see Kate Bornstein, *Gender Outlaw: On Men, Women, and the Rest of Us*. Routledge, London, 1994.

coming out fighting

coming out fighting

an appreciation of the noble art

jill posener

Every three minutes in King's gym in East Oakland a bell rings. Every three minutes it clangs to signify the end of a round, and then again a minute later to start the next. For every aspiring boxer that sound is as much a part of your instinctive boxer's psyche as the gumshield and the feel of your opponent's sweat trickling down your body.

The mythology surrounding boxing is well documented. From real-life heroics and tragedy to gritty docudramas and Hollywood gloss, the sight of two men locked in primeval battle is embedded in our culture. But what if these bodies, dripping with blood, sweat, water and grim determination, are those of women? Women we love, mothers, daughters and lovers?

I once met a tough woman from Watts in Los Angeles. Tyger Trimiar was the lightweight women's champion and she fought with a bald head. She was fearless and feared. Powerful upper body, staring urgent eyes and fists that could deaden your senses. Many people had asked her, with more disgust than curiosity: 'What about your breasts?' With even more disgust she answered: 'That's your first question? Not, what about my head or my brain, but what about my tits? I guess your priorities are pretty clear.'

So, what is it about two women facing each other in the ring, prepared to hurt and be hurt, that both appals and attracts? For those against boxing the answer is easy. But those of us who are deeply drawn towards women pushing at the barriers – of pain, of societal acceptance, of their own achievement – find the idea of watching a woman train, and finally box in a Las Vegas ring, intoxicating – and personally revealing.

Gina Guidi is a thirty-three-year-old California native, who works in the mailroom of a large corporation. Her dream is to fight, just once, in a professional boxing tournament. I choose to see Gina as one of the lines of defence against a world intent on keeping it all pretty. Gina and others like her are women who cannot 'pass' for anything other than what they are.

No one stands around posing in front of mirrors in this gym. In the ring, when 150 pounds of fighting machine are bearing down on you, there won't be much time to check out how good your hair looks, or the exact angle and best light in which to show off your hard-won muscle. There's no fruit bar or wheatgrass drink available here, no plush carpet or expensive cologne. The floor is uneven, the equipment covered in duct tape and the only drink available, aside from the Coke machine by the door, is coffee with powdered milk in Marsha's office. Marsha is boss here.

Marsha Martin is a saint, it seems to me. A woman of immense charm, deep brown skin around the richest smile, a beauty and a no-nonsense angel. No one messes with Marsha, though it isn't her fists they're in awe of. Marsha runs the gym on a day-to-day basis for owner Charles King, and every day, from taking the local punks in off the street to telling champion Julio Cesar Chavez not to spit on her gym floor, Marsha weaves what she describes as 'the United Nations of Oakland quilt': it doesn't matter what colour, age or sex they are, the gym is open for all, every day of the year – and she means every day.

Marsha smiles at the memory of Gina's early days. 'There were no "ladies" facilities, but you don't fret about it – we just built them. You solve problems, you don't wring your hands and hang your head. Cities', she says scathingly as she looks over her gym, 'have it all wrong. If they had any sense at all, every city would fund a boxing gym.'

Men, women, boys and girls pour through this hallowed place all day and into the night. Signed posters from the best and the less cover the walls. All eyes are on the target in front, be it the bag, the ball or your sparring partner. Occasionally, I catch sight of someone's jaw dropping as they see Gina, arms lightning fast, fists curled – lean and extremely hard.

Every day from six to eight in the morning she's here. And every day, the promise of a fight – a real fight with a real opponent – keeps eluding her. Rumours fly. Someone has seen her and wants to set up a fight in Las Vegas. Or a British promoter wants to import some American talent. But, so far, the promises have come to nothing and the training goes on – one day missed means three days of making up for lost time.

Gina knows about lost time, the wrong time. The Olympic Games will include women's boxing for the first time in 1996 – one year after Gina has to turn professional and give up her amateur status at the age of thirty-three. 'I won the gold medal at the Gay Games and it seems sad to me that

I won't get to go to the regular Olympics because I'll be too old. Kinda breaks my heart, you know?' I do know, and I can see those blue eyes welling up with tears.

I have to say, it wouldn't break my heart if professional boxing was banned tomorrow. It isn't like baseball – it isn't 'life' like baseball is. It isn't warm summer days at the ballpark watching grown men or women hit balls, catch balls and throw balls. But there was a time when the sight of a 200-pound man hitting the canvas, felled like a tree, made my blood rush to the surface and I would feel the prickly heat of excitement on the nape of my neck. I haven't watched a live fight since 1986, when I travelled to Las Vegas to see what should have been a glorious World Middleweight Title bout. Instead, it was a fight that saw the beginning of my falling out of fascination with this sport. Sport? I remember crying when Barry McGuigan lost his title on a stiflingly hot afternoon in Vegas. He looked like a wrung-out stick – no dignity left.

As a kid, I'd seen Henry Cooper dump Cassius Clay on his ass and then watched Muhammad Ali get up and 'whup' poor Henry. To see Ali, this giant of a man, now faltering with Parkinson's disease is a painful sight. How my childhood faltered also, and my hero is now a broken man, with only boxing to help him pay the medical bills that only boxing was responsible for. Does any spectator of this sport have anything but an ambivalent approach?

I'm watching Gina and her lover Diane. Diane says her daily drives from San Francisco to the gym in Oakland are a testament to both her love and Gina's 'faith'. Diane holds the punching bag between her face and the dull thud of Gina's gloves as they thwack, thwack into the great wad which embodies the opponent only Gina can see. I can't help but deeply desire that Gina gets to fight – in a ring, with a manager at her side, the seconds removing her gumshield, spraying her with water, the words of encouragement from her people ringing in her ears. This is not training for the sake of looking good. Gina has but one purpose – to get into a ring and beat someone, however she can. Jab and move, wear the opponent down, find an opening, move those feet, keep your guard up, find the gap, put the punches together, impress the judges, watch the referee, knock her out.

Knock her out. That idea is a jolt. Even though I want Gina to win, and even though I know the opponent is every bit as determined as she is, the idea of watching someone I know and like felling someone with a punch, or flying to the canvas herself, is pretty disturbing. 'If I knock someone down, the first reaction is "Yeah, I got her",' says Gina. 'But then if they don't get up right away, you start to get scared. You wanna kill them, but if they're really hurt it's always the other boxer who's the first over there, finding out if they're OK. You always think: "It could be me down there".'

I'm not afraid of violence. I've put myself between fighting women when the heat of their passion turned into the cold rage of anger. I've put myself between the flying fist of a drunk man and my girlfriend's face without a thought for my own safety. I've beaten a teenage boy, who – despite being a lot bigger than me – wasn't expecting his comment about my tits to unleash a fury he had no way of dealing with. I've made the mistake of telling a woman or two that I liked watching boxing, and unwittingly released a torrent of verbal abuse. I've heard all the arguments and I agree with most of them. The film *Requiem for a Heavyweight* (1962), starring Anthony Quinn, charts the fall into degradation and corruption of a boxer at the end of his career. It should be required viewing for any opponent because it's great fuel for the anti-boxing lobby. But it's also a film that speaks to a darker side of most of us: the side which cannot avert our eyes from a car crash, or from the body-bag on the ground; the side that feels an adrenalin rush at the sight of a conflict ahead of us on the anti-war march; the side which won't back down from the fight with our loved one; the pride and the fall. Isn't that side a part of all of us?

The film also speaks to another side: the side that roots for the underdog; that grabs a man from behind as he raises a fist to a child; or stops a car in the middle of the street to pull an injured dog out from the speeding traffic. We yearn for the washed-up old boxer to see through the corruption that dictates his life, and long for him to be able to behave like a human being, to be able to walk away from the ring, but he cannot, and in him, I see the stubbornness, the loyalty, the short-sightedness and the hopelessness that engulfs our inner cities. Boxing, at its best, can be the road to self-respect, to a standing in your community. And boxing at its worst? Is it any worse than the alternatives?

Being the heavyweight champion of the world used to mean something for men like Marciano, Patterson and Joe Louis (the Brown Bomber), who single-handedly changed the way Americans regarded black sportsmen. And then, of course, there was the beautiful Muhammad Ali. These were the best examples of man conquering all fear.

Gina tries to explain just what it is that draws her back into the ring again and again.

> I'm a hurting unit. I ask myself all the time why I do it. That's what you want to know isn't it?

I sparred the other day and I gave the guy a fat lip. But I was hurting. And at the end, when it was over, we couldn't wait to make a date and do it all over again. In the ring there's a focus, a feeling of being at one with yourself, every part of you in tune with every other part, because there's only one thing to do there. I'm not a team player, I don't want conversation in the gym. This is the place where I get spiritual. Within myself, at one with myself. Does that sound weird?

Gina has a life, and she doesn't have a lot to prove. She's healthy, she has a job and she's married to Diane. They have a car, a home and dogs. When Gina trains, Diane sits in the car outside, cigarette smoke curling around her, reading or working while Gina lives her dream. Why the hell should anyone tell Gina that what she wants isn't OK? From male promoters who won't promote women's fights; male journalists who profess some kind of weird disgust (while writing blow-by-blow accounts of the terrible tearing of skin and soul that is inflicted in the ring by men, on men); to male gym owners, who told me they don't want flashes of 'pink and fluff' messing up the drab greyness of their downtown gyms (have these guys ever seen a woman boxer?). And then there are those women, feminists and non-feminists, who occasionally form curious alliances in order to universally condemn some women's choices. Boxing and pornography opponents make the strangest bedfellows I have yet to find. Finally, there are some lesbians who still believe a matriarchy wouldn't involve the throwing of fists or the raising of voices in anger, who still persist in dreaming the 'les-be-nice' to each other dream, and haven't talked to the therapists and the doctors treating lesbian-inflicted wounds.

I like to believe that we are as primal as the next species, but while we don't have an overdose of testosterone flowing through our bodies, we ain't princesses either. Lesbianism is, whether we like it or not, an indefinable continuum of behaviours and desires. I'd love it if another fist never landed, but I'd rather it landed in a ring between two women enjoying the challenge to their spirits, than on the face of the women who share their beds. Joyce Carol Oates, in her classic collection of essays, On Boxing, writes: 'I have no difficulty justifying boxing as a sport because I have never thought of it as a sport. There is nothing fundamentally playful about it. One plays football, one doesn't play boxing.'[1]

Looking into the eyes of a boxer is like looking into the soul of someone who has faced pain and terror, even the prospect of death, and, on pulling back from the brink, eagerly waits for the next hand-to-hand combat. In the ring, you face down your most dreaded demons and go past the point of tolerance to another level of self-awareness. Anyone who has felt the exquisite pain of a hard sexual experience, or a tough physical challenge, will recognize the barriers and the satisfaction of breaking them.

In this gym in East Oakland, boxing is the great leveller. The poorest black from the east side of every city – East LA, East Palo Alto and East Oakland – the puny Hispanic kid from the barrio, the white kid from the mobile home in Yuba County, all find a home here. They all have the same chance to make something of themselves amid the stench of unwashed bodies and clothes, the deafening music, the incessant clanging of the bell and the hurried instructions from the trainer.

So why can't the lesbian from San Francisco make her dream come true? Why can't the sixteen-year-old schoolgirl be given the same chance, when the boom boom of glove on leather ball is music to her ears? In 1987 in Las Vegas, during one of the highest-grossing fights of all time, Tyger Trimiar and two other women boxers staged a hunger strike to draw attention to the unfair treatment of women's boxing. One of the boxers in that contest, Sugar Ray Leonard, had once boasted that he had been forced to eat discarded hamburgers out of dustbins to survive before boxing saved him. Tyger's question is: 'Well, why not me?'

To my warped mind, there's some poetic justice in the ability of a woman to climb into the ring, take blows to her gut, absorb the thud of the gloves to her head, and then walk away from this brutality and return to the rest of her life. Gina will become pregnant by donor, bear a child, go through morning sickness, the strain of the worst backaches, the agony of childbirth, and she'll laugh that the ring never inflicted this kind of pain. It certainly isn't my idea of a good time – neither the ring nor the delivery room.

I have no idea what made boxing so attractive to me as a child. Maybe it was the satisfaction of shocking my mother, and everyone else, with my obvious pleasure at the taste of a good knockout, the sight of a man's knees buckling as his brain momentarily parts from his skull. While I know Gina's three-round bout with head-guards will leave no one reeling, I can see myself in her enthusiasm, in her determination to do what she chooses with her life.

To choose to follow a dream which many men and women so strongly oppose – what an idea! I make no excuses, nor offer any explanation for my love of the 'noble art', even though this love affair has been waning for a long time now. Perhaps the encroachment of early middle age has made me fearful for the first time in my life. I've left it behind a little, but it doesn't mean I don't feel the hair on my neck stand up at the sight of violence. I do. I feel a curious satisfaction at the sight of men throwing fists at each other – hey, at that moment, they ain't throwing them at us. Is this ugly? Is this just too horrible a confession? The anger that drives my hatred of male violence feels too uncomfortably close to the anger that fuels machismo. It's this awful ambivalence, this familiarity with violence, coupled with disgust, which still has a hook in my heart.

As a kid, when I hung a photo of Sugar Ray Robinson on my wall I had no idea that his maleness or his blackness could ever be a barrier for him, or be a barrier between him and me. Maybe as a spectator to this brutal event, I felt the only control over men I've ever felt. At least one of them was going to lose. So long as it wasn't Sugar Ray or Ali or Marvin – poor boys all – who became, through boxing, the scourge of the white man. Rich, successful, wildly attractive black men. I remember I always wanted the black man to win.

Standing in front of the mirror dressed in my father's clothes, with my fists clenched up in that classic fighter's pose, I could dream dreams beyond me, beyond all the wildest possibilities.

NOTE

1. Joyce Carol Oates, *On Boxing*. Bloomsbury Press, London, 1987, pp. 18–19.

d net-sex,

ou. I miss it

pping I'll nev

hat particular

ow was it.

cyber

irtual sex sce

eal-life-like

hing while I

ions to real-

iss it' despe

and I'm kind o

r fall into

pit again. ar

x from merel

dykes

nes to mutual

'tell me some.

asturbate' se

ife sex to 'I

ate, mindless

g afterwards.

cyberdykes

tales from the internet

lisa **h**askel

Along with bars, clubs, glossy magazines and consciousness-raising groups, lesbians are finding another site for connection. Dykes are getting on-line.

The Internet is a global network of computers linked by telephone lines which – with the simplest of equipment – allows the exchange of text either by 'mail' (just like the old-fashioned post, but requiring no paper and with a guarantee of instant delivery to the right address) or in 'real-time' discussion spaces, where a limitless number of users can come together, like a telephone chat-line, but where dialogue is only conveyed through typed text.

The Internet originated in the USA in the 1970s as a military network. It was designed with a multitude of possible routes and connections so that in the event of a nuclear attack it would serve as the last resort of military command and control. Soon other networks began, linking academic computing departments, libraries, then whole universities in the USA and other countries. Commercial services and cheap public access schemes were added and the Internet as we now know it began: a network of interconnecting networks with haphazard growth, ungoverned by any identifiable authority.

What began as a bottom-line instrument of state authority has become a site for more or less open and ungoverned exchange. Relatively low-tech software enables people to run mailing lists on 'special' topics or for particular interest groups, where messages are delivered to a central computer and distributed to every subscriber on the list. Lists can be places of information exchange, controversy and argument, or they can simply provide a forum for making new friends. Not surprisingly there are thriving lesbian lists. Simultaneously, at any one moment there are thousands of chat-lines, with themes from the bizarre and the ridiculous to the impossibly technical. They are open to any browser who cares to join in, each participant inventing a name and a description. The assumed identity can last for just a moment, for an evening, or perhaps for many months, gathering friends and enemies, generating a history and provoking gossip in its electronic social sphere. It can be a world of strangers or a place to meet those most intimate to us.

The Internet may have been transformed from its origins, but it is not ahistorical, and like any other cultural arena it carries within its very structure the values of the world that produced it. The compelling seductiveness of a shrinking world, a myriad otherwise impossible acquaintances and the possibility of divesting ourselves of identities defined by our bodies through a medium of pure text conflicts with a more dystopic tendency. A dystopia of misunderstanding, misrecognition and impersonation, of complex technology and a worrying shift in our relationship to the real world: the panic of addiction, the dislocation of being in many places at once, the schizophrenia of inhabiting multiple personas and the anxiety of all media, namely, who is included and who is excluded? Who speaks for whom?

In the Internet I am immersed in a play of language and a puzzling maze of interconnections: sometimes euphoric, sometimes frustrating, often infuriating, always fragmented, tending to the banal, but nevertheless irresistibly fascinating. This is a 'diary' of my search for connection with dykes on the net. For the sake of authenticity, certain inconsistencies and misspellings have been retained.

I belong to a new nation: a nation without the clutter of landscape, geography, architecture or bodies, the ephemeral nation of cyberspace where upwards of 25 million inhabitants connect their computers by telephone lines to a matrix of nodes, networks and data displays. In my new citizenship, I have no body, no voice, no location. My identity floats as words that flow through my fingers onto my liquid-crystal screen and rush through the telephone wires to flash up on terminals in places beyond my imagining. I'm light and magic.

Something between a dream world of science fiction and the save-all, postindustrial vision of corporate and government executives, the Internet is the closest manifestation of data made space, the nearest approximation of the global information superhighway. Even in its most primitive form – with just the exchange of typed text – the network urgently requires new ways to identify, connect and resist.

sent by: lisa@shelley. daemon. co. uk by smtp mail 00.43
GMT 28.05.94
sent to: euro-sappho, us-sappho

CYBERDYKE

I'm looking to contact dykes who love the net: girls who
use their computers for work, rest and play. Tell me what
you love and what you hate about the net, let me in to your
most intimate moments with your computer.

Do you think the net is changing the ideas of what it is
to be a dyke? Are we blazing the trail for the future, or
are we just a sad bunch of lesbo-geeks?

Please mail answers privately.

I plug my computer into the phone socket. As I dial, my adrenalin starts pumping at the sound of the data crashing through, even though I've done this thousands of times before. A polite 'hello' appears on my screen and I'm in. I'm connected. My message is spreading through the network like tiny cells coursing through veins, electrical pulses travelling thousands of miles, instantly creating pathways through lists and groups, landing on unseen machines and waiting for collection. What do I know about the people collecting my words? They are lesbian enough to subscribe to a lesbian list. Their Internet addresses reveal that they are quite likely to be women. Beyond that I know nothing.

received from nicki r. wegman
received by lisa haskel by smtp mail 18.23 GMT 07.06.94
subject: cyberdyke

Typing is a very much different feeling from speaking or
handwriting because the letters are already there. I
just let the words come out that seem to have been inside
the computer before. I can switch off the screen, so words
flow from my mind into my fingertips without a detour via
the autocensor in my head: the Internet is the best equi-
librium of being 'alone' and 'not-alone' that I have ever
found.

received from Zoe Johnson
received by Lisa Haskel by smtp mail 23.34 GMT 19.08.94
subject: cyberdyke

My lover lives in New York and I live in London. We keep in touch by meeting on the net. It's cheaper than long-distance calling. It brings us close, but somehow also so far away. We meet in the MOO* to 'chat' for hours at a time, a couple of times per week. I know where she's been, what she's been up to, what she's thinking. But I can't see, or hear her, or smell her, taste her or touch her. Sometimes it's as if she is inside my computer and the screen is a barrier. It's my computer that puts me in contact with her and I love it for that. But I hate it too because it withholds her from me. We don't transcend physical distance, it just changes the nature of that distance.

received from lesborg
received by lisa haskel by smtp mail 22.38 GMT 08.06.94
subject: cyberdyke

I come here to experiment, to be someone and someplace else. I can indulge my fantasies here and I can do it all. I touch nothing but my keyboard, but it's not masturbation: there's a person on the other end of the line who responds to me, and I can't predict what they'll do next. We think in words, so this is like a direct line to their thoughts. Pure imagination, a pure connection.

received from nicki r. wegman
received by lisa haskel by smtp mail 21.40 GMT 07.06.94
subject: cyberdyke

Somehow, people on the net are less intimidating because I view them as a part of Zorro [the computer]. I was able to talk on the net about a book I was writing for one-and-a-half years before I was able to do so with physical people. Somehow there are many net-people I don't want to meet in real life, because they might not be as I perceive them now.

Women like my machine. It's not phallic like a flashy mobile phone, but has all its cybernetic thrill. Is the fantasy to master machines and be

* A vertical space for real-time discussion between participants.

mastered by them? Or is it simply childhood memories of visits to my mother's office: clicking keyboards, dextrous ladies at their typewriters, smelling good, looking smooth and soft and so in control? I've always found typing sexy.

In my unity with my computer I am no longer woman as opposed to man. I am an-other. I am fluid, dynamic, a hybrid. I have no essential nature, not because I can act out any social role at will, but because I am no longer just human.

> received from lesborg
> received by lisa haskel by smtp mail 15.34 GMT 08.06.94
> subject: cyberdyke
>
> The net is a first step towards the future. It's not that
> we'll all be playing role-games in this primitive envir-
> onment; in years' time when we can easily see and hear
> each other, we'll laugh at ourselves for taking these
> clunky lines of text so seriously. Technology is going
> to enable us to shift our identities in a million other
> ways. Cosmetic surgery, trans-gender surgery and hor-
> mone replacement therapy are only a beginning. I'm
> looking forward to my computer-controlled silicon
> implanted sex toys. Mix the risky turn-on of body mod-
> ification by piercing and tatooing with the eroticism of
> the cyborg. So yes, we are pioneers. We're using techno-
> logy to mutate ourselves according to our own design. In
> a fully diverse world, gender will become meaningless,
> the idea of the lesbian confined to history.

> received from Frances Lewis
> received by lisa haskel by smtp mail 18.45 GMT 13.07.94
> subject: cyberdyke
>
> I like to think that language will always reveal the
> gender of a person on the net most of the time I feel quite
> confident that I can tell. But on the net there are always
> suspicions: there is nowhere to hide and you're always
> wary of being fooled. You may be being watched and per-
> haps the person you are corresponding with is not the
> person they say they are. However, generally, you can a
> tell a man on the net, not least because they will usually

tell you pretty quickly. The allure of being a woman doesn't last long. But nothing is foolproof and 'talking dirty' on the net provokes anxiety for many women. I'd like to be able to say that if I had an 'intimate exchange' with a 'woman' on the net I wouldn't mind. But unfortunately the net is part of the real world, not above or separate from it, or in advance of it.

received by psycholia
received by lisa haskel by smtp mail 18.40 GMT 07.06.94
subject: cyberdyke

I think these fantasies of slipping and sliding around gender and identity primarily a boy-thing. Women do it all the time anyway; dykes even more so. On the net, I'm something different in different places . . . so what's new? When I go to the clit club I don't play the same part as when I have a meeting at the bank. I subscribe to dyke e-mail lists and find out what's happening all over Europe and the USA; I can discuss lesbian issues there, swop stories, banter, argue, share information. I've got a list of bars in Paris and I've got into fights about my sexual preferences. But then in a chat-space like a MOO or IRC I can play any role that I like. That's why I think the net is something special for dykes: it's like life, but you can afford to play. The dislocation from my 'fixed' identity, my body, is a comforting anonymity.

received from Zoe Johnson
received by lisa haskel by smtp mail 04.05 GMT 07.06.94
subject: cyberdyke

Gender isn't a hat you can take on or off. Assuming identities for play is not the same as the challenge lesbians all face in 'real life', where our very existence challenges everyday, dominant expectations of what a woman is. That's not at all the same as seeing if we can get away with stereotyped behaviour of 'men' and 'women'. Being visible on the street is going to change a lot more than cross-dressing in cyberspace.

I love my computer and I hate my computer. It has hard edges and sharp corners. Why can't it be a nice colour? But it's a lovely size. The size of a biggish book and as weighty, with the same promise between its covers of something new, exciting, thoughtful, colourful. Everything is instantly available. My desire is racing. I want it now.

```
received from saran
received by lisa/haskel by smtp mail 04.05 GMT 07.06.94
subject: cyberdyke

I think my feelings are a bit unnatural because I think of
my computer as being half-way between human and machine.
I enjoy it very much. It is an integral part of my house-
hold and is respected as such. I think of it the same way
some people think of their pets.

received from billie the stranger
received by lisa haskel 01.28 GMT 14.07.94
subject: cyberdyke

I became e-mail addicted about a week into my freshman
year ... i'm now in my third year. I spend as much time as
as possible on the net: up to three hours. Access is
through my college so I don't have to pay. I'm by no means
shy and i prefer faxing and e-mailing over talking on the
phone or going to the bar when it comes to a conversation.
i think that meeting people on the net is about 100%
cooler than any type of personals and computer dating
while still possessing the same type of 'if you have any
free time i'd love to meet you' attitude. I'm an art
student in western new york, and most of the people here
have no other link to the outside world ... so it is
widely accepted to have a 'puter affair. Scarey huh?

DIALLING
ATZ
@0814327986
LOGIN: lisa
password:
protocol: PPP
phase: establishment
time: 19.45 GMT 06.06.94
```

```
net >
WARNING: INVALID POINTER 0x85d30010 ACCESS DENIED LOGIN
ABORTED
```

I hate my computer when it evades my control. How dare it deny me access to my ecstasy of communication? It's an unmanageable frustration: there are lines and lines of tantalizing messages from flesh-and-blood friends, electronic acquaintances and total strangers waiting just for me. My net-world is brought into sharp collision with my 'real world'. I need to dial up on the mother of communications technologies: the telephone. I need to talk to one of the guys on the support desk. I hear the snigger in his voice. A tiny minority of net-subscribers are women. The only lesbians on the net I know, I know through the net. I've no access, so I can't ask for help. I long to hide behind the screen of text. But when I am resigned to a breakdown something in me begins to calm down; I am returned to the pace of blood, not data, and a warmer, fleshier, wetter kind of existence.

received from Deva Aranssen
received by lisa haskel by smtp mail 17.42 GMT 20.07.94
subject: cyberdyke

Yes. Many women are meeting others via this medium. There's often an intense excitement involved. Your screen becomes electric in a very real way. Her name becomes magic, your days are spent in fingering her, talking with her, writing/reading e-mail to/from her. And the intensity builds until the words on your screen become flesh and sound when she reaches over the distance to touch you. . . . Some of these women had met the other woman in real life, some had not. Many of them had started to avoid net-spaces where they had been 'burned' to avoid their former net-partners. Just as in real life? No, there are differences. When the contact comes to an end, the emptiness is much more hollow. You'll spend endless hours asking yourself, 'why?' 'what happened to me?' It's difficult to convince others that something *really* happened to you.

received from Deva Aranssen
received by lisa haskel by smtp mail 19.43 GMT 09.06.94
subject: cyberdyke

I've had net-sex, thank you. I miss it and I'm kind of
hoping I'll never fall into that particular pit again,
and how was it? < sigh > from merely virtual sex scenes
to mutual real-life-like 'tell me something while I
masturbate' sessions to real-life sex to 'I miss it'
desperate, mindless on-line fucking afterwards.

Demons reside in the net. I don't believe in God, but like an evil power
they thwart my intentions and ruin my plans, a bedevilment of technology.
Supernatural forces lurking in a supernatural medium. Often on the net I
feel destined to fall: connections failed; error messages; unknown hosts.
It's as if you reach across an impossible void, brush fingertips but never
clutch hands.

cyberdyke: first MOO meeting 03.09.94

telnet red-pencil.media.tim.edu 9999

welcome to youknowMOO, a space for real-time talk on the
Internet. This is an object-orientated environment: you
can enter different spaces and find different characters
there.

to connect type connect < guest > or connect < character
name > < password >

Connect guest

The LEGO Closet. It's dark in here, and there are little
crunchy plastic things under your feet. Groping around,
you discover what feels like a doorknob on one wall.

Pinstriped_Guest has connected
@join Pinstriped_Guest
you join Pinstriped_Guest
you say 'Hey there. Cool outfit'
Turqoise_Guest has connected
Pinstriped_Guest flows into a glob. The glob slowly drifts
out of the screen.
Guest waves at Turquoise_Guest
you say 'Hello there, Turquoise Guest. Are you by any
chance looking for some people?'
Turquoise_Guest says 'I'm leaving for a moment, nice
meeting you.'

```
you say 'see ya'.
Pinstriped_Guest comes back
Pinstriped_Guest disappears suddenly for parts unknown
you join Violet_Guest
Guest waves to Violet_Guest
Violet_Guest says 'hello'.
you say 'Love the colour. Suits you if I may say.'
Violet_Guest says 'are you a poet?'
you say 'Certainly not. Why did you think I might be?'
Violet_Guest says 'Your language is colourful.'
you say 'Only as colourful as what surrounds me. I'm
looking for some guests, for a kind of a meeting . . . how
about you?'
Violet_Guest says 'I'm just looking around today.'
Guest looks embarrassed
You hear a quiet popping sound. Violet_Guest has dis-
connected.
```

In all this hyper-talk, what techno-dream to buy? Technologically mediated mutable identities, or a lesbian virtual community? So now the free market will let me choose a body. Off the shelf, or tailor-made? McDonalds or Wendy's? Alternatively, with a world to choose from, must I define myself with so much precision?

```
received from paula teixeira
received by lisa haskel by smtp mail 15.27 GMT 06.07.94
subject: cyberdyke

What I like best about the net is that I don't feel so
isolated here. I hate the net when it is down or being
fixed. Sometimes there's too much 'showing off', mes-
sages with words I'm not used to, subjects I cannot
follow because I am too far away from everybody (I am in
Brazil). I am sorry for my English.

received from nicki r.wegman
received by lisa haskel by smtp mail 19.35 GMT 14.07.94
subject: cyberdyke

I have not many other occasions to discuss dyke identity
or almost anything else. And here, I get a 'choice' of so
```

many interesting women. I could never meet so many lovely
dykes physically, because my city is small and I can
hardly travel. In this sense, the net is great for the
differently-abled.

The Internet is said to be a transnational anarchy, and – declare the new
techno-libertarians – information wants to be free. If it is an anarchy, it is
an anarchy of the privileged: everybody I meet here is from a university or
a software developer. If information wants to be free, then why – increasingly – do I stumble on electronic barriers requiring a credit-card number
to break through? The ease of the transaction obfuscating the meaning,
the power becoming more invisible, more elusive with every transformation to the electronic. As power inscribes the network, the question for the
activist is how to resist. How, for the purposes of change, do we occupy the
network as we have seen the crowd occupy the street, the seat of
government, the factory, the academy, the printing press?

received from Monstrous_Gorgeous
received by lisa haskel by smtp mail 16.40 GMT 13.07.94
subject: cyberdyke

A lot of the character Monstrous_Gorgeous is me. People
who know us both say we're pretty similar. She is a lot of
what I would ideally like to be. My ideal image of myself
is confrontational, dedicated to difference, politically active (it's a pretty personal politics) and
working and living with some ideal of trying to change
constructed social paradigms. In my character's interaction on the net I see just how queer I can be. But many
people on the net are very conservative and shocked by
things I do.

received from deva Aransson
received by lisa haskel by smtp mail 25.47 GMT 01.09.94
subject: cyberdyke

I used to be a lesbian activist, but got burned out a
decade ago. The net is, in my opinion, a good place to be
an activist to a tolerable degree. You get to build networks there, if you're so inclined. Political networks
exist, and will be on the increase. However, it will

happen on many levels — from local, smaller networks to bigger ones binding them. I just hope there won't be a hierarchy to these connections, ever.

received from nicki r. wegman
received by lisa haskel by smtp mail 23.37 GMT 23.08.94
subject: cyberdyke

Are we blazing a trail? or just shy and socially inept? neither. Just dykes like other dykes, with one communication medium of many. Alas a privileged one.

received from alex stone
received by lisa haskel by smtp mail 17.36 GMT 4.09.04
subject: cyberdyke

Being on the net does transform my sense of what dyke identity is. I am more intensely dyke because I am touched by the Sappho conversation every work day. Also, I know more about dyke cultures by being net-connected. It expands my world. We are definitely trail-blazing and cutting edge.
DIALLING
ATZ
@0814327986
LOGIN: lisa
password:

SUBSCRIPTION OVERDUE. CONNECTION TERMINATED

heartburn

Dykes don't have problems with food. We're far too sussed. We've read the books, we know about the pressures to look thin, but we have a great attitude towards our bodies.

Of course we have pressures, problems, anxieties, but we talk about them. We don't take it out on our bodies. We don't binge, throw up, eat the fridge clean. We don't have panic attacks in supermarkets and we don't buy diet food.

When you were a child, did you ever go shopping for clothes and catch sight of your full-length reflection in a mirror? Did you avoid your own eyes and pretend that that *thing* was anyone but you?

How did you become so grotesque? When did it happen? Why didn't you prevent it, and why is everyone in the shop looking at you pityingly, including your mother? You determine not to go on any more shopping trips because you can't face the look of disappointment on her face when you walk out of the changing rooms behind all the girls with thin legs. Why does everyone lie to you? Why do you feel different?

When did you start having dreams about taking a knife and digging into your disgusting flesh, cutting it off, disposing of it? Did you pray you would have an accident and be detained in hospital so they would starve you? When did you start pretending you had eaten before you got home from school? When did you start fainting? When did you start cutting diet plans out of magazines and hiding them under your pillow? When did you start keeping a notebook: tomorrow — muesli, apple, no lunch, one digestive, boiled egg. When did you stop writing: yesterday — ate too much, can't eat anything tomorrow.

Picture the scene: you're slumped on the floor and the fridge door is open in front of you. You don't know how you got here or why the fridge door is open, but your stomach has that familiar ache. And you can remember so many years of this moment. Not just this fridge, or this situation, but years filled with this ache in the pit of your stomach. Of feeling nothing, nothing at all.

Your face is sticky, so you wipe the back of your hand across your mouth … it looks like food, but you don't remember eating anything. You don't remember anything, but the fridge is a mess and you're surrounded by empty wrappers. Terrified at what you've done you're unable to move. Is anyone else in the house? Did anyone see you do this? No, of course not. You knew everyone was out this evening — you planned it like this.

You can't stay here all night, you have to clear everything up, work out what's missing and replace it before they get home. Then you remember what you usually do next. You can't let the food stay in your body, a poison seeping into you, becoming solidified, turning into fat. Resigned to the next step, you shut the fridge door and head for the bathroom. It only takes a minute, don't think about it, just do it.

And afterwards, don't try and work out why you're crying, that's not going to solve anything. There's bound to be something on TV and there's nothing left in the house to eat so you can relax.

'Heartburn' is one woman's account of her experience of bulimia during adolescence.

The author prefers to remain anonymous.

5

keeping up appearances

the body and eating habits

valerie mason-john

When you look around the gay nightclub scene you could be forgiven for thinking that most lesbians, in their figure-hugging clothes and weighing no more than nine and a half stone, had just walked out of *Vogue* magazine. Gone is the 1970s principle of non-conformity with the media image of femininity; today the trend is for lesbians to fit in with the stereotype as much as possible. For some lesbians, proving to the world that they can look like the stereotypical heterosexual woman, and yet still identify as lesbian, is a method of coping with their sexuality. Others remain in the closet, while many of us turn to coping mechanisms like drugs, alcohol, food addiction, bulimia and anorexia nervosa.

However, mainstream societys perception of the lesbian stereotype is the 'women's-libber' or 'raging bull-dyke' – women who burn their bras and have little concern for their appearance. Ironically, many people believe our problem is not with eating habits or body image, but with men. As author and columnist Susie Orbach writes in her seminal self-help book for compulsive eaters, *Fat Is a Feminist Issue*: 'Being overweight is seen as a deviance and anti-men.'[1] But the fact is that lesbians are just as prone to developing negative attitudes about their bodies as are heterosexual women. The very idea that, as lesbians, we should be able to rise above the pressure to conform can itself contribute to a low sense of self-esteem, or even to self-hatred – often the root causes of difficulties with food.

The Lesbian Health Workers' Organization, based in London, claims that because of discrimination lesbians already face a higher risk of depression than heterosexual women. A spokesperson from the group says, 'Rejection from society, families, harassment at work and difficulties in finding accommodation can all contribute to a greater stress in our lives.' Both black and white working-class lesbians face an added oppression in that anorexia, bulimia and compulsive eating have been labelled as social diseases of white middle-class women. Therefore, in both communities, such habits are often considered taboo. In African-Caribbean families particular emphasis is placed on preparing and eating food, even when there is a lack of money in the home. Indeed, sociological studies have highlighted that the poorer a family is, the greater the pressure to dress and eat well. It is also expected of black women who have grown up within a black environment that they should be able to cook and enjoy eating as this is perceived as a sign of social status in the community. In *Sisters of the Yam: Black Women and Self-recovery* bell hooks highlights the problems this can cause:

> Though Black women are the most obese group in this society, being overweight does not carry the stigma of unattractiveness, or sexual undesirability, that is the norm in White society. This means, however, that it is very easy for Black women to hide food addiction.[2]

Very little has been written about black women's eating habits and body image, so black lesbians remain an invisible statistic. White lesbians are more fortunate, insomuch as the majority of literature relates to white women; they can at least recognize their problems with food and body image. But *all* lesbians living in a homophobic and sexist society are vulnerable to developing problems with food. Some lesbians believe they have failed the world twice by being both gay and overweight. Such pressures can often trigger the secret eating habit, bulimia nervosa (the 'binge and purge' cycle symptomatic of self-hatred and disgust), or anorexia nervosa (the starvation syndrome associated with the desire to disappear or become a child), or compulsive eating (the bingeing and overeating syndrome which comes from the need to comfort, nourish and reward oneself). All three habits derive from a similar root of self-hatred, self-denial, guilt and the need to control personal worlds.

The advent of 'lesbian chic' in the 1990s has meant an increasing pressure to model ourselves on the images of womanhood portrayed on TV, in shop windows, newspapers, magazines and on billboards. The lesbians of the 1970s and 1980s – those who defied female stereotypes and dared to challenge society by allowing themselves to be fat, who kept body hair on their legs, under arms and on their faces, and who were free of antiperspirant, perfume, bras and high heels – are becoming a phenomenon of the past. Although a stereotype, this type of lesbian is no longer desirable, she is oppressed by the heterosexual community and now by her lesbian sisters as well. This pressure to be 'chic' is experienced by some lesbians as simply a new kind of self-oppression.

For those of us who are feminists, it is surprising that instead of learning to love our bodies we often fall prey to the misogynous media hype. But the myth that we all love our bodies is a potent legacy of 1970s feminism that persists to this day. During a reading of one of my poems entitled 'Our Bodies,'[3] which questioned why women don't love and accept their body shapes, several women in the audience shouted out: 'We do. We do love our bodies'. But afterwards, a number of women said to me that they felt there was not enough said or written about lesbians and their bodies and about eating disorders. One woman summed up their views: 'We're fed up with the assumption that lesbians have it all sussed out about our bodies. There is definitely a need for us to begin to be honest.'

In *Fat Is a Feminist Issue* Susie Orbach writes:

> Feminism argues that being fat represents an attempt to break free of society's sex stereotypes. Getting fat can thus be understood as a definite purposeful act; it is a directed, conscious or unconscious, challenge to sex-role stereotyping and culturally defined experience of womanhood.[4]

It is here that many lesbians run into conflict, as this contradicts everything that has been fed to them through the mainstream media. Although, on an intellectual and political level, some lesbians will agree that being fat is about strength, boundaries, protection, assertion, nurture and rage, on a personal level these same women are terrified of becoming fat, and will do anything in their power to avoid it.

Lesbians rarely speak to each other about their eating habits or body image, and many will deny they have a problem with food. There are a variety of reasons for this. It could be considered politically incorrect to overeat or starve yourself when millions of people in the 'first nation' countries are deprived of food by famine and poverty. Equally, lesbian feminists may view it as unsound to experience uncontrollable eating habits or physical self-hatred. Others hate to be associated with anorexia nervosa or bulimia nervosa because, in medical terms, they are classified as mental illnesses or eating *disorders*. Therefore, I use the term *eating habits*, because we all eat and some of us have developed habits relating to food which help us to survive as women in a sexist, racist, ablist and classist world.

Many women living in the West will adopt eating habits during their lifetimes that fluctuate between anorexic, bulimic and compulsive. Most manage to stay in control, but others lose hold completely and become obsessed with food and body image, their lives dominated by their eating habits. It is not known why some women lose control in this way, while others might become alcoholic or addicted to stimulants, but all addictions come from a state of *denial*, in which we are unable to face the pain and anger in our lives. The addiction becomes the mechanism which allows us to cope with life and avoid breakdown or confinement in a mental institution.

Eating habits may become more of an issue during times of emotional upheaval. There are many of us who undereat or overeat during a life crisis, and many of us have been on diets to reduce weight at some time in our lives. Some of us even belong to groups like Weightwatchers, but never speak about it among our lesbian friends.

The National Eating Disorders Association has no statistics for the number of lesbians with anorexia or bulimia. In the words of one of its spokespersons; '2 per cent of women and 0.2 per cent of men are sufferers. Their sexual orientation is not known.' However, one of the women I interviewed, Carol, says: 'My last doctor told me the number of gay women coming to see her about anorexia and bulimia nervosa is extremely high.' The fact is that incidences of anorexia, bulimia and compulsive eating have increased tremendously during the past twenty years. As it is predominantly women who develop such eating habits, there must inevitably be an increase of lesbian sufferers.

The ABC of eating habits

ANOREXIA NERVOSA

In her *Guardian* article 'Cold comfort on hunger farm', Susie Orbach writes:

> Anorexia is a serious mental and physical problem. But it is also on the continuum with most women's experience in which women use and *abuse* food. When we address the anorexic we are seeing the exaggeration of a response that is common in literally millions of women. . . . A hunger strike, which is after all what is at work in anorexia, is an act of the most extraordinary courage and the most extraordinary desperation.[5]

Few people intend to develop anorexia nervosa when they begin to cut down their food intake. Cutting down is normally a device to get rid of unwanted puppy fat that friends, relatives and carers may have teased us about for years, and the initial food restriction and loss of weight is usually encouraged and praised. Anorexic behaviour varies from individual to individual: cutting down on sweets, potatoes, breads and carbohydrates in general may be just the beginning. Women who become anorexic may already be used to missing breakfast and eating their first meal of the day at lunch-time, and often this situation escalates, from eating one meal a day to, say, one carrot and a cup of water a day. What is common among women who develop this habit is the sheer pleasure at the initial weight loss, as Jill Welbourne and Joan Purgold confirm in their study of eating habits, *The Eating Sickness*:

> They become hooked on the sense of achievement which losing weight gives them. At a time when everything else in their life is messy, confused and going astray here they find a new way of succeeding. Every day the pointer on the scales shows weight loss; that self-same pointer proves how competent and effective they have now become. This seems to us to be the chief reason why anorexics continue to lose weight after they have reached their original target.[6]

Lack of food intake can be coupled with obsessive exercising and the use of laxatives. While this type of behaviour is extreme, it is important to note that there are many women who live on the edge, eating only the bare minimum to survive and who have a ready list of excuses for why they are unable to eat. These excuses range from food allergies and weak stomachs to simply 'forgetting to eat today'. For these women their anorexic behaviour may be supported by social drug-taking, such as smoking marijuana, drinking or taking amphetamines, cocaine or Ecstasy, and there are some lesbians who survive on this cocktail of stimulants.

BULIMIA NERVOSA

The bulimic woman is sometimes referred to as the 'failed anorexic'. In their book, *Women's Secret Disorder: A New Understanding of Bulimia*, Mira Dana and Marilyn Lawrence describe how bulimics are often viewed unsympathetically by society:

> So while the compulsive eater with her obvious 'weakness' arouses our sympathy, and makes us feel better about ourselves, and the anorexic evokes

our wonder and admiration, what of the bulimic? . . . Bulimic women are often treated as frauds and deceivers. The compulsive eater who is unable to control her appetite is at least honest about it and becomes fat. The bulimic, on the other hand, secretly indulges her gluttony and then deceives the world by disposing of the consequences of her weakness. If she then has the effrontery to go to her doctor and complain about how terrible she feels, she is likely to get very short shrift indeed.[7]

Indeed, this is an attitude that many lesbians hold about women who are bulimic. The bulimic's way of coping is often labelled as repulsive, wasteful and self-indulgent.

A bulimic woman's eating habits can swing from anorexic to compulsive – one day she may starve, the next day she may eat compulsively. What is different is the binge–purge cycle. A bulimic woman may binge on frozen foods, uncooked foods or fast foods – anything which can be put into the mouth quickly, eaten and then regurgitated. This 'purging' after a binge may involve vomiting or the use of laxatives: both are equally damaging physically.

COMPULSIVE EATING

Geneen Roth writes in *When Food Is Love*:

Food was love; eating was our way of being loved. Food was available when our parents weren't. Food didn't get up and walk away when our fathers did. Food didn't hurt us. Food didn't say no. Food didn't hit. Food didn't get drunk. Food was always there. Food tasted good. Food was warm when we were cold and cold when we were hot. Food became the closest thing we knew of love.[8]

As with bulimia there is no typical compulsive eater, but what compulsive eaters have in common is the use of food as a coping mechanism, a nurturer, a lover and a friend. Many women who eat compulsively do not link their food intake with their body size. They may enjoy eating a lot of food, but secretly believe they are too greedy for their own good. The eating habit can be quite chaotic, uncontrolled and self-destructive. The intake of food will also vary from one person to the next. What is similar is the high intake of carbohydrate and sugary foods. Compulsive eating is usually carried out in secret or with friends who share the same habit. To her work colleagues and friends a women may appear to be a 'professional dieter', but at home, in secret, she will eat compulsively, experiencing feelings of self-disgust and shame as she becomes aware that her behaviour is out of control.

All three eating habits have physical side-effects: obesity is commonly found in compulsive eaters; a damaged oesophagus, decaying teeth and a ruptured stomach are just a few of the ailments affecting bulimics; and hair loss and the absence of menstruation (amenorrhoea) are problems associated with anorexia nervosa. At their most extreme, all three conditions can be fatal, and women have been known to choke while purging the food from their bodies. Those who work with people with bad eating habits claim the problem cannot be properly addressed unless sufferers seek personal help. Although self-help groups are useful, it seems that success in recovery lies in some form of supported personal therapy.

Personal stories

Lesbian-feminist politics has empowered some women to celebrate and love their bodies, and to be happy describing themselves as fat. These are lesbians who are proud to be big, proud not wearing make-up or a bra, proud that they have not colluded with society's sexism and misogyny, but the influence of lesbian feminism has not been universal. Other women, far from experiencing empowerment, are dissatisfied and angry, and feel out of control and frightened by their bodies.

I have interviewed a number of lesbians living in Britain. Their ages range from eighteen to thirty-six, they come from different cultural backgrounds, and they have a diverse range of eating habits and body shapes. Some were happy with their identity as fat lesbians, others were terrified of being fat and used bulimia and anorexia as coping mechanisms. (Some of the names have been changed to protect individuals' privacy.)

EVA

> I am a very fat lesbian. I rarely associate my eating with my aesthetic look. I eat as much as I want, when I want it. Whatever the place, whatever the company.

Eva believes the term 'eating disorder' has come from men, because it is they who have decided in what ways women are 'well', and in what ways they are 'sick':

When somebody says a woman has an eating disorder it is already defined and pigeon-holed into a serious illness which she can't do anything about. If it was termed as her eating habits being 'ineffective', or 'a problem', it gives the woman more option to do something about it.

Eva is thirty-two, grew up in Athens and came to England in her early twenties. When she identified as heterosexual, her body weight was influenced by her degree of happiness with men. Although she has been a fat woman for the majority of her life, she has always perceived herself to be slimmer and more beautiful than some people have described her:

When I came out as a lesbian, my eating habits were affected. My first girlfriend had a circle of white middle-class friends, who found it a great cultural shock to accept my body size. I began eating a vegetarian diet because of the immense pressure from my girlfriend's peer group. Whenever I socialized with these women they would always try to oppress me. There would be a spare seat on the sofa and as soon as I appeared in the room they would all move off leaving room for three Evas. If I ate dinner at one of their houses, they would put a huge mountain of food on my plate, and small portions on everybody else's plate. When I was alone with my girlfriend we were compatible, but whenever I was in the company of her white middle-class friends, it was clear that she was sitting on the fence. She couldn't quite take people on about their oppressive attitudes towards me being fat.

Eva believes lesbians can be more oppressive than men. In the company of men she felt freer to dress and eat how she wanted, and she did not experience any oppressive gestures or comments. However, when she is around lesbians they tend to make a big fuss if she wears fancy clothes, and often remark 'how much slimmer' she looks. 'I've had lesbian lovers who have touched me, while pretending my body is not as big as it is. This behaviour makes fat women invisible and invalidates us.'

Eva has learned to make herself feel comfortable on the lesbian scene by dressing extravagantly, wearing lots of jewellery, adopting a hard glare and acting cool. She has been forced to assume this persona in response to a lesbian and gay scene that has not made fat people welcome. She knows there are plenty of fat lesbians out there because many of them turn up at conferences, demonstrations and poetry readings. But most of her female friends stay at home, and whenever she goes out clubbing she regularly bumps into the same three fat women.

Eva is also tired of being treated like an intellectual. Whenever she chats up a woman, the conversation inevitably moves to the areas of social work or politics. She believes that while fat women are looked upon as interesting people to talk too, it's still the slim women whom people want to go to bed with.

Yet Eva's relationships during the past six years have been successful. She has had slim lovers who have loved her body as much as she does, and who have challenged other lesbians about their oppressive behaviour. She says, 'It would be a lie to say that I have everything sorted out about my body, but I am comfortable with it.' There are some parts of her body that make her wince when she sees them in a photograph – like her bottom. Sometimes, she may catch sight of her body and feel: 'That doesn't look like me.'

There are changes that Eva would like to see: for a start, she would create a new fashion range for fat lesbians because shop clothes are never made big enough; she feels that promotion of images of fat lesbians is important because they are never visible on posters, in films or in the gay media; and, of course, there should be larger dodgems at fun-fairs. Eva would only lose weight if it was 'a matter of life and death'.

SHARON

> I've always had a thing about my body. I never liked it. I always felt I ate too much, and that I didn't have a right to eat chocolate.

Sharon is thirty-three and grew up in a Roman Catholic family in England. She became bulimic two years ago. At first she didn't realize what was happening to her. She had overeaten during dinner with a friend, and when she returned home made herself sick. Then this behaviour grew into a habit. Whenever she ate too much, she purged, and in a matter of weeks it had escalated to such an extent that she was vomiting up everything she ate. As Sharon became thinner she became hungrier, and so the eat–binge–purge cycle dominated her whole life. She felt that she was going insane.

Although Sharon experienced lesbian relationships in her late teens and early twenties, she found it very difficult to accept. If anyone asked if she was a lesbian she denied it, and while working as a nurse she routinely joined in with homophobic jokes. It wasn't until she returned to study that Sharon began to feel confident about her sexuality, and while at college she met two other lesbians who were proud to be out. However, just the realization that she was a lesbian triggered off the bulimia, as she found it very difficult to acknowledge something that she had always experienced as shameful: 'For me bulimia was ultimately linked to me coming to terms with being a lesbian. I used bulimia as a coping mechanism to cope with my sexuality.'

Sharon believes bulimia represented her silenced voice from twelve years earlier when she had been unable to come out to her family and friends:

> Coming out was so stressful that I hid behind the bulimia. Going out on the lesbian scene was stressful; coming to terms with loving women was stressful. Bulimia was very much linked to my sexual identity. Although I couldn't have control over my thoughts and feelings, I could over my body.

Sharon was scared of becoming a stereotypical bull dyke – big and butch with cropped hair, big boots, jeans and a baggy jumper. She was so terrified of this image that it delayed her coming-out process, and prolonged the bulimic behaviour. To Sharon, her bulimic and anorexic behaviour guaranteed that she would remain slim and feminine.

Since seeking help with her eating problems, Sharon has attended a self-help group affiliated to the National Eating Disorders Association, and follows a food plan of three meals a day. She describes herself as a 'recovering bulimic'. Although she has regular eating habits most of the time, she has experienced occasional relapses – often triggered by homophobic attitudes. Sharon believes that, eventually, as her self-esteem about her sexuality improves, the bulimia will disappear altogether.

ANGELA DE CASTRO

> I describe myself as a small, round lesbian, but people call me a small, fat lesbian. Fat or round, I feel good about my body. I like it, my lovers like it, and I enjoy dressing up.

Angela is a thirty-eight-year-old Brazilian and a professional clown, performing with, among others, the Mammas and Pappas, Ra Ra Zoo and the Right Size theatre company. In Brazil, being fat is considered a social stigma and body culture revolves around slimness, beauty and youth. When Angela walked the streets people would often shout out 'Fatty!', and she was repeatedly told she was a lesbian simply because she was fat:

> Brazil is a Latin culture, therefore it is very macho. People assume women are lesbians because they can't attract a man, or because they are ugly, fat or bad

women. Because it is so difficult to be a lesbian in Brazil, women support each other. We do not oppress each other over size, or body image.

Before leaving Brazil, Angela was part of a theatre production which explored traditional Brazilian Indian culture. In the show everyone appeared naked for most of the performance. When the production closed Angela received letters from three women who described how much easier they felt about their own bodies after seeing her shameless performance on stage. She realized that as a performer she had a role; to expose her body so that more women could feel proud and positive.

When Angela moved to England over ten years ago she found a new freedom, which allowed her to express herself artistically, sexually and individually: 'It was like paradise, after living in a Third World country with Third World attitudes.' During her years in England she has been able to celebrate her body and sexuality without fear of persecution or stigma. She believes it is much more acceptable to be fat in Britain, and a lot easier to be an out lesbian.

In August 1993 Angela made history on the lesbian scene when she performed on stage at Heaven nightclub. She was the first fat lesbian to perform in a bikini in front of over 1,500 women. I was there to witness the gasps of shock and desire when Angela appeared on stage:

> In nightclubs I have a responsibility to put a good show on. If I have to be with my belly hanging out and dancing, I will do the best I can do. Of course there may be lesbians who will be shocked when they see me perform, because people have the idea that all dancers should be trendy, have a nice body and be beautiful. I'm not a media stereotype, but I have a good body, and I'm beautiful, sensual and a very good performer.

She believes that too many nightclub promoters are narrow-minded when they choose performers. 'I know some lesbians think I'm outrageous dancing around in a bikini. Rather than see that I am representing other women, they think: "Look at that fat woman" '.

To survive the onslaught of the image of the stereotypical woman presented in the media, Angela believes that fat lesbians should feel secure about their bodies, and cultivate a strong personality; otherwise they will continue to assume that they are somehow inferior to the rest of society. Above all, Angela would like lesbians to enjoy their bodies. Her message to fat lesbians is: 'Don't be intimidated by the scene; go out. Fat is beautiful.'

BERNIE

> When I became anorexic I felt strong and powerful. If I couldn't have control
> over my sexual desires I could over my body. The rigid routine of an apple for
> breakfast, Ryvitas for lunch and cream crackers for tea, plus a five-mile run
> every day, gave me a sense of exhilaration, excitement and happiness.

At the time of writing, Bernie is an anorexic–bulimic, that is, she
alternates between weeks of starvation and weeks of bingeing and purging. She is twenty-two, of African-Caribbean descent and was born in
Britain. In Bernie's household homosexuality was a taboo word, something which only existed in white society. Condemned by the Bible, Bernie
believed it must be wrong, but her sexual urges for women would not go
away. She prayed to God for forgiveness, and asked him to take away her
'evil' thoughts. But at the age of eighteen she fell in love with a woman,
and her feelings became so overwhelming that she lost her appetite. In the
space of a month she had cut down her food intake to a minimum. She
lived on this diet for six months until, gradually, she began bingeing and
starving herself:

> On the one hand I was so elated that I could be sexual. I was raped as a child
> and sexually abused, and knew that I didn't want to be sexual with men. On
> the other hand I was disgusted with myself for having, what I then believed to
> be abnormal behaviour. This was also supported by the fact that I didn't know
> any other black lesbians. The bulimia was a relief from this terror.

When Bernie first started going out to nightclubs, she felt a pressure to
be beautiful and slim. She convinced herself that although her face could
never be beautiful, as she was black, her body could be the desirable size.
Her anorexic behaviour returned, compensating for the large amounts of
food she had been bingeing on and throwing up. She recalls: 'I wanted to
fit in. I couldn't be beautiful, but I could be slim. Starving myself was the
best way I knew to keep myself thin. My body weight seemed to stay the
same as long as I purged after I ate.'
Since then, Bernie has begun to build up her self-esteem around her
sexuality through therapy. Meeting other black lesbians has made her
more confident, and she believes the anorexia and bulimia will become a
thing of the past. However, she would like the space to talk about this part
of her life on the lesbian scene, because keeping these issues hidden
makes it difficult for women to be honest about their eating habits. It has
been the white heterosexual community that has supported Bernie with

her anorexia and bulimia: 'Among my white heterosexual female friends I am able to be honest, without being judged or guilt-tripped.' In contrast, both the black and lesbian communities have denied this part of her personality. She believes the black community finds it difficult to understand black women who have problems with food, and that lesbians are too busy trying to be right-on to admit that they are as vulnerable as anyone else to problems with self-image. Bernie's black family told her: 'Grow up – black women don't get things like anorexia or bulimia nervosa,' and the lesbian community either pretended nothing was wrong, or tried to make her feel guilty for eating so much food.

SANDRA

> Witnessing what my slim sisters have experienced does not make me want to rush out and be a galloping hairpin. I'm a very fat woman, and I am happy with my body. It defines who I am. Being fat gives me more control over my environment. Doctors say, 'If you're too fat you will die'. I say, 'If you're anorexic you will die sooner'.

Sandra is of mixed racial heritage, with a white German mother and black African father. As a child she was classified as medically overweight and spent the first twelve years of her life in and out of hospital, being pumped with steroids and prescribed over a hundred different diets. Consequently, her metabolic rate has been irreparably affected, making it very difficult for her to lose weight. Although Sandra's body size is partly related to medical problems she still loves her body, enjoying the strength and power which goes with being a very big black woman. Nobody will threaten her, and she feels completely safe walking down the street late at night. However, she is aware that there are medical issues associated with being extremely fat. Fat women have a higher propensity to hip and spinal problems, varicose veins, diabetes, heart disease, osteoarthritis, breast cancer and hysterectomy.

Sandra is fully aware of other people's negative attitudes about her body. Both men and women perceive her to be non-sexual, though heterosexual orientation is assumed, and she has received equally oppressive treatment from other lesbians:

> The lesbian community was never welcoming of me being a very fat black woman. It was considered that I was obese because I was sloppy. It was also assumed that I was stupid because I was so fat. One of the first lesbian parties

I went to, the women dropped their heads and never said anything. A few minutes later I heard hoots of laughter from another room. I felt a tremendous sense of isolation. If I hadn't been with my lover I would have broken down and cried.

Sandra believes the lesbian scene is only welcoming to those who are slim, beautiful, young and available for sex. Sandra's lover Eileen is often irritated by lesbians' attitudes towards her lover. 'There is a lot of prejudice in the lesbian and gay community against fat women and men. It is very insidious; often you catch a glance or hear a snigger. Some lesbians have been very antagonistic.'

CAROL

Carol is twenty-one and became bulimic at fourteen. As a teenager growing up in a large Protestant Irish family in the countryside of Northern Ireland she had little self-esteem, was unhappy at school and felt isolated from her peers. Eating and purging became something to relieve the boredom. After a year or so of this bulimic behaviour, the bingeing and purging began to take control, until it became something she felt 'compelled' to do. As a result, she withdrew from her friends, cutting herself off from the people around her. Ever since, her eating habits have fluctuated between anorexic and bulimic.

When Carol began her first relationship with a woman she fell in love and quickly became obsessed. The affair was a temporary distraction from the bulimia, but it soon crept back into her life:

> I became comfortable and relaxed, but once the novelty wore off, and the relationship became familiar, I found my old habit of bingeing and purging entering my life again. I think it was me not being able to say to my lover when I was angry. My bulimia is the only way I know to express anger.

When she isn't bingeing Carol often feels an overwhelming sensation of fury which is sometimes directed at her girlfriends. She describes her bulimia as 'being seven stone with anger'. She explains: 'I'm unable to get in touch with what I am angry about. I think I am too scared to face it.'

Carol is surprised at how many of the young lesbians she knows have problems with food. She believes the lesbian scene has an artificial image of itself:

> When you look around the night clubs most women range from slim to skinny and there is a lot of pressure on image and looks. The gay scene is a very competitive arena. I think it is one of many triggers that encourage young lesbians to develop eating disorders and low self-esteem.

She rarely confides in her friends about her eating habits, because most women, lesbian or heterosexual, find it difficult to grasp what bulimia is about. Women seem to find it more disgusting and disturbing than anorexia:

> When I lived in a lesbian communal household, the women thought I was crazy. At meal times I would sometimes feel the urge to instantly flee the table, and often I was unable to eat with them. Bulimia is a lot more invisible and harder to detect than anorexia.

Although she purges most days, Carol describes herself as a 'recovering bulimic'. She is aware that recovery is a long and difficult process, but is confident she will succeed. She is also adamant that her sexuality is not the cause of her bulimia. In fact, it is one of the few things in life she feels confident and secure about.

It would seem that there is plenty for lesbians to discuss about body image and eating habits. All the women I spoke to said they were pleased the subject had finally been put on the agenda. Lesbians come in all shapes and sizes. We are far from being immune to anorexia nervosa, bulimia or compulsive eating, and it is important to explode the myths surrounding these conditions. Bad eating habits are not necessarily an issue only for large women. There are many fat women who are not overeaters, and many thin women who are, a point that Angela de Castro feels should be emphasized: 'It is important to remember that you can be fat, fit and healthy, while many thin women are unfit and are unhealthy'.

By creating a culture which emphasizes youth and beauty, lesbians are rapidly going down the same road as gay men, whose culture promotes the 'perfect V-shape' body – slim waist and broad muscular shoulders. This is fast becoming a uniform look, which is just as popular on the lesbian scene. The 'ideal' of white, slim and beautiful is so limiting that only a few of us will ever fit into this category. When so much emphasis is placed on the external, physical aesthetic, ignoring the emotions we hold inside ourselves, it is hardly surprising that many lesbians develop eating habits such as anorexia, bulimia and compulsive eating.

Lesbian culture in the 1990s is undergoing rapid, sometimes bewildering, change. Whatever this new climate is that we are moving into, one thing is certain: men are looking at lesbians more and more, and lesbians are watching themselves being looked at. In 'Love me, love my doppelgänger' in the *Sunday Times*, Christa D'Souza discussed this development:

> 1990s dykedom – or part-time dykedom, as many are calling it ('because if you are a part-time dyke, you don't have to buy into all the politics and say I'm never going to shave anything again') – seems to be less about hating men than hating men for not noticing.[9]

Whether lesbian chic is a new destructive pressure in the lesbian community is debatable. But what is clear is that many lesbians fall prey to unhealthy eating habits often simply in order to conform to an image that is ultimately acceptable and non-threatening to men.

NOTES

1. Susie Orbach, *Fat Is a Feminist Issue*. Hamlyn Paperbacks, Feltham, 1978, p. 17.
2. bell hooks, *Sisters of the Yam: Black Women and Self-recovery*. Turnaround, London, 1993, p. 71.
3. At Oval House in London on International Women's Day 1993.
4. Orbach, *Fat Is a Feminist Issue*, p. 18.
5. Susie Orbach, 'Cold comfort on hunger farm', *Guardian*, 13 March 1993.
6. Jill Welbourne and Joan Purgold, *The Eating Sickness*. Harvester Press, London, 1986, p. 30.
7. Mira Dana and Marilyn Lawrence, *Women's Secret Disorder: A New Understanding of Bulimia*, Grafton Books, London, 1989, p. 25.
8. Geneen Roth, *When Food Is Love*. Piatkus Books, London, 1992, p. 18.
9. Christa D'Souza, 'Love me, love my doppelgänger', *Sunday Times*, 7 February 1993.

RESOURCES

The Eating Disorders Association
PO Box 474
Norwich NR3 1QE
Tel. 01603 621 414

better by
design

better by design

creating the perfect body

sheridan nye

The primary focus of attention in sport as a whole is the body and its attributes – its strength, skill, endurance, speed, grace, style, shape and general appearance are tested and/or put on display. This need not imply that the mind is not involved: judgement, motivation and aesthetic awareness are integral to physical performance; but it is the body that constitutes the most striking symbol as well as the material core of sporting activity.

Jim Hargreaves, *Sport, Power and Culture*[1]

Tie a bandana around a woman's head, show off her thighs in a pair of shorts, tease me with her biceps in a short-sleeved shirt and that's what I call a good game.

Robbi Sommers, 'From the sidelines'[2]

Power games

Power is a dirty word. Its associated terms – corruption, exploitation, tyranny and greed – make a craving for power into a guilty secret. In a different context, power can offer autonomy and freedom of choice and as a liberating force, it is a prize to be seized by the disenfranchised majority from the oppressive minority. In the physical body, power is potential energy – the potential to act, resist or overcome. A powerful body signifies what it is capable of and says: 'Anything you can do I can do better.' Power feels like sex and is certainly an aphrodisiac.

For lesbians the strong woman is a seductive role model. From Martina Navratilova to Madonna at her pumped-up prime, the strong woman is contemptuous of male harassment, unbowed by period pains, a metaphor for liberation and self-reliance. But for those of us who are inspired to test our own bodies' limits, the interplay between personal growth and personal politics; self-confidence and ambition; health and danger; desire and narcissism; can be as confusing as it is exhilarating. The point at which weight-training becomes body-building, where determined effort becomes competitive sport, is blurred as the first target is achieved only to give way to the next.

The first reaction to a female body-builder is often disgust at such a 'grotesque' physique, rather than an appreciation of her skills, talents and dedication. In lesbian culture, we rarely discuss our feelings about physique at all,[3] but I believe it is worth putting the body centre-stage for once, as its role in lesbian culture offers interesting insights into our complex relationship with our physical selves. In this chapter I examine some of the common criticisms of and misconceptions about body-building and talk to the women who push themselves to the limit.

Eroticizing power: taking control

For women and queers, physical strength, like wealth or education, can offer an easier path through the obstacle course of life. But while strength can be empowering and inspirational, blatant muscularity in women is an uncompromising challenge to society's ingrained gender roles. Life in the West in the 1990s may appear to offer a plethora of social and sexual roles to chose from, but society still has a stake in imposing 'what girls should do' and 'what girls shouldn't do'.

What girls aren't supposed to do is celebrate, idolize or covet huge, muscular, sinewy female bodies, but someone forgot to tell Ruth Jordan. At forty-two, but looking ten years younger, Ruth packs eleven stone of muscle onto her five-foot-three-inch frame, an image that is belied by her soft voice and slight south London twang. Ruth recalls how, after some initial doubts, she was persuaded to switch from casual weight-training to competitive body-building by a friendly instructor who recognized her talent for self-motivation and muscle-building:

> I thought: 'What me? No way. Never'. I'd never been a weakling, but I'd never been that much into exercise either. I just got into the idea that I was getting stronger. Some people would come to the gym and just go through the motions, but I liked to lift a bit more than I did the last time.

After three years of intensive preparatory work she reached competition standard, going on to win the British over-35s EFBB[4] Women's Championship three years running from 1989 to 1991. She describes to me the thrill she gets from the competition:

> Competing is a challenge and it's great to feel yourself getting stronger. I can't stand training light. If I've got an injury or something I'd rather not train at all. And I get a real kick out of winning, definitely. There's absolutely nothing like it. You ask yourself when you're dieting before a competition: 'What the hell am I doing this for?' When you're up on stage and you win that's when you realize.'

Ruth rejects any notion that female body-builders ultimately want to be men. 'No. Absolutely not. I'm a strong woman with muscles. Maybe there are certain qualities that society likes to think are intrinsically male, but I don't believe they are. Women can be strong and women can be powerful.'

After taking third place in the 1990 World Championships and her third British Championship in 1991, Ruth retired to concentrate on her career as a fitness instructor, training body-building wannabes in Jubilee Hall gymnasium in London's Covent Garden. Another factor that influenced her decision to quit was increasing pressure to use steroids. The stigma of steroid abuse has dogged the image of body-building more than that of any other sport, and often distracts attention from the sheer hard work involved at competitive levels. Although opinion on the competition circuit varies, one thing is clear: it is difficult to compete 'naturally' against heavyweights who believe in their right to supplement their training with science. Ruth found the dilemma difficult to resolve, but in the end chose not to get involved. 'It's a personal choice whether you want to take them or not. I'm not condemning anyone, I just didn't want to take it that far.'

Despite the popular image of female body-builders as fulfilling the ultimate butch-dyke stereotype, Ruth says she rarely trains other lesbians and, as far as she knows, she is one of the few, out or otherwise, involved in the sport:

> I don't think weight-training is that popular with lesbians, I don't see that many in the gym. There are a few now who are getting interested in training and getting fit, but it used to be that it wasn't quite right-on to pay that much attention to your body, and there's still a bit of that attitude around. Most lesbians, I have to say it, are very lazy about exercise. Apart from the ones that are particularly sporty, and they are usually into team sports anyway, there are very few that will dedicate themselves enough to become competitive body-builders.

So what motivates a lesbian to give herself over to a lifetime of training, if her achievements are likely to be scorned, or more often ignored, by other lesbians? As in any competitive-level sport, body-building demands dedication, time, energy and cast-iron will-power. In the months prior to competition, a typical training regime starts with an hour and a half of heavy workout with weights, followed by an hour of aerobics, six days a week. And the devotion doesn't end in the gym. Food intake is strictly regulated, if not exactly frugal: five or six meals a day – maintaining the all-important balance of proteins and carbohydrates – is the usual pre-season fare, followed by a bucket of vitamins and other supplements for dessert. Having adjusted to this Schwarzennegger-scale appetite, male and female body-builders alike crash diet in the weeks before competition, cutting out fluids, salt and fats, encouraging muscles to the surface unobscured by body fat. Becoming a body-builder doesn't happen by accident.

The tangle of motivations behind a passion for muscle is not easily unravelled. Some lesbians cultivate the ripped and hard look as casually as adopting a style of clothing, using the body to express an image and minimal amounts of clothing to set it off. Others are inspired by the competitive edge and the promise of 'being good at something'. Ruth testifies to a variety of benefits:

> One of the best methods of taking out your stress, taking out your anger, is to go to the gym and have a workout. Whether you want to take that to the level of being a competitive body-builder, and whether you want that look, is an individual thing. For me, I like winning competitions. I like being strong and, yes, it is very sexy.

An intrinsic part of weight-training to any level is that the pain barrier becomes a familiar friend. Years of training have given Ruth an intimate understanding of her body's natural pain reliever – endorphins – and she is matter-of-fact about the pain-pleasure principle at work in the gym.

> Obviously training past your strength is painful, but it's a nice kind of pain, the same as if you're masochist. The sexual pain is a similar feeling. It can be scary, especially doing squat-lifts. You've got all this weight on your back and you're not sure if you're going to be able to get up again. Sometimes your life does flash before you. You're definitely pushing against your pain threshold. There's the physical pain of S/M sex, you go past your pain barrier, but there's also the mental thing of pushing yourself emotionally and that correlates with what happens in the gym.

On a superficial level, strength and muscularity are strictly the domain of the 'butch top', but Ruth turns this assumption on its head.

> I never used to wear make-up until I got into being strong and being a femme. I think in my lesbian-feminist days, in the long-distant past, I was trying to look butch and it wasn't really me. But as I got stronger I liked to have some things about myself that were more femmy. It wasn't just to soften the muscle or to conform – I just liked the contrast.

This identification continues in the bedroom:

> I'm a stereotype really. [She laughs] I like butch women and I like to be a femme. I'm kind of 'top in the gym and bottom in bed'. It's not how strong you are but how you use it. Although I'm strong my girlfriend could pin me down. It's a matter of attitude. I like feeling very powerful and assertive in the gym and then being very vulnerable and submissive in sexual relationships. Being vulnerable is just a different kind of power. To be a bottom you don't just give up and let the other person do it. The myth is that the bottom is the victim. That couldn't be further from the truth. You're consenting to being that vulnerable. I think you have to be emotionally strong enough to do that.

Some lesbians prefer to appreciate the sexual allure of female muscle from afar. In 'Sex and the single gladiator' Donna Minkowitz expresses her fascination with the female comic-book caricatures on *American Gladiators*, which she describes as 'the only TV show where women with big muscles are celebrated as the living gods they are ...':

> She has her legs clamped tightly around the legs and lower torso of the flailing contender. . . . No way can she escape the hard-bodied Ice. As the girl writhes and tries to hold on, Ice's legs scissor her down to the ground.[5]

Making explicit the link between physical power and the sexual undercurrent of SM, she expresses her confusion: 'I don't know if I'm watching a sport or reading Pat Califia.'[6]

Strong dykes are also a popular muse for lesbian photographer Della Grace. Her notorious chronicles of lesbian sub-cultures include 'lesbian lads' of various shapes and sizes in defiant poses of sexual and gender ambiguity. Grace says she enjoys the spectacle of muscularity in women as representing a challenge to compulsory feminity:

In my work and life, and in terms of how I personally feel about my body, the bodies I want to be sexual with are usually harder, less feminine. I think a lot of the women I photograph, and that I also fancy, have a sort of ambivalent relationship in some ways towards their gender rather than their sexuality. I think there's an element of equating being a woman with weakness, and resisting that by making their bodies hard. But I think it's wrong to see weight-training as a repudiation of feminity or anti-female. That really bothers me because I don't see it as anti-female but anti-stereotypical female.

Even though the importance of appearance and style in sub-cultures has been a preoccupation of cultural commentators, and photographers, since the 1970s, the sexual element of muscularity has been largely overlooked from critical positions outside lesbian culture. In their book on the previously neglected phenomena of women's fetishistic practices.[7] Lorraine Gamman and Merja Makinen stop short of suggesting that some aspects of lesbian culture, in terms of our clothes and bodies, may be rooted in fetishism, saying, 'Some lesbian dress-styles owe as much to ideas about "resistance" and "protest" as to ideas about sexual fetishism,'[8] while concluding that more research into the subject is needed.

Lesbian academic Elizabeth Wilson has also pondered the sexual and subversive meanings contained in fashion and clothing. She maintains that the function of clothes, in a high-tech, sophisticated society where functionality is divorced from practical necessity, is to translate our culturally 'invisible' bodies into cultural artefacts: 'Dress is the cultural metaphor for the body, it is the material with which we "write" or "draw" a representation of the body into our cultural context'.[9]

But does the body need a metaphor to communicate some of its more basic messages? Could a fascination with muscularity, with its characteristics of pleasure through (self) objectification, and gratification through a masochistic relation to pain, fit the model for female fetishism offered by Gamman and Makinen? Strictly speaking no, as sexual desire in this case is not for an inanimate object, but for an attribute of the body itself. Their distinction is between fetishism and 'fragmentation': 'Fragmentation is related to objectification (and to fetishism), but over-emphasis of parts of the body is not the same thing as not wanting physical contact with the body ...'[10] This suggests that the woman who admires muscles on other women is not a fetishist as such, because she desires the body as a whole.

But the complex motives behind a woman's fascination with her own muscularity suggest desire working at a deeply symbolic and unconscious level. As Della Grace suggests, a desire to be 'hard' could mask a desire for the protection denied by a feminine body; a denial (or 'disavowal' in Gamman and Makinen's terms) of women's vulnerable position in society, and of lesbians' invisibility in mainstream, popular culture. We may have 'lesbian chic', but as yet we are not part of any advertising agency's customer profile. This disconcerting visible/not visible, female/not female status is reaffirmed every day in our absence and presence in magazines, newspapers and on TV. Eventually, the individual is forced to take defensive action: to deny the circumstances causing the confusion. So, if we can't contort our bodies and style to fit the bill of compulsive femininity, then we'll damn well go the other way. In a way, in lesbian mythology, a worked-out body is like a Harley Davidson in *Easy Rider*, a representation of the owner as an outlaw free from the tyranny of (feminine) convention.

Gender trouble

While the sexual connotations of muscularity have been underplayed, accusations that 'strenuous' exercise and 'obsessive' body-building are symptomatic of neurosis – the result of society's conditioning of women to dislike their bodies – are not uncommon. As feminists from Susie Orbach to Naomi Wolf have stressed, the female body has become constrained at every turn to aspire, through spending, diet and exercise, to the prescribed ideal: the 'beauty myth'[11] in Wolf's terms. Women's bodies are habitually starved, shaved and surgically altered in the name of compulsory femininity, and few women living in the Western world can confidently say they are above the pernicious influence of the 'slim ideal'. As Gamman and Makinen point out: 'The thin erotic aesthetic is so central to the Western beauty ethos that for women, eating has become associated with sinning.'[12] They estimate the diet industry in Britain to be worth at least £850 million a year, while the number of women suffering with some kind of eating disorder in the West has reached 'epidemic proportions'.

Female body-builders upset the beauty-myth applecart by, firstly, refusing to accept the dominant ideology: where compulsory femininity demands women make themselves smaller and less obtrusive, body-builders dedicate themselves to becoming larger and taking up more space. Secondly, female body-builders disprove certain 'essential' attributes of the female body in relation to the male body: namely that women are naturally smaller and weaker than men. In fact, pound for pound, women's muscle is identical in strength and structure to men's and according to Carol L. Christensen: 'many highly trained women athletes exceed the abilities of most men'.[13]

As lesbians exist at least partly outside the confines of gender-role conformity, perhaps it is surprising that most competitive women body-builders are straight. In the women's glossy magazine *Options*, Rebecca Gardiner interviewed three top British body-builders: Kimberley-Anne Jones, Beverley Hahn and Loretta Lomax.[14] While Gardiner commends their decision to pursue their careers at the expense of male approval, she avoids questioning their heterosexuality or attributing fetishistic narcissism as a motivation. Body-building is presented as a laudable, if extreme, way for women to claim their independence from men, rather than as a radical rethink of the boundaries of physical possibility, or simply as a sport.

In the accompanying photographs the women are undeniably muscular, but all three sport rather incongruous bleached blonde perms, and Gardiner grants them each a confirmation of their feminine credentials: 'Beverley insists that she cries if she sees an animal in distress; Kimberley-Anne loves putting on her Garfield pyjamas and spending a quiet evening in with her cats; and Loretta enjoys pampering her boyfriend.' Yet in the photographs the women forgo high heels for Timberland boots. By rejecting some aspects of compulsory femininity, but not others, could it be that women body-builders are genuinely surpassing the oppressive ideal by pursuing their own individual style, rather than, as they are often accused, trying to soften their 'masculinity' for the sake of conformity?

Even so, one line of feminist thought maintains that the 'fitness industry' is simply capitalism's response to women's growing awareness of the futility of dieting. Women's magazines, especially those aimed at a twenty-something readership, have tended to drop articles on diets as women have become increasingly cynical about the whole diet industry. But the slim ideal, and the need to encourage women's spending, remain and so the miracle diet is resurrected as the miracle diet-and-exercise programme. As the underlying aim is fundamentally the same – to lose weight – some women have argued that the moralistic drive for fitness is simply a 'corset of muscle',[15] another method of restraint.

Elizabeth Wilson draws on Michel Foucault for a connection between maintenance of the disciplined body and of an ordered society, and between care of the self and the need to create ethics in a time of crumbling moral standards. Jim Hargreaves describes the goal-oriented pleasure at work in 'the jogging cult' in terms of similar scale:

The drive within this culture to transform the body into a receptacle of continuing sensations is a powerful drive to give meaning to one's life in certain terms: to do something about one's body in this context is to do something about one's life.[16]

But if, as Wilson claims, clothes are 'disguising the recalcitrant body we can never entirely transform'[17] and the gospel of fitness is ultimately found to be a lie, then the case for latent influences at play behind the current popularity for working out carries greater authority. The fact is that strenuous exercise often does give women significant control over the size and shape of their bodies, even within genetic and age constraints (larger women tend to develop muscle more easily, as do older women, owing to the drop in oestrogen that begins after the age of about thirty), and fitness promotes feelings of well-being quite apart from the satisfaction of achieving set aesthetic aims. The question of whether women should *want* to make this transformation is difficult to answer. Western standards for separating pleasure from pathological impulse – distinguishing between 'want' as an active choice and 'need' as an uncontrolled obsession – are stamped through with cultural subjectivity.

Nevertheless, some feminist commentators are unequivocal in their condemnation of 'the cult of the body, a preoccupation that is both obsessive and destructive.'[18] Here, Jean Mitchell makes a distinction between acceptable and 'excessive' exercise, but fails to define where this borderline might lie. Falling back on the concept of women's 'natural' lack of muscle tone, she claims that body-builders 'steadfastly deny the bodies that they were born with and try to emulate a masculine ideal.'[19]

It seems women cannot win: a feminist charges those who change 'what they were born with' with idealizing men, while newspaper commentators, who, after all, are the chief instigators of the feminist backlash, can dismiss one of the world's fittest women, Elle MacPherson, for making 'a grand living showing off what God gave to her'.[20] The message is that women should be satisfied with, or grateful for, their bodies, but they have no business claiming any credit for their achievement, hard work or talent in developing them.

When Mitchell describes women body-builders as 'unnatural', her views curiously echo those of the early opponents of women's participation in sport. In *Out of Bounds* Helen Lenskyj charts the emergence of women's sports in the early part of this century against a backdrop of ominous warnings from commentators and doctors about 'unnaturalness' and the risk to women's reproductive well-being:

> There are numerous activities suitable for girls and women, but let these be of the type that will be suitable to their physical and mental natures. ... The tendency for girls to ape the activities of boys is regrettable. In most cases, it is physiologically and psychologically unsound and may be definitely harmful.[21]

> Excess exercise is more harmful to women than to men. ... It must of course be axiomatic that nothing can be good for a girl's body which renders her less capable of motherhood.[22]

Temporary amenorrhoea (loss of periods), as the body shuts down competing energy drains to compensate for the stress of strenuous exercise, is common among women athletes. This is the root of the 'unnaturalness' debate. But how 'natural' is it for women in the West to have to take a day off work, or handfuls of painkillers, at the onset of their period each and every month? Hormones guru and former features editor of *New Scientist* magazine, Gail Vines, quotes new research from a team at Harvard University led by anthropologist Peter Ellison suggesting regular, heavy periods may be anything but healthy or natural:

> Increasing numbers of scientists think our [Western women's] high levels of sex hormones can be linked to the increase in cancers of the breast, ovary and endometrium. ... Epidemiologists now suspect that the fewer these hormonal highs – i.e. the fewer menstrual cycles a woman's body is exposed to over her reproductive lifetime – the better.[23]

Ellison found that a combination of high-quality nutrition and lack of exercise among women living in the West tended to raise oestrogen to 'poisonous' levels, with an accompanying increased risk of cancer. By comparison, in less affluent countries, women's bodies tended to 'shut off' fertility during times of physical stress by reducing levels of oestrogen and progesterone, the result being that menstruation, with its risk of unwanted pregnancy, becomes lighter or ceases altogether. Ellison suggests that strenuous exercise (comparable with the physical hardship experienced by women working the land in developing countries), combined with a well-balanced diet, would help women in the West bring their hormone levels down to 'normal'. It is worth noting that although *prolonged* amenorrhoea can cause a permanent reduction in fertility, this is only one

way of measuring women's health, and for most athletes this phenomenon is temporary, for example during the build-up to competition.

Grievous bodily harm

'The current fitness vogue has little to do with health . . . on the contrary,
it is a sign of psychological ill-health.'[24] Although Jean Mitchell's equation
of body-building with neurosis is rather blunt, her contention that ' . . .
anorexia nervosa and compulsive exercising can fulfil the same function:
to force the body into moral submission'[25] is an important insight into
how self-discipline and self-destruction can become linked, with dangerous consequences.

Leigh Newton is a thirty-two-year-old journalist living near Inverness in
Scotland. Her father left home when she was sixteen and she was left to
look after her mother who had multiple sclerosis:

> I was faced with having to leave school and look after my disabled mother at
> a time when most kids are still growing up, so I was forced to grow up too
> quickly. And compounded with the stress of having to look after a severely
> disabled person was the fact that I wasn't too keen about my body.
>
> I think all teenage girls go through a phase of dieting. I think everybody at
> some stage in their teenage years looks at themselves in the mirror and they
> don't measure up. They think if they lose a couple of pounds here and there.
> It's a bit like the advert for aspirin: not only does your headache go but your
> whole surroundings, everything changes, life is better, there's new furniture.
> . . . If your life is going out of control the one thing you can control is your food
> intake and your weight. Eventually this becomes an addiction.

When aerobic exercise became part of her pilgrimage to lose weight
Leigh set up a mini-gymnasium in her bedroom:

> You could say I was *driven*, as I drove my mother up the wall with the noise.
> I thought nothing could stop me in my quest for perfection. Unfortunately, in
> my mind's eye 'perfection' resembled an underfed stick insect. As a result, at
> eighteen years of age I found myself under a Mental Health Act order. Yeah,
> they literally did 'come to take me away', minus the 'ha, ha'. At that time, I was
> considered to be a danger to myself, and the doctors told me that if I carried
> on living like I was then I could expect to remain on the planet for around a
> week.

Leigh was admitted to hospital weighing just four and a half stone.

> I came out of hospital about a stone heavier, but nowhere near cured. I went to a local sports club and took to weights, and at the same time I took to writing for music magazines. I thought I could add weight in the form of muscle, not fat. At this time I considered myself a body-builder, despite the fact that I weighed under six stone and had seven-inch biceps and fifteen-inch thighs.

Leigh combined her new-found enthusiasm for weight-training with her writing experience and began drafting articles for body-building magazines:

> The turning point for me came when I arranged to interview a top female body-builder, Carolyn Cheshire, at Gold's Gym in London. I didn't actually have an outlet for this article at the time; that didn't matter, I was about to meet and talk to my first real body-builder. I remember sitting across the table from her and I couldn't take my eyes off her. The part of me that I most wanted to develop as a female body-builder was my upper chest, the pectorals. She had on this zip-up top that was just zipped to the pec line. I could not take my eyes from them. I thought: 'I want pecks like that'. And I realized that I could have a body like that, all I needed to do was what she did.
> The fact was that the interview cured me. I was so inspired I headed straight for the gym, told anyone who would listen, and actually got up in the middle of the night to have something to eat without feeling guilty.

Leigh decided to start on the slow climb to competition standard, eventually entering a couple of regional shows in Scotland. As she got more involved with the serious side of body-building she discovered that not everything she was learning would help with her recovery:

> Drug use was widespread and accepted if you wanted to reach the top. Female athlete were taking large doses of male steroids, anabolic steroids, developing body hair and deep voices. The use of recreational drugs was widespread as well. Speed when dieting for a contest, blow to come down after workouts.

Leigh is disparaging about competitors who get into dieting and drugs. From her perspective as a former anorexic she has little time for unhealthy obsessions, whether in the name of sport or anything else. Her disenchantment became final when she realized that anorexic and bulimic behaviour was also part of the body-building scene:

> Dieting body-builders train hard, eat little and sometimes smell rather than eat food, or even put food in the mouth just to get the taste of it and then spit it out, which all seems like 'acceptable anorexia' to me. Of course, body-building is a much healthier form of control for those who seek it – anorexia can kill you, body-building, unless you're talking steroid abuse, only serves to make you healthier. But when you see body-builders on the day of a show they are as weak as kittens. They're dehydrated and starved of calories. They call it 'ripped', I would just call it unhealthy. Some people think these women actually walk around looking like road-maps 365 days of the year, but most of the pictures you see in magazines are taken in the days immediately following a contest when they are in condition. The rest of the year they are usually at least two stone heavier and look like beach-balls. Of course, not all female body-builders are drugged-up yo-yo dieters, but unfortunately, these women are often ridiculed.

Although Leigh recognizes that body-building helped her out of the self-destructive anorexic cycle, she has decided to distance herself from the sport – to train for herself rather than for competitions:

> I don't follow rules any more. I train as often as I want with as many sets as I want. I still train six days a week, but I do it because I enjoy doing it. I don't need a crutch. Body-building for me was a replacement addiction, albeit a healthier one.
>
> To me now I look normal in the mirror. Training has given me more self-confidence about my body, whereas as an anorexic I was ashamed of it. It's not a power trip, it just gives me more confidence in myself. Most people have got bits of their body that they're self-conscious of, y'know, either their nose is too big or their bum's too big. Someone once asked me, Is there anything about your body that you'd change? and I said, 'No, there isn't. I'm very happy with the way I am now.' And if there was anything then I know I can just do it by training a certain body-part a certain way.
>
> If I had taken body-building to its maximum it wouldn't have been healthy. It's not a sport, it's a life. You find yourself doing everything around the gym, and around meals. Your daily food is monitored in terms of fat, protein and carbohydrate instead of calories. So it's another form of monitoring. It really is reverse anorexia.

Leigh's salvation through managing to control and redirect her talent for self-discipline is not unique: the reigning world champion female arm wrestler, Katherine Monbiot, is also an ex-anorexic, and Leigh herself knows of anorexics who have become triathletes. But it would be too simple to say that body-building is a cure-all for women with eating disorders, or to say that the former anorexic's inclination toward self-destruction reduces anything she puts her energies into to just another symptom of her illness. The dividing lines between sport, ambition, obsession and determination can be so fine that differences become a matter of semantics. Even using long-term health as a bottom line is unreliable – as a sport, body-building is hardly alone in involving an element of danger.

The sporting life

Sport is an expression of strength, skill, self-discipline and the will to win, but whereas the muscular, flexible body is a by-product of most sporting activity, body-building incorporates these values in the physique itself. Cutting out the need to put a ball in the net, or to restrict individual flair for the greater good of the team, the product of the body-builder's labour is there to behold.

Body-building as a sport is a controversial concept and even the British Sports Foundation refuses to recognize it as such. In Britain, regional heats are held in theatres, town halls, community centres and sports halls across the country, while the glamour of the big event under bright lights is saved for the EFBB championships in October in London.[26] National and international competitions attract big prize money and sponsorship from food supplement and equipment manufacturers, but little in the way of publicity outside the specialist body-building magazines. Although promotional deals can be lucrative, few women earn enough to turn professional.

Without the financial incentive, exhibitionism and narcissism, the sheer pleasure of being looked at, must surely play a part in persuading contenders to flaunt it in such a public arena. But most body-builders claim their reward is informed recognition for the months of training, dieting and nutritional expertise. Even so, respect for the judges' criteria has been a thorny subject ever since Bev Francis's highly publicized defeat, at a physique show in New York in 1983,[27] for her 'excessive' development. Francis's alleged unfeminine appearance was thought a potential danger to the sport, as advertisers would shy away from association with such a 'masculine' woman.[28]

As body-building's ruling bodies grapple with the competing aspirations of athletes and advertisers, the goalposts in women's competitions continue to move. Ruth Jordan has found this both irritating and yet par for the course:

> I feel very frustrated by it. You don't know what they're looking for half the time. One year they'll say you mustn't be overly muscular – it's not 'feminine' – then the next year it's all right. To win a British championship you've got to be quite big, then when you go into international competitions you might get marked down because they'll be looking more for shape, definition, proportion, that kind of thing. It kind of goes in waves. Every now and then the powers-that-be decide women are getting too big and they want them to look more marketable. The only thing you can do is be the best you can and have a combination of size and good condition. If you've got it all they've got no excuse not to place you.

To work so hard and yet ultimately depend on such subjective judgement, is one of the paradoxes of body-building as a sport. US feminist Gloria Steinem equates women's willingness to submit to this kind of scrutiny with a need for approval:

> In bodybuilding contests, as in corporate and academic settings, victory can be negated – and discipline reasserted – through the highly subjective process by which a winner is selected ... the experience that any high school girl who ever tried out for cheerleader remembers: being chosen.[29]

Others might say that subjectivity in sport – from line calls to penalty decisions – is a necessary evil which underpins its entertainment value, and which is neither unaccountable nor peculiar to men judging women.

Either way, the parallel Steinem draws between work, academia and body-building is interesting because it reveals not only similarities between the feudal mechanisms for success, but also the need for acknowledgement that lies at the root of the activities themselves. But if these different 'contests' that women put themselves through are so similar, why is it that physical strength is often considered rather base when compared with career or academic status? The French theorist and sociologist Pierre Bourdieu has identified a mechanism he terms 'distinction', whereby some cultural activities are valued above others, and so confer class status. In 'How can one be a sports fan?' he suggests how this strategy is manifest in sport:

> ... a strong body, bearing the outward signs of strength – this is the working-class demand, which is satisfied by body-building – or a healthy body – this is the bourgeois demand, which is satisfied by a gymnastics or other sports whose function is essentially hygienic.
>
> ... weight-lifting ... in the eyes of the aristocratic founders of modern sport, symbolized mere strength, brutality and intellectual poverty, in short the working classes.[30]

It is through such deeply ingrained cultural values that the body expresses its rich symbolism. Changes in popular culture and political environment brand themselves onto the body: the 'survival of the fittest' climate of the Reagan/Thatcher years inspired the fitness boom of the mid to late 1980s and the popularity of muscle-man icons Schwarzenegger and Stallone; and in the post-recession gloom, the 'waif' period of high-street fashion mirrored youth's uncertainty about its immediate future. As a cultural artefact, it is unsurprising that the body is as susceptible to divisions of value as art, lifestyle or fashion. Inevitably, 'brutal' physicality with its working-class, unsophisticated connotations comes low on society's scale of worthiness.

Some schools of feminist thought are also uncomfortable with sport's association with male boorishness and unsisterly competitiveness. But Greta Cohen disputes the assertion that competition among feminist women is a contradiction in terms:

> Competition creates opportunities to master the very skills feminists find essential when creating a co-operative model. ... Strong bonds of friendship exist among sportswomen everywhere. ... That is why Chris Evert and Martina Navratilova could sit together and share a bagel in the locker room just prior to an all-out competitive effort at Wimbledon's centre court.[31]

A less cosy picture would be that, at their level, Evert and Navratilova were both well paid and respected in their profession and so, although the stakes were high, the match was hardly a matter of survival.[32]

In less well-paid events, success ultimately relies on someone else's failure. Sport releases the power of the body as kinetic energy and, in its purest sense, this energy is apolitical and immoral, expressed through being faster and stronger than the opposition, and setting the pace for the rest to follow. Avoiding the mythologies of essentialist thought, there is no reason to expect the average sportswoman's competitive instinct to be any less deadly than the average sportsman's. The soap-opera appeal of truly competitive sport – the shifting fortunes of familiar faces – parallels life's everyday, mundane battles, and is what makes it such compulsive viewing. As Jim Hargreaves describes it: 'Sport can thus constitute regular public occasions for discourse on some of the basic themes of social life – success and failure, good and bad behaviour, ambition and achievement, discipline and effort ...'[33]

Body talk

Somewhere along the line, fitness and body-awareness have become associated with a doctrine – a doctrine with a whole baggage of moralistic dogma attached. Perhaps adverts such as the original compaign for home-fitness courses featuring Charles Atlas, with its catchline: 'You too could have a body like mine', and underlying implication: 'You too *should* have a body like mine', are to blame. But it's no coincidence that advertising in the 'fitness industry' still takes a moralistic tone – what better way to sell magazines, courses, supplements and equipment than to spread a fictional fear of underachievement?

With no other terms in which to discuss the body (other than bar-chat sexual objectification) it's no wonder lesbians tend to avoid the subject. Consequently, a set of destructive beliefs has evolved: that thin lesbians pity fat lesbians; fat lesbians resent thin lesbians; fit lesbians despise unfit lesbians; unfit lesbians are disgusted by muscular lesbians; and tall lesbians look down on everyone.

In the course of collating these interviews I have found very little in the way of judgemental attitudes, and the purpose of this chapter is to suggest that lesbians' bodies can be a site of expression rather than oppression. Of course, this transition is difficult because it demands a way of seeing that is somehow removed from the pressures and values of mainstream society.

Della Grace is well aware of the contradictions inherent in making aesthetic judgements about physique:

> I want to get a tattoo done around my waist, a chain to sort of symbolize the chain of body fascism [she laughs]. I can't be dishonest and say it doesn't exist because it does, and there's a part of me that has bought it.

I've got a little bit of muscle now, not a lot, and I've always been strong and I like that. It's about being sexy, and about being able to accept the attention of women. Y'know, I want to look like one of the women that I would turn my head for. It's about saying that your body matters. This vehicle that carries you around matters and what you put into it and how you treat it matters.

If a line has to be drawn, as some have tried to do, between a healthy and unhealthy preoccupation with the body, then perhaps it should also address the level of genuine enjoyment involved. As a last word on the subject, former triathlete and out lesbian Jackie McConochie sums up her enthusiasm for her sport and the demands it makes on her:

I don't think of it as a chore; I enjoy it too much. I can cycle fifteen miles into town if I want to, I can run for a bus. It feels so good to be able to run, it's real exhilaration. I know I can climb over anything, do and go where I like. That makes me feel great and it's not something I'm about to just give up.

NOTES

1. Jim Hargreaves, *Sport, Power and Culture*. Polity Press, Cambridge, 1986, pp. 12–13.
2. Robbi Sommers, 'From the sidelines', in Susan Fox Rogers (ed.), *Sportsdykes*. St Martin's Press, New York, 1994, p. 209.
3. A recent exception is Megan Radclyffe, 'Big dykes', *Diva*, issue no. 2, 1994.
4. English Federation of Body-Builders.
5. Lily Burana, Roxxie and Linnea Due (eds), *Dagger: On Butch Women*. Cleis Press, San Francisco, 1994, p. 38.
6. *Ibid.*, p. 39.
7. Lorraine Gamman and Merja Makinen, *Female Fetishism: A New Look*. Lawrence & Wishart, London, 1994.
8. *Ibid.*, p. 67.
9. J. Ash and E. Wilson, *Chic Thrills: A Fashion Reader*. Pandora Press, London, 1992, p. 6.
10. Gamman and Makinen, *Female Fetishism*, p. 62.
11. Naomi Wolf, *The Beauty Myth*. Chatto and Windus, London, 1990.
12. Gamman and Makinen, *Female Fetishism*, p. 10.
13. Carol L. Christensen, 'Basic exercise physiology', in Greta L. Cohen (ed.), *Women in Sport*. Sage, Newbury Park, CA, 1993, p. 130.
14. Rebecca Gardiner, 'Pump it up'. *Options*, March 1994.
15. Ash and Wilson, *Chic Thrills*, p. 10.

16. Hargreaves, *Sport, Power and Culture*, p. 218.
17. Ash and Wilson, *Chic Thrills*, p. 9.
18. Jean Mitchell, 'What's healthy about the current fitness boom?', in Marilyn Lawrence (ed.), *Fed Up and Hungry: Women, Oppression and Food*. Women's Press, London, 1989, p. 156.
19. *Ibid.*, p. 162.
20. 'In search of the brain', ES *Magazine*, the weekly supplement of the *London Evening Standard*, 15 July 1994, by an uncredited writer.
21. Arthur Lamb, in Elmer Ferguson, 'I don't like Amazon athletes'. *MacLean's Magazine*, issue 51, 1938. Quoted in Helen Lenskyj, *Out of Bounds: Women, Sport and Sexuality*. The Women's Press, London, 1986, p. 36.
22. Dr Geoffrey Theobald, 'Emancipation of women', *American Journal of Public Health*, September 1936, p. 871. Quoted in Lenskyj, *Out of Bounds*, p. 38.
23. Gail Vines, 'Oestrogen overdose', *Vogue*, September 1994.
24. Mitchell, 'What's healthy?', p. 157.
25. *Ibid.*, p. 170.
26. At the Wembley Conference Centre.
27. See *Pumping Iron 2: The Women*, 1985, distributed by Virgin.
28. Volkswagen has not been so sheepish. Its advertisement featuring Kimberley-Anne Jones, 'built like a Vento', was designed to illustrate the car's indestructibility. Then again, as the product is a car rather than a body-building supplement, there is no implied association between buying it and developing Kimberley-Anne's physique.
29. Gloria Steinem, *Moving Beyond Words*. Bloomsbury, London, 1994, p. 117.
30. Pierre Bourdieu, 'How can one be a sports fan?', quoted in Simon During (ed.), *The Cultural Studies Reader*. Routledge, London, 1993, p. 352.
31. Cohen (ed.), *Women in Sport*, pp. 315–16.
32. A common criticism of the women's tennis circuit is that some competitors are content to maintain their top-ten ranking rather than challenge the top seeds. See Michael Mewshaw, *Ladies of the Court: Grace and Disgrace on the Women's Tennis Tour*. Warner Books, London, 1994.
33. Hargreaves, *Sport, Power and Culture*, p. 12.

Bibliography

Juliet Ash and Elizabeth Wilson, *Chic Thrills: A Fashion Reader*, Pandora, London, 1992.
Lily Burana, Roxxie and Linnea Due (eds), *Dagger: On Butch Women*, Cleis Press, San Francisco, 1994.

Carolyn Cheshire, *Body Chic*, Pelham Books, London, 1985.

Greta L. Cohen (ed.), *Women in Sport*, Sage, Newbury Park, CA, 1993.

Simon During (ed.), *The Cultural Studies Reader*, Routledge, London, 1993.

Bev Francis, *Bev Francis' Power Bodybuilding*, Sterling Publishing, New York, 1989.

Lorraine Gamman and Merja Makinen, *Female Fetishism: A New Look*, Lawrence and Wishart, London, 1994.

Jim Hargreaves, *Sport, Power and Culture*, Polity Press, Cambridge, 1986.

Marilyn Lawrence (ed.), *Fed Up and Hungry: Women, Oppression and Food*, Women's Press, London, 1989.

Helen Lenskyj, *Out of Bounds: Women, Sport and Sexuality*, Women's Press, London, 1986.

Michael Mewshaw, *Ladies of the Court: Grace and Disgrace on the Women's Tennis Tour*, Warner Books, London, 1994.

Susie Orbach, *Fat Is A Feminist Issue*, Hamlyn, London, 1978.

Susan Fox Rogers (ed.), *Sportsdykes*, St Martin's Press, New York, 1994.

Gloria Steinem, *Moving Beyond Words*, Bloomsbury, London, 1994.

Naomi Wolf, *The Beauty Myth*, Chatto and Windus, London, 1990.

roadkill

7 roadkill

aileen wuornos's last resort

karena rahall

Lesbians make up the largest percentage of women awaiting the death penalty in the state of Florida. The most recent addition is the infamous Aileen Wuornos, a prostitute working the highways of the Florida Inter-state system, who was charged with killing seven white middle-aged men. In some cases she unloaded her gun into them, took their money and belongings, then left their bodies (sometimes covered, sometimes naked) in the woods. She was finally apprehended when Tyria Moore, her lover, co-operated with police and led them to her.

This chapter aims to explore the ways in which Wuornos has been represented in the legal system and the media. The focus will be on her demonization and the exploitation and erasure of her sexuality. In the first months that the story was covered by the media, Wuornos was portrayed as a ruthless lesbian who hated men and killed for pleasure. As the story of the crimes unfolded, the media rarely mentioned her sexuality but began instead to portray her as a prostitute with the mind of a child. The fact of her alleged lesbianism seemed to be ample cause for society's alarm, according to many in the media and legal system who regarded it as evidence of her hatred of men. But, in the media, Wuornos was also a prostitute: a remorseless, violent prostitute who never displayed regret for the murders, which she claims were committed in self-defence.

Wuornos's reluctance to accept a lesbian identity is another issue I would like to address. A born-again Christian, she was adopted by a married woman who claims to be in love with her, and who has strongly influenced her resistance to the claim of lesbianism. In this case, what is a lesbian? How do lesbians regard this woman who appears to be one of them, but who rejects the possibility of her lesbianism?

I believe there are two systems of representation at work here, and I hope to examine both closely. The first is the patriarchal system, which at once consumes and rejects the lesbian killer. The second is a system within which she is accepted by some lesbians and rejected by others.

In order to discuss lesbian reaction to Wuornos, I find myself in a position that leaves me feeling both uncomfortable and hopeful. When I first heard about the case it never occurred to me that some lesbians would reject Wuornos. Her connection to the lesbian community seemed assured somehow, whether she viewed herself as a lesbian or not. I found her case fascinating precisely because of the many stories that focused on her apparent 'gender confusion'. When I began to dig a little deeper into the legal realm of the case I discovered even more startling declarations about her sexuality and its supposed link to violence. This information led me to believe that lesbians would soon vehemently attack such representations, if not for Wuornos's sake, then at least for their own. The fact that no unified group mounted a counter-attack against the handling of the case came as a surprise to me. Further investigation uncovered some of the fears and deeper meanings behind lesbian identity and its inter-relationships with dominant culture and intra-relationships within the lesbian 'community'. Discussions about ideological division should take place and although they may be difficult, they will do more to unify any political progression we may seek than ignoring the existence of such divisions. I believe the institutionalized vilification of one lesbian based on her sexuality affects us all: those who would distance themselves from the Wuornoses of the world do so at their own peril.

The relationship between the law and the woman who rejects both her place within it and the social order will be examined. It's not necessary to show admitted resistance to convention by the resistant woman because women are taught, generationally, never to admit to their resistance. I will demonstrate how the lesbian in court is either sexually erased, or hyper-sexualized. It is also my intention to show, through historical analysis, how she has been represented as a demon, a man-hating aberration for which there is no reasonable explanation. The law regarded her as mentally sick from the outset, and, importantly, not really a woman, but rather a child. For the woman who chooses to use man's traditional weapon – a gun – cannot be a real woman. In a patriarchal system, real women fall apart at that fatal crossroads between killing and being killed. A real woman will succumb. So what does the law do with the prostitute who is a lesbian who kills?

The media has been adept at labelling Wuornos a calculating killer, as well as a child incapable of complex thought. In her interviews, Wuornos projects lucidity, level-headedness and, the worst crime of all, anger. If a woman kills a man, she must show remorse, regret and above all else, extreme self-hatred for the deed. The prevalence of this notion is exemplified by the media's overt and collective shock at Wuornos's inability to feel such self-hatred and remorse.

At the time of writing, Aileen Wuornos is awaiting death by electrocution on Florida's Death Row. To date, she has stood trial for the killing of one man, Richard Mallory. Her plea is 'no contest' to the killing of five other men, and she remains uncharged in the case of one more: the body of missionary Peter Siems has never been found and, therefore, Wuornos cannot be charged. She awaits the outcome of one last effort to appeal the Mallory trial, based on evidence discovered since her sentencing regarding his past conviction record.[1]

During her trial for the death of Mallory, the prosecution hoped to prove that Wuornos acted maliciously and with premeditated intent to kill. They sought a verdict in accordance with the state's charge of first-degree murder. In so doing, the state had to prove, beyond reasonable doubt, that Wuornos was a predatory killer, that she actively sought her victim and planned to kill him. Since there were no witnesses to the actual killing, the state put together its version of truth based on physical evidence and supposition.

In attempting to prove Wuornos's guilt, the state presented very little evidence to demonstrate conclusively her intent. None of the expert witnesses were able to pinpoint either Wuornos's or Mallory's exact position at the moment before his death, and therefore, could not testify as to whether a physical struggle had occurred. What has not been disputed is that Wuornos shot Mallory four times with her .22 calibre pistol in December 1989 and left his body covered with a rug in the woods near Ocala, Florida. Beyond that, the truth slips and slides between two possibilities. Either Wuornos was a cold, calculating, brutal, man-hating lesbian who killed for the 'thrill' of it or she was a childlike, helpless victim, the product of an abusive childhood with the moral capacity of a four-year-old. No alternative explanations for her actions were offered. I will discuss further the implications of the insanity, or pathology defence later in this chapter.

During the course of the trial the state argued a motion which would allow evidence from the other six killings to be admitted in court. Such a ruling is not unusual in a multiple-murder case where the defendant is being tried on all counts. However, in this case, Wuornos was only being tried on one count so the possibility for future trials to allow this evidence would seem something like over-trial: six juries hearing six murders in six trials, one for each murder.[2] Judge Blount's decision to allow the state to present such evidence may be grounds for a retrial if the defence can successfully argue to a jury[3] that the information is unduly prejudicial. It must be said that such grounds are highly unlikely to be constituted by an appeal court in this case.

John Tanner, the lead prosecutor for the state, began his opening statements by educating the jury about the motives of not only Wuornos but all prostitutes.[4] This tactic of drawing on stereotypical representations of prostitutes and lesbians would be employed by the state throughout the trial. In the following excerpt Tanner makes his first attempt at supposition of truth and actually speaks for Wuornos.[5]

> He [Mallory] didn't know he was about to pick up a predatory prostitute who'd had sex with over 250,000 men ... [T]hey began to move towards the *alternative* act of having sex, but he wouldn't take his clothes off. He just wanted to unzip his pants and she didn't like it that way and they began to argue and struggle. She got out of the car and said, 'No, you're not going to just fuck me, you're gonna pay me!' And then she shot him as he sat behind the wheel. Aileen Carol Wuornos liked control, she had been exercising control for *years* over men – *tremendous* power possessed through prostitution.[6] (my italics)

The 'alternative' of which Tanner speaks evokes several images: were they preparing to have anal intercourse? Could he be referring to oral sex? Or is it that, since Wuornos's profession is seen as the means by which she attains power, the 'alternative' sex is really a reference to Wuornos herself: as a predator engaged in the profession of sex for sale, is it she who represents the alternative to 'normal' femininity?

Her prostitution might well be the reason for this representation, since prostitutes are routinely seen as transgressors of feminine sexuality. Of course, prostitutes share this act of transgression with lesbians, and, indeed, there was no shortage of conflation in Wuornos's trial. Prior to her arrest, and during the period of the killings, Wuornos lived with Tyria Moore. The two women were openly lovers, and their relationship only came to an end when Moore – as part of a deal with police that provided immunity from prosecution in return for her testimony – persuaded Wuornos to confess to the crimes during a wire-tapped telephone conversation.[7]

Although Tanner refrained from using the word 'lesbian' throughout the trial, he did portray Wuornos as a man-hating predator who lived with a female 'room-mate'. However the fact of their sexual relationship was revealed by both Wuornos and Moore, making his own revelation unnecessary. More recently, since she became a born-again Christian, Wuornos sometimes denounces her lesbianism, although she has always maintained that she loved, and still loves, Moore and does not regret their relationship.[8]

The question of her sexual orientation is, in fact, rather difficult to ascertain, but what is certain is that she lies outside the socio-symbolic order, and that ensures her vilification.

Tanner relied on the fact that most jurors were able to make an historical and cultural connection between lesbianism and prostitution. In other words, it was unnecessary for Tanner to extrapolate Wuornos's sexuality since the signifiers of prostitution fit neatly into patriarchy's notion of lesbianism. The nineteenth-century sexologist Havelock Ellis pointed to this relationship while researching criminality and lesbianism. Ellis's theory is not so different from Tanner's assumptions made almost ninety years later:

> The prostitute has sometimes been regarded as a special type [of lesbian], analogous to the instinctive criminal ... [her] homosexuality [is] due to the following causes: (a) excessive and often unnatural venery; (b) confinement in a prison, with separation from men; (c) close association with the same sex, such as is common in brothels; (d) maturity and old age, inverting the secondary sexual characters and predisposing to sexual inversion; (e) disgust of men produced by a prostitute's profession, combined with a longing for love.[9]

Tanner fills in the blanks with his repetitive assertion of the average prostitute's need for control and domination. In so doing, he sets up, for the jury, the opposition between female sexuality as either seeking control or as being a passive receptacle of it. Women who seek control are dangerous, and women who specifically seek control through the use of their bodies are beyond contempt: they are evil. For Ellis and Tanner, prostitutes are characterized by an 'instinctive criminal' nature when coupled with homosexuality because they seemingly use men solely out of a desire for control. Another study, conducted in 1987, arrived at a similar conclusion:

The most criminalistic, feministic, aggressive, and homosexually active women were those whose first gay experience preceded their initial arrest ... [they] may also exhibit [less] traditional femininity in other areas such as aggression, and given the proper causative circumstances, criminality.[10]

I would also like to suggest that the two identities of 'lesbian' and 'prostitute' rely on each other to create a sense of common hysteria. The fact that Tanner did not use Wuornos's lesbianism more frequently suggests that if she had not been a prostitute, her past relationships with women would likely have become primary evidence to prove her motive for killing these men.

The prostitute, like the lesbian, is the object fixed in the gaze of the subject, and the subject is usually defined as male. Yet there is something disturbing about this object: it transgresses the rules of the social order, thus limiting or controlling the subject's gaze. Luce Irigaray submits an account of woman as commodity which sheds light on how the value of women is defined through the gaze and is dependent on competition.[11]

The body of the commodity is not where value is determined, but rather outside of the body and in accordance with a paternal standard by which all commodities/bodies are compared. The binary between the 'good woman' and the 'bad woman' is contingent on this comparative value. Irigaray points to the specific importance of 'use-value': the prostitute has a particular value precisely because she is used; she has been purchased before, and therefore given value to be sold to the next customer. The lesbian is valuable only in so far as she can be used and compared – as a transgressor – to other women; both heterosexual women and other transgressors. The lesbian and the prostitute are useful in securing the good woman/bad woman binary by assuring the value of the not-prostitute/not-lesbian. But, because the male gaze cannot be assured, the commodification of women relies not on exposure but upon restraint of the visibility of prostitutes and lesbians.

The value placed on the object of woman demands her participation in the appraisal, and every woman is at least a potential commodity (the prostitute through the sale of her body, the lesbian through her potential sale, for the lesbian is valuable so long as she may one day be set 'straight'). As members of the opposition in the binary, prostitutes and lesbians hold a very important resistant power to this value system: their visibility and subjectivity are the carriers of this power. In other words, when women become participants in the exchange or resist the exchange of their bodies, they disrupt the structure which would confer value upon them. Consequently, their power is kept under restraint by oppression, devaluation and invisibility. John Tanner, in his closing statement went so far as to explicitly confer a sort of mystical power on Wuornos and all prostitutes: 'Her appetite to control men, and that's what most prostitutes are about besides money, it's control; tremendous control to take all the man has, physically. Some say spiritually.[12]

This kind of power accorded Wuornos indicates her breech of contract. Her value as a prostitute was tolerated because men received goods. But if what Tanner said is true, then prostitutes are in the business of stealing men's souls. The absolute terror invoked by the product that comes to life and demands to be part of the exchange is demonstrated by Tanner in his statement. And, of course, this very insistence on her subjectivity means that the gaze is necessarily turned back upon the male. Such an act is seen as more than evil; it is incomprehensible. Wuornos failed to recognize her place as goods to be exchanged, and in so doing disrupted the social order. In fact, this disruption may be seen as one of apocalyptic proportions, since all men are in the business of the exchange of women. Woman's desire to take on the role of the subject creates a deadly force – something approximating a disease – which, unchecked, can turn into murder. Tanner does not just present Wuornos as a 'soul thief', but accuses all prostitutes, which in turn implicates all lesbians.

Interestingly, according to Havelock Ellis, this evil bubbles just beneath the surface: women who work together are prone to lesbianism, as the simple absence of men encourages women's propensity toward same-sex relationships. If prostitution is just one more instance of abnormal feminine sexuality, then all women must be protected or restrained from this approximate menace.

This conflation of lesbianism and prostitution extends to the law, and is central to understanding how the criminal-justice system works to define women and their value. If we say that the law is simply an extension of society and, hence, adjudicates with the same sense of right and wrong, it is only to be expected that anyone not involved in the construction of the legal or social order will be confronted by linguistic barriers. Even when the law attempts to bridge this gap – for sometimes it sees clearly the delineation of power – the words to describe truth within the legal structure are bound by a strict code of usage that permits only those with power to speak. As women are beyond the language of the law, they are unheard and will always remain so until the entire structure of the social order is reconstituted.

The justice that purports to be served is really another word for protection from what lies outside the structure. Resistance to the system of law has only ever led to the ejection of the resister: the death sentence. Wuornos refused to play by the rules and, rather than succumb to them, holds tightly to her own death.

Wuornos wanted to assert self-defence as her reason for killing Mallory, but since the evidence from all the killings would be admitted, her attorneys decided that her past abuse and childlike nature should be presented as well. They were well aware that no one would believe that a woman could kill seven times in self-defence, even with the evidence that Mallory was convicted of sexual assault. The jury in this case was asked during the selection process whether they believed it was possible for a prostitute to be raped: they all answered affirmatively. It remained for the defence to convince them that the possibility was an eventuality.

Rape has come to represent the symbolic victimization of women, but when it comes to *proving* rape the task is much more difficult because the language of law protects men. Because the perpetrator speaks in the male language of the law and because there are almost never any witnesses to rape (the law works on the premise that doubt is all one needs for exoneration), the male voice takes precedence. In this case, the male voice was silenced and the state, as a male institution, proposed to speak for it.

The defence only permitted one witness to speak on Wuornos's behalf: Wuornos herself. In fact, they tried to dissuade her from speaking at all, believing that her testimony would do more harm than good. If she had not spoken, the defence would have called no witnesses; this can hardly be called defence. A number of witnesses were prepared to testify as 'experts' on subjects ranging from child sexual assault to violence against prostitutes, but the defence turned them down. What power Wuornos exercised in this decision is difficult to determine since the attorney–client privilege prevents the disclosure of any conversations between Wuornos and her counsel. Even Jackie Davis, Mallory's ex-girlfriend, offered to testify as to Mallory's violent past, but she too was never called. Davis also informed the police about Mallory's conviction in Maryland, but neither the defence nor the prosecution followed it up. Since the trial, yet another witness has come forward to express his astonishment that he was not called.[13]

The action, or inaction, of the defence is unusual considering this was a first-degree murder charge, and it would seem they simply felt Wuornos was not worth the effort, or that her crimes were so incomprehensible that nothing they did would save her from death. Certainly, nothing Wuornos said in court could be valuable:

> Even as stories unfold in the courtroom, the value of the 'facts' the court will call evidence has been predetermined by the social mechanisms that privilege certain forms of communication ... it means that the simple and direct recollection of the facts [a woman gives] in court would stand against the enormous collection of documents already recording the events of the crime and her life.[14]

Convinced she could persuade the jury that she had acted in self-defence, Wuornos insisted what she be allowed to testify. Her insistence made the use of an insanity/pathology defence impossible because such a defence would require Wuornos to give up her voice and refrain from telling her side of the story. Her attorneys, however, seem to have disregarded her wishes by resorting to pathology explanations which directly contradicted her own testimony.

The insanity/pathology defence

This defence is used to show that an abnormal reaction on the part of the defendant was exercised, and that because the reaction fell outside 'normal' standards of behaviour, the court should judge the defendant differently. The defendant is forced to rely on the institutions of law and science to speak for her, since her own voice is unheard. Because 'normal' standards of behaviour are male, the pathology defence suggests that women are inherently unreasonable: their actions are not reliable based on patriarchal standards of behaviour, but their transgression – their crimes – may be forgiven if they prove their worth as a commodity to the court.

The woman who transgresses the law must feel remorse and see the error of her ways; she must not recognize that she has disturbed the order but may only admit to having stepped outside her place and, in order to maintain her value, she must quickly show restraint. The pathology defence shows the court, and hence the social order, that the woman has not really disturbed anything because she was not in her right mind.

This assertion failed to work for Wuornos for several reasons. Firstly, she stepped out of her place so many times that not even a plea of insanity could bring her back to the court's satisfaction. Secondly, she has never shown remorse; instead she has continually stated that her behaviour was justified. No insanity defence will help – or allow to remain in the social order – the woman who believes in her actions and thus places her own value on herself.

If Wuornos were indeed insane – and she must be so if part of the definition of insanity is to be outside the social boundaries of reasonableness – then she has given value to her imagination which tells her that her actions were correct. Her actions, both before and after the crimes, constituted a response to danger that her imagination convinced her were very real. What she saw in her mind directed the actions of her body: she resisted these men physically by ending their lives. She took away their bodies before they could penetrate her, and hence, take her. Rather than using reason to distance herself from her imagination, Wuornos didn't view her actions as unreasonable. If she had killed them and then reverted to remorse or sorrow by rejecting the danger she imagined, would she be judged sane? It is unlikely, because of the repetition of her crimes and the added terror evoked by her profession and gender.

In the event, Wuornos was judged to be sane. Her crime was to exist outside social boundaries, yet the ruling of sanity relies on the conclusion that she existed within them. Wuornos was deemed to be within social boundaries (sane) so that she could be punished – for existing outside them – with death: the ultimate exclusion.

Residing both inside and outside the social order is key to understanding the logic of the court in its decision to kill her. The logic holds that a person must be judged sane in order for execution to go ahead. Sanity suggests that a person exists within the structure of social boundaries in so far as she understands the rules of that structure. When the court finds a person to be insane, that person is kept alive, and often given the prospect of freedom one day, but the sane person, by virtue of guilt, is sentenced to death because she is not fit to live within the structure of the society that she understands. It is precisely because she understands the structure that she must be executed, for she is understanding and yet resisting.

In a court of law the determination of sanity is based on a very simplistic notion.[15] Does the defendant understand the concept of right and wrong and/or did she at the time the crime was committed? This very basic question limits the legal system in its efforts to determine the complexities of psychic reasoning. The fragile state of the social order is further propped up by countless psychiatrists and psychologists who are brought into the courtroom to testify for either the prosecution or the defence.

Some will say the defendant is sane while others will claim insanity, yet the notion of truth, which the court seeks to define, is undefinable and subject to arbitrary interpretations.

Motives and marginalization

Wuornos herself displays an ambivalence regarding the issue of her life and death. When she feels any glimmer of hope she expresses a willingness to fight, but when she feels hopeless she injects all of her energy into condemning what she believes are the widespread systems of corruption which have tried and convicted her. At times, exposing those who, she believes, are involved is more important to her than life. This energy is directed most strongly when she is being judged or questioned about her motives:

> WUORNOS: I'm not going to allow them to put me in prison for life when I've been viciously raped, viciously tormented. I've suffered a great deal. I've been raped numerous times even before I got the gun. Why should I allow you to say, 'Oh, we're sorry, we'll overturn the sentence and give you life.' Then you're just ... you're just putting me through the torment again, when I did something to keep myself alive. I'd rather die.
> GERALDO RIVERA: You'd rather die in the electric chair?
> WUORNOS: I would rather die in the electric chair, a natural death, than to live life in prison and be tormented continually for the rest of my life when I don't deserve it. I ... it's either acquittal or death, because I did what anybody would have done.
> RIVERA: But when you give the state a kind of defiant declaration – acquittal or death – don't you know what side the cards are likely to fall on?
> WUORNOS: Yeah, corruption, death.[16]

Wuornos believes that her story can help other women who may find themselves in similar positions. Whether it will be heard is another story. It is worth noting that since her first interviews Wuornos has become quite worried about how she will be interpreted. For this article I would have liked to provide a number of quotes from her letters specifically addressing her desire to warn women and to describe her ordeal, but she has come to distrust anyone who uses her words. Her fear that they will be taken out of context and distorted are warranted, but most importantly, she fears people are only using her story for financial gain. I've done my best to contextualize some of her most adamant public sentiments but, unfortunately, because I am unable to use her words directly, I run the risk of perpetuating any misrepresentation. This further illustrates the successful silencing of Aileen Wuornos.

While it would seem obvious that Wuornos shares a bond of marginalization and vilification with lesbians, a great many women in the lesbian community find her situation completely beyond the scope of their own oppression as lesbians within a dominant culture. Reasons for this may vary: some find the story of self-defence in so many instances unbelievable, others perhaps feel that a woman so prominent in the media will only increase the negative representations of lesbians. Whatever the reasons, it is clear that Wuornos is not a woman many lesbians want to be associated with.

This split within the community is indicative of how complex and heterogeneous the lesbian community is today. Most gay and lesbian publications ran stories on the case which countered the mainstream media's representation of Wuornos as a cold-blooded lesbian killer and man-hater. Groups were also formed to combat those characterizations and to provide legal support for Wuornos.[17] Providing such support was very difficult in light of the heavy sentences which had already been handed down. Beyond those difficulties, those supporting Wuornos were faced with harsh criticism from some lesbians. At the 'March on Washington' for lesbian and gay rights in 1993, the Coalition to Free Aileen Wuornos placed a banner along the route which read: 'Free Aileen Wuornos, Support Dykes Who Fight Back'. Literature was also handed out explaining some of the facts of the case and detailing many of the questionable statements made by the media, prosecutors and police about Wuornos that would seem to implicate all lesbians. Some women cheered the banner and took the literature, while others expressed disdain for the group's actions.

While the 'March on Washington' might generally be considered a mainstream event, even radical groups had difficulty endorsing support for Wuornos. Some members of the Lesbian Avengers in New York, with which the Coalition was affiliated for a time, were hesitant to back Wuornos, some believing that she may not be a lesbian and others that there were women more worthy of the group's support. Aside from the very disturbing issue of competing oppressions, the difficulty in accepting Wuornos as a lesbian presents some important problems to do with identity and politics. Whether Wuornos identifies as a lesbian or not, she has been labelled a lesbian. The references made about her crimes have been directly linked to her sexuality, so that the disclosure hardly matters; she has literally had no voice. It is important for marginalized people to understand the thread that connects those who disclose their identity and those for whom no choice exists. We are inextricably bound together in the same space: a site of attack. Therefore, it matters very little whether Wuornos chooses to express any sexual identity – she is a lesbian.

Beyond insanity

Before Wuornos was ever arrested for the killing of Richard Mallory, news stories abounded with tales of the first female serial killer, dubbed the 'Damsel of Death'.[18] At this point, all that was known of the suspects (at first, Moore was also assumed to be involved) was that they were female and travelled along Interstate 75 throughout the counties of Florida. The dead men were sometimes found clothed and sometimes unclothed; condoms were discovered at some of the crime scenes. From this 'evidence' the label of serial killer was pinned to the suspect(s). No further evidence or information ever changed this categorization, even though further information might have led to a closer examination of the definition of a serial killer and at least an acknowledgement of the differences between Wuornos and those who were given the label before her.

Significantly, serial killers have been described as existing 'beyond insanity'. In other words, they are considered to be so far out of the reach of 'normal' structures of behaviour that they cannot be defined. And yet most 'experts' who study serial killers suggest that at least 500 are still at large in the USA and many more are waiting to follow suit, not yet beyond the control of their fantasies.

One expert – Norris, a psychiatrist – describes the serial killer as a victim of abuse, unable to relate in any 'normal' fashion to his/her sex objects. The killer fantasizes about ridding the world of what he/she sees as demonic representation, but when the killer has finished the task of murder, he/she finds the object is not what he/she thought it to be. The object/victim no longer represents the evil; the serial killer still feels the rage the killing was supposed to defuse, so he/she kills again. Norris describes the interim period, between murders, as a phase of deep depression that lasts until the killer murders again.

So, what does it mean to be beyond the reaches of science and society? Serial killers have been interviewed over and over again by these experts and their stories are told repeatedly in an attempt to see inside the mind of these aberrant creatures. Investigators and psychiatrists profile these murderers, and often successfully profile criminals at large, based on what they learn from the interviews. A distinctive pattern has apparently emerged, with a structure that wavers only slightly from killer to killer. Yet Norris, and many other experts, contend that these people are beyond imagination, that they represent anomalies; that they can never be understood. The repetition of the evidence they present and the striking similarities that exist between serial killers suggest that the experts are overlooking something important and are failing to take the credit that seems due them.

Most serial killers, to date, have been white, heterosexual and male. The FBI's Behavioural Science Unit was specifically created to profile serial murderers. This is what they have discovered so far: most kill and/or mutilate and/or rape (dead or alive) their victims; the victims tend to be members of traditionally oppressed and 'valueless' groups, such as homosexuals, women (prostitutes), children and the elderly;[19] they often feel powerless and helpless, so they gain power by killing those they believe are responsible for their incapacity; they strike back at their victims and remove what they interpret as the power being exerted over them; their motives vary, depending on, in the experts' view, their childhood memories of abuse.

How 'experts' define abnormal and normal behaviour is very important in the profiling and labelling of people as serial killers. How they view the killer and his/her victims is also a major factor in attempting to establish motives and patterns. When these experts analyse their findings and create theories about the killers, they look to those societal patterns of acceptability which are currently considered to be 'normal'. These theories become definitions which are followed by law enforcement and the media, in most cases, without question.

Carlton Gary, a black man from Atlanta, was haunted by memories of the wealthy white women for whom his mother had to work when he was growing up. Gary represents an anomaly in that he's not white and there's a reversal in the social status of his victims. What is most striking is the way in which one expert has theorized about Gary's motives:

[The women's] power in the community was unchallengeable, and in Carlton Gary's view they comprised their own pantheon, making the economic and social decisions that translated the lives of Gary's relatives into hope or hopelessness. But most frustrating of all to an abused but intellectually gifted black child ... he was absolutely invisible to the matrons. ... Not that they weren't kindly, churchgoing, charitable women; they were all that and more. They were the epitome of what a Southern lady should be, but the antithesis of what Carlton Gary's mother actually had been.[20]

In other words, there was nothing abnormal about these 'ladies' who oppressed Gary and his family. In fact, their victimization is doubly regrettable because they are 'real' women, not members of oppressed groups, and the blame seems to rest squarely on the shoulders of Gary's mother, who could not be like these women. Blatant racism aside, the reference to the serial killer's mother is not unusual in this kind of theory. Time and again, the mother is scapegoated, analysed and found to be the prime cause of her child's behaviour and violence. From that point, all women become the cause and the mother is displaced onto any other woman the killer encounters. The experts are complicitous in this displacement: the fear of the feminine becomes painfully apparent in their analyses.

The abuse Wuornos says she suffered at the hands of various men, including her father, has been all but ignored, however. (This is because there is no need to explain her symptoms – she's a woman so she embodies them.)

In his analysis of motive, Robert Ressler, one of the original members of the FBI's Behavioural Science Unit, comes very close to asserting that serial killers are actually not as anomalous as might be assumed:

> I had long argued that the aberrant behaviour of killers is in some ways only an extension of normal behaviour. Every parent of an adolescent girl has observed that teenage boys will repeatedly walk or ride their bikes or drive their cars by a girl's house, or hang around as close to her as they are allowed, and engage in impetuous, spontaneous behaviour.[21]

In this case, stalking women is regarded as normal behaviour: men are *expected* to watch women, to size them up, to get as close as possible until stopped, not until they stop themselves. Men are expected to be predatory. It's the woman's responsibility to draw the line, but she should be aware that the line rests between voyeurism and rape or death. In other words, all men fit the profile of serial killers – before the killing begins – if they engage in this sort of behaviour.

Ressler's normative explanation demonstrates the existence of the serial killer within social boundaries; what pushes him over the line is the woman/mother. It's she who forces him to kill the girl he should simply be objectifying in a normal manner. Ressler is sitting directly atop the explanation for male violence against women and he does not even know it. His acceptance of woman as always already 'other' and responsible for male terror is precisely evidence that serial killings of women are not an anomaly.

The media have swallowed these theories readily, happily quoting the authoritative experts responsible for the profiles. Even though Wuornos does not fit the profile – for no serial killer has ever claimed self-defence – she does fit the structure in other ways. Since women are so readily blamed for the behaviour of serial killers, it makes sense that a woman who is not really a woman could play both roles. She is both responsible for her actions as a woman and yet, as a lesbian, she is 'male-identified'.

The complicity of the media indicates how easy it is, given the right circumstances, to slide the female killer into the mould of the male killer. In Wuornos's case, as soon as it became known the killer was a woman, news stories were obsessed with the notion of the male-identified woman. In a story printed days before Wuornos's arrest, Steven Egger stated: 'If it turns out that women are involved, I won't be particularly surprised given the changes in the female role.'[22]

Other statements given to the press by these experts indicate that the real fear is not the gun of the killer, but her sex: if women were to begin killing men, the social structure as we know it would fall into disarray. It's the notion of women's power – of women as subjects – that contains the real threat. Men would no longer be able to count on women to be their victims, because those victims might not succumb so easily. The logic here points to women's changing roles: the more aggressive and autonomous women become, the more they begin to resist their place as objects of men's desire. To resist such male objectification is implicitly anti-male, and anti-male has always been understood as lesbian. Hence, the killer of men, always aggressive, is male-identified, since 'real' women know their place. In an article on Wuornos, Susan Edmiston drives this sentiment home. Quoting Robert Ressler and Dr Kathy Morall, Edmiston relays a warning to all women:

> There may be an intrinsic hatred of males here, as well as an identification with male violence which helped push her across the line into what has been considered a 'male' crime. (Ressler)

> I think you can go one step further. You might not expect a woman of clear sexual identity to do this. I see her as a woman whose sexual identity is

> distorted. This woman's motivation could be a psychological challenge to the
> male – 'I'm more masculine than you.' (Morall)[23]

Therefore, a sexual identity which is unclear – read homosexual – in women is directly linked to the hatred of men. Women who hate men must be sexually confused. Also, since she is not a man, but not really a woman, she is a failed copy, a woman striving to be like a man. She can never really assimilate all that maleness entails, so she can only strive to attain the identity through male action and violence; but she will never succeed. Her body prohibits her, so she becomes mad and terrorizes men in a vain attempt to be like them. She is a failure in her madness. She has failed to disengage from her girlish homosexual desire, to accept her lack; she has failed to be inscribed by male desire, and most importantly, she has failed to properly acknowledge these failures.

But in this failure she has become resistance itself. From beginning to end, Wuornos has remained steadfast, she has never renounced her actions. Even after becoming a born-again Christian she has not admitted that what she did was wrong. This is one site of resistance that no amount of terror, threat, religion or insult can dislodge, and it is this resistance that threatens the socio-symbolic order. Wuornos represents the autonomous woman in many ways: not only did she resist her object status, but she continues to do so and still claims victory: 'I'm going to heaven and you're all going to hell.'[24] She portrays herself as a martyr, a sacrificial lamb – seductive images to say the least. What if killing her does not purge her being from the world? If she is remembered by others as having stood tall and proud, if she is not broken, she remains a threat after her death. Ressler quickly attempts to refute this possibility, and in so doing makes a startling admission.

> Wuornos isn't a trend, she's an isolated case. Males are definitely the killers among us. But I think the numbers of female murderers will increase during the nineties, and the fact that women are getting involved at all is alarming. Women have always provided a balance to male violence, and I'd hate to see them tip that balance.[25]

The balance Ressler clings to is that of male violence against women. If women start killing back, there will be a shortage of male perpetrators and a shortage of female victims to keep the balance. What's so important about this balance anyway? If men stop killing women the balance will be tipped as well.

Another feature of the case points to this balance of female and male violence: it took police only nineteen days to capture Wuornos once they suspected her. Contrast this to Ted Bundy's treatment. He was arrested twice, based on descriptions and several pleas from his fiancée and one of his professors, but was freed because he was engaged in a 'normal heterosexual' relationship and seemed 'more in control than [his fiancée]'.[26]

The comparison between Wuornos and Bundy occurs quite frequently in news accounts of the case. Images of Wuornos luring her victims to their deaths are compared to Bundy's enticement of women through his wit and charm. Wuornos is never described as charming, witty or alluring, so the question remains: why would all these men go into the woods with her? Reporters have speculated as much as the police. Even with the existence of condom wrappers as evidence of sexual encounters, many journalists concluded that she 'hitched a ride, as she was known to do, and then turned on the men who were good enough to offer help'.[27] Such speculations arose before Wuornos's confession was made public and the hysteria around the crimes was heightened by the disclosure that she had a female lover; hating men, then, became a given, and closed the discussion of motives for ever.

News reports also focused on the oddity of a woman who should have been a victim. Short of claiming her victim status outright, reports indicated that Wuornos, if she were a 'real' woman, would have become the victim rather than the predator. One story reported that women are usually self-destructive and that this case marks a departure in that 'normative' behaviour, making Wuornos the first female serial killer.[28] The paradox in the reportage is striking: at one and the same time the reporter admits that women are victimized by men and tend to succumb rather than fight back, and then only a few sentences later, calls the woman who does fight back a serial killer.

What most of the news stories have in common is a complete disregard for anything Wuornos says on her own behalf. Instead, reporters have trusted literally anyone claiming to know her, printing their stories without question. When Wuornos's voice is actually heard in these stories her words are scrutinized and the truth consistently questioned, even when evidence proves her statements to be true. There is nothing unusual in this scrutiny: most murderers are treated with some suspicion. However, there seems to be a need in this case to prove that Wuornos was not, and never will be valuable as a human being. When stories point to her 'troubled past' they include instances of abuse only as evidence to prove that she hates men, not how or why this situation could come about. While travelling from one courthouse to another for a hearing, Wuornos was taped by the officers in the car in the hope that they might catch her in a lie or confession: 'For the first time in her desperately troubled life, what goes on inside Aileen Wuornos's head now matters. Her words finally have value.'[29]

Ultimately, however, those words only have value in so far as they can prove she is evil and so act as a warning to other women. The value represents fear and an almost hysterical attempt to 'know' her. The hope is that in knowing her, she may be restrained, kept at bay and prevented from doing any more damage to the very social order that never permitted her to speak. But she has spoken now, and it's too late to stop her words and her actions. Her speaking body has already ruptured the space that refused to let her inside.

NOTES

1. Mallory spent ten years in Maryland's penal facility for its most violent offenders. He was convicted of assault with intent to rape and sentenced to four years, but the doctors and officials at the prison held him for ten because they believed he was too dangerous to women. Neither the prosecution nor the defence uncovered these facts. The information was first revealed on NBC's *Dateline*, 10 November, 1992.

2. The state relied on the Williams Rule, otherwise known as Similar Fact Evidence. This covers the admissibility of specific criminal acts to prove a particular issue and relates to specific incidents of conduct, if relevant to a purpose other than to show propensity or bad character. If the sole purpose of the introduction of evidence is to show propensity, then it would be ruled inadmissible because it creates prejudice and acts like a trial within a trial. For example, the evidence can be used to show a unique *modus operandi*. For the exact citation and precedent, see the following sources. *Williams* v. *State* 110 So. 2d 654 (FL) and Florida Statute, section 90.404(2). Ironically, the prosecution attempted to use this rule to enter the testimony of three women who claimed to have been raped, in exactly the same way as the accuser in the William Kennedy Smith trial, but were denied.

3. *Ibid.*

4. John Tanner acted as Ted Bundy's spiritual counsellor while he awaited the electric chair, and pleaded for his mercy in an attempt to delay the execution. 'When a "Bad" woman kills', *Progressive Women's Quarterly*, summer 1992, p. 30.

5.   The insertion of Wuornos's voice by Tanner should have been rendered inadmissible because it constitutes evidence, true or false. In fact, his re-creation of the scene is also inadmissible because he presents it as fact. He might have said: 'The state will attempt to show. . . .' However, evidence is not permitted to be shown in opening statements, but the remark was not objected to by the defense and so was left in the court record. It is important to point out, perhaps rhetorically, that even when an objection is made and the remarks stricken from the record, the jury has heard it. Lawyers know this tactic all too well.

6.   Court TV (New York), *Trial Story: Serial Killer or Victim?* November 1993.

7.   In fact, technically she was not granted immunity from the state, nor did she plead out her case. Moore was never investigated after the officers attempted to involve her in a movie deal with Republic Pictures, even though one of her alibis was false and she was found in possession of several items stolen from the victims. She was never charged with any crime at all. The police handling of Moore is now under investigation by the state Attorney's office.

8.   Aileen Wuornos, letter sent to The Coalition to Free Aileen Wuornos, 30 March 1993.

9.   Havelock Ellis, *Studies in the Psychology of Sex*. Random House, New York, 1910, p. 212.

10. Lindsy Van Gelder, 'Attack of the killer lesbians', *Ms.*, January/February 1992, p. 82. Quoting study at East Tennessee State University, 1987.

11. See Luce Irigaray, *This Sex Which Is Not One*. Cornell University Press, Ithaca, 1985, p. 179.

12. Court TV, *Trial Story*.

13. Tom Evans in an interview with Michele Gillen said that he spent a week with Wuornos after she killed Mallory. His testimony would have shown that Wuornos did not kill every man she hitched a ride with, as the state would have the jury believe. *Dateline* NBC, 10 November 1992.

14. Kristin Bumiller, 'Fallen angels', in Martha Albertson Fineman and Nancy Sweet Thomadson *At the Boundaries of Law*. Routledge, New York; 1991, p. 103.

15. First established in *M'Naughten's*, 10 Clark & F. 200, 2 Eng. Rep. 718 (H. L. 1843). Later adopted as precedent under *Durham* v. US, 94 U.S. App. D.C. 228, 214 F.2d 862 (1954). Referred to as either the M'Naughten or Durham Rule.

16. *Geraldo Rivera*, CBS, 23 March 1993.

17. The Coalition to Free Aileen Wuornos was established in New York City in 1993. Since its foundation, other groups have formed around the USA and continue the work of countering stereotypes about lesbians and prostitutes with regard to the Wuornos case.

18. Mike Clary, 'A mother's love', *Los Angeles Times*, 17 December 1991, p. E1. Several other news sources, including The *St Petersburg Times*.
19. Robert Ressler, *Whoever Fights Monsters*. St Martin's Press, New York; 1992.
20. Joel Norris, *Serial Killers*. Anchor Books, New York; 1988, p. 31.
21. Ressler, *Whoever Fights Monsters*, p. 78.
22. Mike Clary, *Los Angeles Times*, 7 January 1991, p. A12. Quoting Steven Egger.
23. Susan Edmiston, 'The first woman serial killer', *Glamour*, September 1991, p. 325.
24. Court TV, *Trial Story*.
25. Quoted in Edmiston, 'First woman serial killer', p. 325.
26. Norris, *Serial Killers*, p. 81.
27. Chris Lavin, *St Petersburg Times*, 18 January 1991.
28. Cathy Shaw, 'Slaying case defies theories on gender', *Miami Herald*, 25 August 1991, p. 3B.
29. Lavin, *St Petersburg Times*, 2 June 1991.

s together:

from my crotch to m[

...derful.

...damn it, yeah,

...fuck me, anything . . ."

...used

...st a wall

...e muscles of her neck

...up to make a wind

...back to my mama's cheek

...her's arm.

...ver and over how I

...ing in such a wind?

...like my mama

...in a dra[

o I forge
Deny all that?
Preten I am not
my ghter
my
Pretend
at least as much
in my life   as pain?

*p*ublic *r*elations, *p*rivate *h*ell

Where   then   will I f
where women never w
where we will sit kne
finally listening
to the whole
naked truth
lives?

8 public relations, private hell

lesbian domestic violence

belinda hollows

> I grabbed her by the hair and punched her in the face, I've got this thing where I put my hands around her throat and try to choke her, and I slapped her around the face and threw her on the bed. She was crying and saying 'Stop it'. When I think about it now it makes me really sad. She had to go to work the next morning: she was totally shook up, a nervous wreck, and she couldn't stop crying. This didn't go on for a few minutes, this was like a three-hour torture session. I kept her on the bed and I kept hitting her.

Helen is a lesbian in her late twenties. Violence has dominated eight out of ten of her relationships to date, but despite the continuing physical and emotional abuse, she tells me that her current lover, Carol, has recently moved into her flat:

> I've sat down with her and said: 'Look, I don't love you. Do you still want to go ahead with it?', and she does. She's prepared to go through anything because she loves me, and I just get more angry because she's so pathetic. All I wanted to do was sleep with her, and then it went from one thing to another. She won't take responsibility for herself, but maybe I'm not letting her. I feel stuck with this woman now, and I'm waiting for it to end. There'll be a point where it will blow up and she'll just go. I'll get so pissed off that I'm trapped with her that I'll get even more angry. I don't understand it, because I would never go out with anyone like me. I don't agree with it or condone it.

Ten years ago this account would not have appeared in any publication claiming sympathy with the lesbian movement. Reports of lesbian domestic violence were strictly the property of the tabloids, who revelled in stories of butch dykes wielding hammers in the bedroom. In an attempt to counter such examples of negative representation in the mainstream media, the gay press remained quiet on the subject.

I believe that this period of protectionism, while at one time necessary, must now end. In order to make progress lesbians need to be open about their lives, past and present. Women who batter and emotionally abuse their female lovers behave like the men feminists rally against, the men from whom women sought to 'reclaim the night' in the 1970s and 1980s. Whether aggression in men was biologically determined or socially constructed didn't matter: we protected ourselves from the harm it could do by building national and international networks of shelters, crisis lines, campaigns and support groups. Women's Aid and other feminist organizations cited sexual inequality as the main cause of domestic violence: 'Women's Aid recognizes that violence against women results from the unequal position of women in society'[1]. As lesbians, who supposedly 'love' other women, we felt above it all, and self-righteously extolled the virtues of our egalitarian partnerships. And as lesbian and feminist orthodoxy strengthened, it became harder to speak openly about those 'off' days in our relationships, despite evidence from research conducted in the USA that domestic violence was as prevalent in lesbian relationships as in their heterosexual equivalents.[2]

My motivation for writing on this subject is twofold. Firstly, I want to ensure that the reality of violence in lesbian relationships is not dismissed as 'lesbian punch-ups' or 'lovers' tiffs'. Secondly, I would also question why the women's movement and the lesbian community have censored the existence of lesbian domestic violence for so long, and point out how this has resulted in an inferior support network for lesbian victims or survivors of domestic abuse. I believe there's nothing to be gained from remaining silent. Silence is denial and denial obscures the issue, which ultimately leads to the perpetuation of violent relationships.

Abusers can always find excuses for violent incidents, and often these excuses are accepted by both the perpetrator and the abused partner. Jealousy, drunkenness, frustration, depression, her lover's weakness and the violent relationship she shared with her sister as a teenager are all reasons given by Helen to explain her abusive behaviour. In her study of lesbian partner abuse in the USA, Claire Renzetti identifies three key areas that determine the likelihood of conflict in lesbian relationships: dependency versus autonomy; jealousy; and the balance of power between partners. The women I spoke to in the course of my research confirmed that, mostly, their experience of violence could be traced back to these three root causes.

Domestic violence comes in many forms, all of which are used to exert power and control over others. Apart from physical and sexual abuse (including sexual withdrawal), perpetrators may use property destruction, economic abuse (running up debts and controlling assets), psychological and emotional abuse and homophobic control.[3] In the latter case if the abused partner is in the closet, the abuser has another lever with which to widen the power gap. She may even play on the victim's discomfort with her sexuality, demeaning her self-image and suggesting that she deserves punishment because she is a lesbian. Whatever her partner's vulner-abilities, the abuser will exploit them to manipulate and hurt her, as Helen's relationship with Carol demonstrates:

> Carol is really overweight. That isn't a problem for me, I'm quite big myself. But I say things like: 'You're really fat; why don't you lose some fucking weight? You really embarrass me. I can't take you anywhere 'cause you're so ugly. Why don't you get a life and get yourself together instead of going around in that state? And your daughter's as ugly as you are, you're both horrible, ugly people.' I can't remember the exact words. Everyone's said that the actual hitting isn't anywhere near as bad as the verbal stuff. I really dig deep and say the most horrible, nasty, disgusting, abusive, insulting things to people. All the things they really hate about themselves I magnify and exaggerate.

Helen admits that she's entirely responsible for the violence in her relationship, but the power she wields over her partner is so extensive that Carol accepts blame:

> The morning after [the incident of verbal abuse] she sat down and said: 'I can't blame you for feeling that, because I *am* fat and ugly. You want a partner who's attractive to you, and I'm obviously not attractive to you.' Partners try to change when I criticize them; they don't tell me that I'm talking rubbish, because then I punch them.

Helen describes how the climate of fear created by the constant threat of violence manifests itself in Carol's behaviour:

> She goes really quiet and tenses up, and she'll say: 'Come on Helen, don't start', and I'll say: 'Don't start? Don't tell me not to start, you're starting it.'

Then she'll try and avoid making the situation worse, so she won't say the wrong things and she won't look at me the wrong way, but it doesn't matter. If she just sits back and watches the telly I'll say, 'Don't ignore me', and she'll say, 'I'm not ignoring you.' Or she's got this habit of sitting by the window and looking out. She won't look at me because she doesn't want to look at me the wrong way. So I'll say, 'If you don't want to fucking look at me why don't you just go out? Don't sit there and show me the back of your head. Am I so repulsive to look at?'

I'll just make an issue out of everything. It doesn't matter what she tries not to do, she'll do something wrong. If she gets up to go out to get out of my way, I'll say: 'Oh, so you're walking out on me now, are you?', so that would be wrong as well. Once I'm in that frame of mind there's nothing that they can do right, and that's where the violence starts because I can't compromise on anything. Things that you think are just little eccentricities become real faults – like leaving the top off the toothpaste. I feel like I want to hammer them into the ground and make them so insignificant. I want them to think that I hate them and despise them and that there's nothing worthy about them. Then when I've done it and I'm back to normal, I just cry and think 'How can I have been so horrible?'

The reasons given for staying with an abusive partner are similar for both lesbians and heterosexual women, but one explanation that has more significance among lesbians is the belief that the abuser will change.[4] Women, after all, are not supposed to be inherently violent. The abuser constantly plays on her partner's optimism, offering promises of peace, pledges of love and explanations for a particular bout of violence. Indeed, it's quite likely at this time that the abuser will feel genuine remorse and believe that she can fulfil these promises, but in fact this is merely another element of the power play which only reinforces the imbalance within the relationship. The honeymoon period that follows an incident of abuse exploits the victim's love and dependency and distorts her perceptions of the severity of the assault:

The morning after is horrible, you feel like killing yourself. I'm not saying it for sympathy. When you look at the mess, there's broken glass everywhere and holes in the doors, and there might be blood on the floor from a cut on my hand or somebody's lip. And then this person you live with gets up and they've got a massive shiner or a split lip, or they're bruised and they ache because I kicked or hit them so much. I've been really good the last few days because she's got this black eye and she's really cut up, so I'm on my best behaviour, to prove to her that it won't happen again. But I know it will, and so does she. When I apologize and promise, I really mean it. The morning after you feel like you'll never do it again, but only for a couple of days when you have to face it, and then by the third day I think: 'Get real', it is going to happen again because there's a pattern to it.

Helen may feel she can't control her violent temper, but why should she when, in effect, it serves her purposes? The connection between violence and control has been clearly identified in both heterosexual and lesbian relationships:

Like male batterers, lesbians who batter seek to achieve, maintain and demonstrate power over their partners, in order to maximize the ready accomplishment of their own needs and desires. Lesbians batter their lovers because violence is often an effective method to gain power and control over intimates.[5]

Helen has realized that although she may not have superior personal or physical power over her partners, she can gain that power by force:

In most of my relationships my partners have been the main earners and the main home-makers. I just feel like I'm a sex object really. . . . I provide them with sex and they provide me with a nice home and make sure there's food in the cupboard: they do the washing and I provide the violence. Even if they're not very domesticated to start with, when they live with me they have to be; they become moulded into this thing. The power's not there to start with, then I intimidate them and I'm aggressive and they learn not to say or do certain things, so the violence is used to bring on the power. I feel that if I don't hit them then they are going to hurt me. In any relationship there's always one who's got the upper hand, who loves the other a little more, and that sways the relationship. I've been one down in a relationship and I really hated it, so I always try to be one up so I'm not hurt or affected by their decisions. I think the violence is part of getting the upper hand, being the one who can make decisions. I am a very selfish person. I can care about people and look after them, but underneath I think I'm doing it because I can get something out of it, or in some way it's going to better my life. I'm quite pathetic really, I get my own way by threatening violence.

Although Helen is frequently drunk when she abuses her partners, most studies conclude that there is no simple causative relationship between alcohol and violence – the former merely facilitates the perpetuation of the latter.[6] Alcohol not only lowers the drinker's inhibitions but it also allows an abusive attack to be dismissed as a drunken fight. Such virtual exoneration may also be reinforced by friends and relatives, who can defer their guilt and responsibility when they walk away from the situation in the belief that 'it was just the drink'.

Acknowledging the danger of a situation marks a crucial step in the passage from victim to survivor. Heterosexual women who have experienced domestic violence are now more able to identify their situation thanks to the relatively high profile of the issue in politics and the media. Violent lesbian relationships, however, remain relatively unacknowledged.

I spoke to two women from Pain and Strength, a support group established in 1991 for survivors of lesbian domestic violence, who agreed that ignorance within their own particular social groups hindered their ability to escape abusive partners:

> I felt there was a real denial about how serious it was among my friends. Everyone treated it like a lover's tiff rather than that I was actually being harassed. I was sharing a flat with three other women at the time, and it was evident that it was going on. I didn't say anything but nor did they, so telling them wasn't an issue; I shouldn't have had to say anything, and I didn't. I left the country to get away and I succeeded. I needed people to acknowledge it, without having to say: 'This is what's happening'. I wasn't strong enough. I feel people don't want to know because then they will have to make judgements and decisions and choices about who they are going to stay friends with. I lost touch with every single woman who was a mutual friend of ours. I wasn't in a position to make demands and say 'fucking support me', so they didn't.

The silence within the women's movement is intended to combat societal homophobia and disunity within our own ranks. Lesbians don't wish to add fuel to the homophobic fire, and we have problems admitting, even to ourselves, that the lifestyle once held up as an ideal is, in fact, fallible.

While denial minimizes support within the lesbian community, homophobia discourages the victim from seeking help elsewhere. The message that all batterers are straight men and all victims straight women is implicit in the posters and leaflets for crisis lines and women's shelters that are displayed in nearly every library, town hall and community centre in Britain. This, coupled with the low expectations of the abused lesbian –

the belief that her situation lacks credibility – further limits her chances of finding appropriate help.

Increasingly, white heterosexual women who experience domestic violence are turning to the police. While it's equally valid for a lesbian to report a domestic assault, the police's history of homophobia, as well as sexism and racism, does little to encourage women in a vulnerable situation to seek their help. Equally, lesbians have little faith in the power of the courts. This is partly because of their notoriously ineffectual record in heterosexual cases of domestic violence, but also because of a reluctance among feminists to see women fight it out in what is still regarded as a patriarchal institution.

If a lesbian is discouraged by friends from turning to the police for help, it may reflect the friends' inability to deal with the situation rather than any genuine concern for the welfare of the victim and the community. At the very least, making a decision to turn to the police tells the batterer that the victim has identified the abuse for what it is and intends to hold her accountable for her actions. The police may be able to put an end to the violence by placing an injunction on the abuser, or in some cases imprisoning her. However, it would seem that the lesbian community often finds this recourse to legal action more offensive than the acts of abuse themselves.

In the face of homophobia lesbians in abusive relationships might also avoid seeking help from their families, limiting their sources of support to gay rather than straight friends.[7] It's important to stress here that this creates a twofold dilemma: the victim of abuse is less able to leave and the abuser, if she recognizes her behaviour as a problem, is less able to seek help.

Instances of lesbian abuse smash two powerful myths: firstly, that lesbian relationships are more egalitarian than straight ones, and secondly, that women are non-violent. Cases of husband-battering, child sexual abuse, violent crime, serial killing, killer carers, teenage street gangs and female terrorists all demonstrate that women are not inherently non-violent. Alix Kirsta's book *Deadlier Than the Male: Violence and Aggression in Women* was written in an atmosphere of increasing awareness of women's violent potential.[8] She argues that 'qualities such as anger, dominance, competitiveness and the basic killer instinct' have always been part of women's make-up and, at one time, were crucial to basic survival.[9]

The different ideological stances taken by feminists in the 1970s and 1980s were established in opposition to men's oppression of women. A clear association was made between violence and men, while women were the combatants or victims of such behaviour. Whether the differences between men and women were defined in essentialist terms (based in biology), or whether gender behaviour was seen as socially constructed, there was a general acceptance that feminists and lesbians were trying to create alternative personal relationships. To acknowledge the violent potential in women tears down that safety barrier behind which women could shelter and organize, and the ideal of the unquestionable safety of a women-only space can no longer be relied upon. For lesbians who believe their sexuality is a choice – whether personal or political – rather than a predetermined fact, the acknowledgement that lesbian battering exists creates a problem: the notion of lesbianism as a 'superior' alternative suddenly becomes contentious.

Throughout the history of the women's movement, differences between women – and specifically between lesbians – were minimized to exaggerate the differences between women and men. Emphasis on the nurturing and caring nature of women – expressed to its logical end in the egalitarian bliss of lesbian relationships – removed us even further from any association with violence. Kirsta describes these attitudes as 'fatal flaws permitted to remain undetected deep inside the heart of feminism', and she goes on to point out the harm this ignorance has done:

> A wilful refusal of the modern women's movement throughout its twenty-five-year history to address, let alone attempt to understand, women's own acts of violence and desire for power over others, while succeeding in covering up the extent and nature of women's abuse and brutality towards other women, children, the elderly, male and lesbian partners and prison inmates, simultaneously devalues these victims and invalidates their suffering. Which amounts to just the sort of betrayal for which men have traditionally (though often justifiably) been blamed.[10]

While it is understandable that lesbians facing the dual oppression of sexism and homophobia might seek to present a united front, the setting up of rules and the policing of behaviour according to political correctness meant that problematic identities were suppressed, and consequently the chances for open debate depleted.

A large amount of lesbian theory, debate and action centred on the theme of violence against women – by men – as a manifestation of the unequal position of men and women in society. This movement was a great unifier: it gave women a cause with a tangible enemy, and the success of the shelter movement bears testament to this. It's ironic therefore, that these bastions of feminism and political correctness, many of which were set up by lesbians and most of which have lesbians on their staff, have been guilty of homophobia by exclusion.

Shelters offering help to survivors of domestic violence usually stress the availability of their services to *all* women (through commitments to equal opportunities and anti-discrimination), but in reality lesbians do not consistently receive a service equal to their heterosexual counterparts. Caroline McKinlay, of Women's Aid Federation England (WAFE), admits that there is still work to be done in this area:

> If you look at WAFE's constitutional position and statement of aims and principles, a very good service is offered to lesbians who want to use refuges and refuge services. However, that's just on paper. If you're actually talking about what services lesbians receive if they actually approach a Women's Aid group, then I would say that it varies depending on the awareness and abilities of individual Women's Aid groups.

Targeted outreach work is required to change lesbians' perceptions of domestic violence, while the services that exist for victims and survivors should appear inclusive rather than exclusive. But homophobia within the shelter movement *is* being tackled: a resolution was passed by WAFE in 1991 which recommended that all workers participate in sexuality-awareness training.

Concerns that have delayed progress to equal services include the fear that heterosexual women who have been encouraged to leave their husbands or male partners to escape an abusive situation may be reluctant to share communal accommodation with lesbians. Also, the safe space that a shelter traditionally provides may be compromised by knowledge of its location within the lesbian community. In small towns there is often a close relationship between women's support services and lesbian social life: lesbian socials are often held to raise funds for shelters.

If any refuge groups are not tackling these problematic areas it is merely because the issue has been given low priority. Heterosexual victims are given precedence as part of a cycle of homophobia which delays the shelter movement from opening its doors to lesbians. This is compounded by the belief that if a shelter openly offers its services to lesbians their funding will be cut, as has been the case with some projects in the USA: the Georgia Network Against Domestic Violence lost three-quarters of its funds – all its state funding – after adding sexual orientation to its anti-discrimination policy.[11] In spite of these threats many projects in the USA are now successfully providing services to battered lesbians within previously existing women's services, as well as specifically designed new projects.[12]

The movement to provide help to lesbian victims of domestic violence also faces another, more ideological, obstacle. Here, clear-cut issues of 'them' and 'us' do not apply, because the 'enemy' lurks within the assumed safety of the lesbian community, and it is from here that the problem must be tackled. Women's Aid are caught between efforts to tackle homophobia within refuges by presenting positive images of lesbians[13] and confronting the brutalities which some women face at the hands of their female partners.

An independent movement does exist to help the survivors and victims of lesbian domestic violence in Britain, but it's very small. At the time of writing, there were three or four support groups in existence, all of them London-based.

Pain and Strength has faced some specifically 'lesbian' obstacles to the expansion of its support and campaign work. For example, the difficulties involved in welcoming new members to the group:

> It's been difficult because when new women come in there's all the issues around safety again. We try to make sure that abusive women don't try and join. We meet in different places under different names so that nobody can see where we are. Our greatest fear is that someone will track down a woman they've been abusing. We always meet a new woman first before introducing her to the group, and talk through her experience. We have this screening thing where two of us meet women who want to join the group and we ask them straightforward questions. After a while you can see that they get tangled up trying to get out of the questions. We always find out.

Three years on, Pain and Strength have instituted a campaigning drive – distributing leaflets and holding workshops – in an attempt to raise the level of debate and awareness of lesbian domestic violence among women's support and shelter organizations, and within the lesbian community itself. They are optimistic about potential achievements at a grass-roots level, despite negative responses from some quarters of the lesbian community:

> At Hackney Pride I had people coming up to me and saying: 'What are you saying, that everybody should leave their relationships, or what?' People get

all hyped up and really defensive, it's quite scary. Before, I probably would have immediately said: 'Oh, she's probably abusive', but now I think maybe she's in an abusive relationship and she's getting oppressed herself. OK, they're bitching at me, but I feel quite good in the end because at least something happened; they might not come to a group or change, but maybe in a year's time.... Basically we want people to start talking about it. We want debate; so that people don't say: 'What are you talking about?' when we raise the subject, a really basic level of debate. I think from that would come: 'What can we do?'

It would be wrong to suggest that lesbians never receive any help from the established services. Pain and Strength report the example of one woman in their group for whom the efforts of Women's Aid secured the imposition of an injunction against her partner and subsequent rehousing. My intention is not to discourage women from seeking help from these organizations, but it is important to stress that this help depends upon the individual branch. Pain and Strength believe that Women's Aid's philosophy – on the causes of domestic violence and its relationship to inequality is too simplistic. They stress that discussions should be widened to include an understanding of the issues of power and control in abusive same-sex relationships:

I don't think it's that simple, because going by that argument, if you had a relationship between a black woman and a white woman, or a middle-class and a working-class woman, you'd expect the more privileged socially to be the abusive one, and that's not the case. You have to look far more broadly at what this society teaches us about power. I think in the end it's your choice how you use the power you have. Coming from a feminist background, I think that having that big man/woman division doesn't really work that easily any more. We have to look at the fact that these people make choices and we make choices.

Personally, the partner I was with came out as an incest survivor during our relationship, and she had a lot of physical problems. I was young and dynamic and sporty, I was quite successful and outgoing, and she had a hard time going through that. When you look from the outside, she had less power than me, was the incest survivor and the one who couldn't walk around that easily, but still in the relationship that was turned around.

In the 1980s I think at one point in my head I had all that bullshit that women are better than men; I don't think I really believed in it, but I was surrounded by so many who did that I was influenced. In the feminist, or lesbian-feminist movement, there were a lot of vibes around that. Through going through this relationship I have realized that women aren't any fucking better than anybody else. I think I would have learned that anyway. That's my personal political point of view, but I think it's really important to realize that just because we are lesbians doesn't mean there aren't abusers around us. The man/woman thing, or the stronger woman/weaker woman thing, isn't the way to explain power dynamics in a relationship.

In the USA the debate around lesbian domestic violence predates the debate in Britain by about ten years. The New York City Gay and Lesbian Anti-Violence Project's poster campaign, which promoted its services very publicly on every subway, is a testimony to the advances being made in the USA in terms of education and outreach work. Apparently, fears in New York of feeding homophobia have been overcome.

Naturally in a movement dealing with such emotionally charged issues, there's a certain amount of internal struggle, but it may be useful for British lesbians to learn from the heated debates published in the pages of the American lesbian and gay press in the late 1980s.

Among the themes that emerged was that of 'sleeping with the enemy': the dilemma of split loyalties over the treatment of abusive lesbians. The argument runs on two levels: how should abusers be treated socially within the lesbian community, and how should they be helped to change, if at all? When Beth Zemsky wrote an article in *Gay Community News* suggesting that batterers should not be ostracized, her words provoked impassioned responses. She argued that exiling batterers from the community would not put an end to lesbian battering, and pointed to the danger of creating 'good guy'/'bad guy' divisions. These false categories, she claimed, obscured the fact that *all* lesbians had the potential to be abusive:

> When we categorize women who are abusive as 'them', we make them 'other'. We transform them into objects. Objectification of any person or group replicates the abuse structure of the larger society that fosters sexism, racism, classism, anti-semitism, homophobia and interpersonal violence.[14]

In short, Zemsky was calling for an 'abuse-free' response from the lesbian community in its approach to domestic violence.

When anything approximating sympathy is expressed for the abusers there is bound to be a barrage of attacks, and indeed, reactions to Zemsky's article were wrathful.

Beth Leventhal emphasized the importance of safe spaces. She argued for the right of lesbians to fully participate in the community without threats of abuse and harassment, and she blamed the 'us' and 'them' split on the abusers themselves. The issue is, perhaps, one of balance – to avoid a rift in the community while ensuring the safety of women. Leventhal did concede, however, that exclusion is not the answer:

> Perhaps ostracism is not the best long-term approach to ending lesbian battering. I don't think any of us really know yet. There's not been enough safe space, both literal and figurative, for battered lesbians to get together, share our experiences and develop an analysis of lesbian battering and strategies to end it.[15]

At one extreme we can imagine pub doors carrying notices declaring 'No batterers', and on the other a lesbian social structure which apparently includes everyone, but in effect excludes the victims and survivors of abuse, too afraid to go out for fear of meeting their abuser. In this scenario the abuser apparently emerges with the privilege of unmaligned social status, while the meagre and unfair choice for the victim would seem to be 'get over it, or stay at home'. But if batterers *are* ostracized, the prospect of defining new categories of 'good' and 'bad' rings a tortured echo of divisiveness last heard during the 'No SM gear' battles of the 1980s.

The idea that abusive lesbians will change their behaviour either by 'learning their lesson' when their lover leaves, or through long-term voluntary counselling, is an appealing one. When we talk about ending lesbian abuse, the ability of the abusers to change must be taken into account. Unfortunately, throughout the history of the battered-women's movement the experience has been that very few male batterers reform. We tend to harbour a falsely optimistic notion that violent women are more redeemable than men because of ingrained ideals about the nature of women. Of course, it would be wrong to allow pessimism to create a self-fulfilling prophecy, but what real reason do we have to suppose that women have more potential to change than men? Real change will only come about once women's abusive behaviour is fully acknowledged and widely debated. The dilemma we face is how to focus on batterers without denying the needs of victims and survivors, needs which most people believe must be given priority.

Lesbian abusers do not constitute a clear-cut category of women. They do not wear a uniform. They exist across class, age, race, ability and location, but they all behave in a way that demands censure. To maintain the position of self-righteous judgement that has characterized the community to date is only exacerbating the destructive effects of abuse: lesbian batterers may taint our image of the ideal lesbian partnership, but they cannot be made 'non-lesbians' simply by virtue of a moral judgement made against them.

As we have seen, women can be violent in their relationships: every bit as violent as men. To be confronted with the fact of lesbians abusing other women is to recognize the abuse that you or your friend is suffering. It is to name your own abusive behaviour. In so doing, we make the first tentative steps required to leave a situation or seek help. The initiatives I have described in this chapter signify the beginning of a potentially seminal movement: there is much to be learned about the nature of power, oppression and violence and its relation to gender from the study of domestic violence in lesbian relationships.

Research in the USA suggests that the problem is widespread; as to its prevalence in this country, we can only begin to ascertain its scale once debate reflects the seriousness of the issue. Although I'm unable to offer statistics, my conviction about the size of the problem in Britain was backed up circumstantially during the writing of this book: friend after friend suggested lesbians I might talk to who had been victims of violence; previously I had known only one.

NOTES

1. Women's Aid Federation England, Statement of Aims and Principles, 1994.
2. Claire Renzetti, *Violent Betrayal*, CA Sage Publications, CA, 1992, p. 17. 'Coleman (1990) studied the prevalence and severity of violence amongst 90 lesbian couples who were recruited through advertisements, newsletters, fliers, contacts with psychotherapists, support group facilitators, and community organizations, and by snowballing. Based on participants responses to a 12-page questionnaire, Coleman characterized 42 couples (46.6%) as violent and 48 as non-violent. Loulan (1987) arrived at a considerably lower figure of 17% in her survey of 1,566 lesbians, whereas Lie, Schlitt, Bush, Montagne and Reyes (1991), in a survey of 169 lesbians, found that 73.4% reported experiencing acts defined as physically, sexually, or verbally/emotionally aggressive in at least one previous lesbian relationship and 26% reported experiencing such acts in their current relationships.'
3. Kerry Lobel (ed.) for US National Coalition against Domestic Violence Task Force, '*Naming the Violence: Speaking Out about Lesbian Battering*'. Seal Press, Seattle, 1986, p. 188.

4. 'The rationale most frequently cited was love for one's partner (67%) followed closely by, "I thought my partner would change" (64%).' Renzetti, *Violent Betrayal*, p. 78.
5. Lobel (ed.), *Naming the Violence*, p. 174.
6. Renzetti, *Violent Betrayal*, p. 60.
7. *Ibid.*, p. 100.
8. Alix Kirsta, *Deadlier Than The Male: Violence and Aggression in Women*. HarperCollins, London, 1994. Kirsta's research coincided with the first-ever conference on female violence, organized by the Forensic Psychiatry Department of St George's Hospital in London, 1991.
9. *Ibid.*, p. 9.
10. Kirsta, *Deadlier than the Male*, p. 5.
11. Katrin Snow, 'The violence at home' *The Advocate*, 6 February 1992.
12. Renzetti, *Violent Betrayal*, p. 122. 'In my survey of service providers, 96.4% of those who responded said they welcomed battered lesbians as clients, yet just 37% reported that they do outreach to lesbians.'
13. 'WA [Women's Aid] groups should actively encourage lesbian involvement and promote positive images of lesbians.' 1991 Annual Conference Resolution on Lesbians in Women's Aid.
14. Beth Zemsky, 'Lesbian battering: a challenge to our community', in *Gay Community News*, 4–10 December 1988.
15. *Gay Community News*, 15–21 January 1989.

RESOURCES

Pain and Strength
c/o Wesley House
4 Wild Court
London WC2B 4AU

Lesbian Survivors of Lesbian Violence
c/o West Hampstead Women's Centre
55 Hamstel Road
London
NW6 2AD

excuse **m**e **m**adam, **a**re **y**ou looking **f**or **a** **g**ood **t**ime?

excuse me madam, are you looking for a good time?

jackie james

This chapter was inspired by a new and unprecedented classification in the personal ads section of the popular gay press: 'Female Masseurs and Escorts'. This public manifestation of what is, in reality, woman-to-woman prostitution indicated either a new demand for such services or an increasing acceptance of them.

Several lesbians I know have questioned the existence of woman-to-woman prostitution, either because they'd never heard of any instance of it, or because they didn't realize that lesbians were willing to pay for sex. However, research assures me that there are women who make money on their backs, or fronts, or dangling from a leather swing, without ever having to set eyes on a penis.

The idea of lesbian prostitution is anathema to many lesbians, especially those who came out in the 1970s and 1980s. Symptomatic of postmodernism, and evolving from the increased gay visibility of recent years, it would appear to be yet another example of how women have achieved equality, but not in quite the way most feminists would have wanted. In fact, there is evidence of woman-to-woman prostitution going back as far as the eighteenth century.

At a time when the sex trade was burgeoning in fashionable London society, high-class brothels of many kinds existed. In her book *Whores in History*, Nicky Roberts relates a time, in the 1770s, when Mother Courage of Suffolk Street and Miss Frances Bradshaw of Bow Street were just two of the notorious madams catering for the lesbian trade.[1] She also names sisters Anne and Eleanor Redshawe, the discreet proprietors of the dramatically named 'House of Intrigue', in Westminster. Probably run along the same lines as any other brothel of that period, the only difference was the absence of men.

Most London brothels would provide obliging young men for society ladies, but far fewer establishments specialized in accommodating women whose tastes were less conventional. A shrewd minority of madams probably recognized that other, wealthier women, who shared their own sexual preference but could not obtain satisfaction as easily as men, would pay handsomely for discretion. Undoubtedly, some of the prostitutes themselves chose women as their sexual partners outside working hours. Think of Cleland's *Fanny Hill*, a novel which accurately depicted the eighteenth-century sex trade.[2] Fanny earned her living and her independence by enslaving men with her sexual technique. But her first sexual encounter was with an older woman, also a prostitute, who taught Fanny to recognize her own desire and give pleasure to herself and her partners. Then, as today, some women's personal circumstances or inhibitions curbed their ability to meet partners of the same sex or to live as they would have wanted. Isolation, even within a wide social circle, is just one reason why lesbians may appreciate the existence of prostitutes who cater for their needs today. My intention was to discover more about the women who placed the personal ads, why they were working as prostitutes and how they knew that there was a market of women who would pay them for sex.

Nickie is in her mid-twenties. She sells sex to other women. Our first meeting surprised me. Tall and slim with a shiny red-blonde bob, clear-skinned and slightly freckled, in her red wool blazer and Armani jeans she looked like a lesbian you might meet in a West End women's bar. Although I hadn't expected a peroxided chain-smoker with peeling white stilettos and bare legs, I must admit that my subconscious image was more along the lines of a sharp-talking, glam-butch babe in leather and lipstick.

Nickie immediately came across as an intelligent, self-assured woman, happy to discuss the politics of her unusual professional status. I was intrigued to know how she had entered the business. Surely such an articulate person, possessed with a friendly manner and smart appearance, would have no trouble holding down a good job? Listening to Nickie, however, I soon discovered how keen she was to dismiss the label of victim, and promote her lifestyle as a combination of easy money and a sense of vocation:

> I am not a victim of society. I didn't become a prostitute because I was desperate for money. People have asked me this many times, and I always say

that if I had no other option than having sex for money, then I would have done it with men, not women. Let's face it, it's not difficult to find men who'll pay for it. It's an easy way to make money if that's what you want. I got into it unintentionally, so I didn't intend to finance myself by having sex. As it goes, I discovered a kind of freedom I could never have as a forty-hour-week wage slave.

Nickie came to London from the provinces in her early twenties. Living alone and working in temporary jobs as a secretary, she concentrated on building a social life and making friends on the gay scene.

I was quite shy and had never been to a club or even a party on my own before, but I was desperate enough to force myself to go out and explore. I was shocked to find that the scene was so cliquey, and to see the same cliques in every pub and club I went to; it was disheartening to realize that I'd have to seek out people's acceptance even though I was one of them, and they knew it.

After a few one-night stands, which she had hoped would lead to lasting friendships of some kind, Nickie once again found herself plunged into the anonymous throng milling around the scene:

Most of the women ignored me, and the ones who didn't scared the living daylights out of me. Having one-night stands was unsatisfactory, but I never said no – at least I felt I was connecting with someone. All I really wanted was for someone to fall in love with me so I wouldn't have to go out on my own any more.

I noticed Jo because she was older than most of the crowd. She was about thirty-five, very attractive, a bit butch, although she was very well dressed. At first I thought she must be a tourist. She had a winter tan and was obviously wealthy.

She'd noticed me looking at her and she came over and introduced herself. I felt very *gauche* and thought of her as way out of my league, she was so sophisticated. I went home with her that night in a brand new Golf GTi convertible. She had a flat in a huge Georgian house in Bayswater; it was all worlds away from what I was used to. She ran a bath for me, lit by candles, and we drank chilled champagne. I was well and truly seduced!

According to Nickie, this was her first taste of being financially rewarded for sex, although nothing so distasteful as money ever changed hands. She was quickly moved in to Jo's flat, given her own bedroom and bathroom, and rent and bills were never mentioned. Her own high-street wardrobe was gradually phased out by gifts of more expensive and restrained garments. The relationship was harmonious, if imbalanced. Nickie was to all intents and purposes a kept woman, although she continued working as a temp.

Within a year, however, the relationship lost its emotional momentum. Jo travelled across Europe a great deal as her own business became more successful. She hinted that Nickie should feel free to see other women. Nickie now had a network of friends through Jo, but rarely took the initiative to contact them when Jo was away.

Then Jo asked Nickie to have dinner with a friend of hers, an American woman who was in London on business. They dined together in her hotel near Hyde Park, and Nickie was not surprised when they ended up in bed together. It seemed that Jo and her friend had made some kind of prior arrangement about Nickie.

The success of this meeting was the catalyst for Nickie's future. More and more often she found herself 'entertaining' her girlfriend's associates, and her co-operation did not go unrewarded: 'Every woman Jo arranged for me to go out with would buy me dinner and drinks at the very least. Often I met them more than once and they would give me presents, always expensive with an impressive label.' Did she not question these payments in kind, assuming that's what they were, I wondered? How did she feel about her girlfriend acting as a kind of pimp for her?

> Ha! I loved it! How many twenty-two-year-olds do you know who wear Chanel jackets and cashmere sweaters? Seriously, OK, I was naïve about it at first, but it didn't take long for me to see the pattern forming. The first time it happened I thought Jo wouldn't have known about it unless I told her – I still felt guilty about sleeping with one of her friends. I don't think I would have done it if I hadn't been drunk. When I told her about it she laughed and said she already knew. She said she knew a number of gay women who would be glad to take me out. I thought she must have me down as a proper little gold-digger, but she said that it was a good time for me to meet new women. So that's how it started. After a while I knew pretty well that I was being paid for sex and that Jo had instigated this – but I could have walked away. She wasn't some low-life pimp keeping me locked up with a serious drug habit, for God's sake! She wouldn't have forced me to do anything I didn't want to.

Now Jo has moved away to live permanently in another country, where she has developed a relationship with a woman older than herself. Nickie remains in the same Bayswater flat, paying only for the bills and council tax, supporting herself by temping and having sex with women for money. She has maintained contact with some of the women Jo introduced her to, and who still visit her for sex, although Nickie claims they are more like friends to her these days.

With the experience gained from her sole and unusual lesbian relationship, Nickie came to the conclusion that there were probably plenty more women living in, and passing through, London who would be glad of the company of a discreet, attractive female companion. She decided to advertise, and her instinct paid off: she began to receive calls from curious women wanting to know exactly what was on offer:

> I usually charge £50 for sex; that's about one to one and a half hours. I have no qualms about asking for that kind of money – if the customers couldn't afford it they wouldn't come to me, and most of them visit me more than once. I get a lot of calls from women who claim to be straight but want to experiment. They feel self-conscious about their sexual technique, or don't know how to achieve orgasms. Some women feel intimidated by me, but I try to help them relax by touching them gently and admiring their bodies. Most of my lesbian clients are closeted because of their work or family life. They are the ones who visit me most regularly, purely for sexual relief.

The financial element of woman-to-woman prostitution is at least as controversial as the sexual aspect. It is widely accepted that women use sex as a commodity with which to acquire money and empowerment, but what is more difficult to countenance is that women are now using their power and money to buy sex. It's the issue of power that poses the most problematic questions in the consideration of women buying sex from each other. Is this a triumphant subversion, born of a new freedom, or is it merely equality manifesting itself in the adoption, by some women, of another aspect of traditionally male behaviour?

Interpretations of woman-to-woman prostitution in terms of equality and power depend on whether prostitutes are viewed as victors or victims in the game. Victorian society leaders – in other words, men – reinforced the image of the prostitute as victim and outcast, in an attempt to dispel the theory that the prostitute had power and financial independence. The legal persecution of prostitutes during this period is well-documented.

In the 1970s and 1980s feminists worked against this idea of the prostitute as victim and criminal. Indeed, prostitutes themselves began to organize, establishing groups like The English Collective of Prostitutes.

Although male clients were the source of income for these working women, men's need for anonymous sex was, on the whole, regarded with contempt by feminists: if they weren't exploiting women, they were a pathetic species whose sexual weaknesses were exploited for money by female prostitutes.

We have long since overcome the idea that there is something wrong with women who want sex badly enough to go looking for it, but paying for it is another matter. Ruth is a lesbian in her early thirties who describes herself as a feminist and has paid a woman to have sex with her.

In 1994, Ruth had just come out of a particularly significant and long-standing relationship with another woman:

> Cathy and I bought a house together two years ago and I never, ever thought we'd be unhappy. We broke up last year. Cathy had been having an affair with a woman she worked with, and I found out about it. It ended our relationship, even though the affair was over. Cathy had been bored and dissatisfied, and my trust in her was completely shattered.
>
> I began to get over it, but the last thing I wanted to have to do was go out there again and meet women I didn't know – I couldn't face it. My friends were also Cathy's friends, and I found it difficult to spend time with them knowing that they had to divide their social lives between me and her.
>
> I decided to go to a prostitute because I missed having sex and I didn't want any emotional involvement. I suppose that's why men visit prostitutes. I'd seen women advertising in the gay papers, and I thought it would be the answer to my problems. I didn't tell anyone what I was planning to do – there was still a part of me that said there was something a little un-feminist about paying to have sex with another woman.
>
> I rang a woman who advertised as a lesbian escort in a gay magazine. Her name was Sarah, and I thought that sounded very safe and normal. That was my only criterion for making a choice from all the adverts I'd seen! I'd envisaged actually going out on a date with her, but when I rang she just told me what she charged, and what for, and asked if I wanted to make an appointment to see her that evening. I said yes, otherwise I would have lost my nerve and chickened out.
>
> I went across London to the address she'd given me. I was quaking with nerves, probably more so than if I'd been going out on a date. She told me she charged £100 for a two-hour session, so I stopped at the cashpoint on the way. When I did that, I started to feel more confident because it reminded me that this was my decision, I was in control. All I wanted was to have sex with another woman, without any of the emotional crap that goes with it.

That's what I talked to Sarah about for the first half-hour when I arrived at her flat. I was quite surprised at how detached she was – I suppose because I'm used to having intimate conversations with women, I'd expected the same from her. I also thought there would be empathy between us because we were both lesbians, but she was very passive and only asked me to tell her what I wanted.

I found it hard to relax at first, so she started by giving me a massage. I got turned on quite quickly and my embarrassment went straight out of the window. It had been so long since I'd felt remotely sexual, so it was a relief to know that I could respond to another woman – any woman. I didn't really mind that she didn't talk to me during sex. Then she asked me if I wanted to touch her, and I did. I couldn't tell whether she was faking her orgasm – I don't really want to think about it! What I found most strange was not talking and being close after the sex was over.

It makes me think of that joke: 'What does a lesbian bring along on her second date? Answer: her suitcases.' I couldn't have sex with a stranger without feeling as though there should be some emotional connection, even though I'd put cash in her hand. I just don't think women can have anonymous sex like men can, and yet we deride men for it all the time.

She was very sweet and concerned that I'd enjoyed myself, but she got straight out of bed, put a bathrobe on and made it quite clear that I wasn't expected to hang around. I paid her, and she thanked me and told me to call her again soon. I said I would, but I haven't yet. I think I probably will go back, because I'm still not going out much and I have no interest in starting another relationship. Plus, she was very good in bed and I still think about it more than I think about the last time I slept with my ex-girlfriend!

Did she, I asked, consider the political and moral aspects of paying another woman for sex?

Well, it does feel strange to pay for it, for a lot of reasons. I always think of other women as my equals, whether I know them or not, and this applies especially to lesbians. I like to think we're all in the same boat, and we've achieved a lot over the past decade. But when you pay a woman to do something for you, whether it's cleaning your house, cutting your hair or having sex, that immediately changes your roles; it makes you unequal.

This is true to some extent, but if a woman is establishing her financial independence by charging money for a service of some kind, does it necessarily follow that she is exploited or vulnerable? Surely women can empower themselves and other women in this way? Where prostitution is concerned, there are other factors to consider. The social stigma of prostitution is extremely powerful. I wanted to ask Nickie how this stigma had affected her, and in what way her life was different from those of other women.

This time I visited her at her home. When Nickie answered the door I noticed a marked change from the woman I had met only ten days before. She was dressed quite formally for eleven o'clock in the morning. She looked older and more glamorous than at our first meeting, but also far less pretty and approachable. There was an air of defensiveness about her, as though I had come to pass judgement on the way she lived.

As I expected, she was less keen to reflect upon the negative aspects of her lifestyle, but she did concede that sacrifices had been made on her part in exchange for financial reward:

When I was living with Jo I didn't find it demeaning to be kept, although I knew it made me unequal to her. Because she was older than me and more worldly, I had placed her on a pedestal anyway, and was too besotted to question her behaviour. When I look back I wish our relationship had been different in some respects. I would have liked to build a career for myself like she did. We could have been equals, two successful women instead of one successful woman and her girlfriend. If she really had wanted to give me my independence she could have just given me a job, I suppose. But I think she was planning on phasing me out.

I had become hooked on the luxuries. She offered me an instant change of lifestyle. As I say, I could have achieved that for myself over a period of time, but when something you've always wanted is handed to you on a plate it's not easy to question the reasons why. For my part I've sacrificed normal relationships and friendships. There is a lot of stigma attached to being a prostitute – I'm not ashamed of what I do because there are plenty of women happy to pay me for sex, but I don't like the idea of being judged for doing it by the moral majority. Lesbians nowadays are very open and blasé about their sexuality, but I'd bet you anything that most of them would be shocked if I told them about what I do.

I still work part-time, for quite a lot of different companies, I'm always on the move. When you're not a member of staff you don't really get to know people at work, and they don't get to know much about you. That's a perfect situation for me because I do need to have a steady income that I can rely on, but if I had a regular job with the same company it would make things rather awkward. It's impossible to befriend someone if you don't want them to know about a major part of your lifestyle.'

Nickie is an honest, articulate woman whose opinions make for interesting conversation. I suspect she suffers, more than she is prepared to admit, from leading a double existence. Since the end of her first relationship she has only ever had sex with strangers or with women who know her as a prostitute. While this appears to fulfil her requirements for a comfortable lifestyle, surely it leaves an emotional chasm which ought to be filled by friends and lovers?

> I do have friends, of course, I'm not a complete social outcast. It's just that I have to be careful about who I confide in. Very occasionally I might bump into one of my clients in a club, and if that happens then I don't acknowledge them unless they make it clear they want to speak to me. Confidentiality works both ways, you know.

For the time being, Nickie clearly plans to continue this existence. She is young and independent, and does not want for company. Would she, however, still hold the same priorities in five years' time?

She appears uncertain how to answer this question:

> I don't think it's a case of changing the way I feel about what I do. I don't feel guilty about earning money this way, and the law doesn't affect me. Prostitution is not a legitimate job but who's going to give me away? I couldn't and I wouldn't solicit on the streets – can you imagine a lesbian streetwalker! The women who pay me for sex don't really want to think about the sordid aspect of it; they treat it more like sex with a therapist than anything else.
>
> Perhaps my attitude to relationships will change. At the moment I don't want to be in a relationship, but one day I'm sure I'll meet a woman and fall in love. When that happens I'll know that the time has come to stop sleeping with other women altogether, so I will no longer be a prostitute. My situation isn't desperate. I know I can work in the real world, although I won't be as free or earning nearly as much money. I suppose I'll be happier about some aspects of it: living a 'straight' life and being more open about myself. Conforming will be quite a novelty for me.

Perhaps women like Nickie will become more commonplace. In another ten years it may be widely accepted that women pay for sex, and many of those women are likely to be lesbians.

Historically, the overwhelming prejudice has been against the prostitute herself. Kate Millett defines this attitude in her book, *The Prostitution Papers*:

Prostitution is regarded as humorous, inevitable or convenient. [The prostitute] is derided, castigated, to blame. For centuries, a tremendous moral and sociological confusion has surrounded the entire issue, a phenomenon one can only account for by considering the monumental sexual repression within our culture, its inability to recognise the prostitute as human.[3]

It may be that one reason why lesbian prostitution is relatively uncommon is that as a community we *do* see one another as human, that we don't observe others with the same detachment which a male viewpoint affords. First and foremost we can empathize with other women. But lesbians are capable of exploiting and abusing one another and there is little justification for assuming that lesbian prostitution takes place on a higher ethical plain than heterosexual prostitution.

Some people may see woman-to-woman prostitution as a breakthrough, enabling women to earn money in the sex industry without the involvement of men; others will always view prostitution as exploitation and a violation of basic human rights. It is, I acknowledge, probably an irresolvable argument. At least by studying the growth of woman-to-woman prostitution we may succeed in throwing some interesting light on the general discussion, especially on theories which see prostitution as a symptom of gender inequality.

NOTES

1. Nicky Roberts, *Whores in History*. Harper Collins, London, 1992, pp. 160–161.
2. John Cleland, *Fanny Hill* or *Memoirs of a Woman of Pleasure*. Penguin Classics, London, 1985. First Published 1748.
3. Kate Millet, *The Prostitution Papers*. Paladin, London, 1975, p.56.

getting **h**old

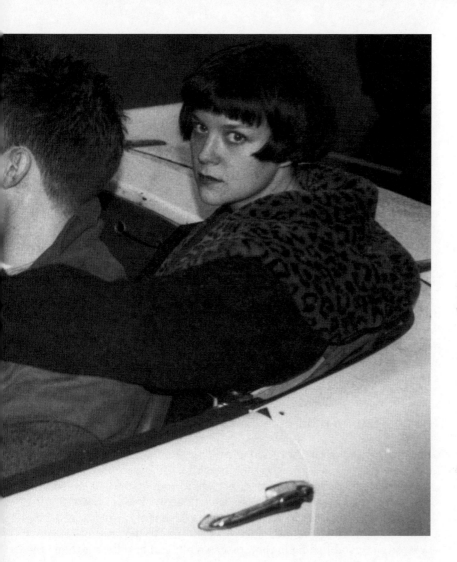

of **t**he **p**hallus

10 getting hold of the phallus

'post-lesbian' power negotiations

charlotte ashton

As a single, all-encompassing definition of what constitutes a lesbian becomes increasingly difficult, this chapter looks at how a new broader definition of lesbianism – post-lesbianism – is being negotiated in and through the mainstream media. Looking at how post-lesbianism has developed out of the turbulent histories of both the lesbian and feminist movements, I intend to show how the resulting new trend in dyke life – to ape the acts and aesthetic of straight women – is creating for lesbianism a new politics of closet heterosexuality.

The post-lesbian is born: lesbianism repackaged for the 1990s

Once upon a time in the good old days after Stonewall, but before Madonna, there was a thing called a lesbian. She wore dungarees and clumpy boots, had cropped hair, didn't wear make-up and never, NEVER slept with men because to do so was treason. Today, however, the situation is not so clear-cut. In the 1990s the advent of the bisexual boom, lesbian chic and the reclaimed queer has put paid to the separatist sisters of yesteryear, establishing in their place an altogether different thing: the post-lesbian. This is a woman who wouldn't be seen dead in dungarees or without her make-up, who has taught straight women to wear clumpy boots and approves of sleeping with men because it is the ultimate reversal of power, the ultimate plurality. Dogma and dungarees have been traded in for fashion and femme.

Marketed mainly in the mags under the brand name of 'lesbian chic', the defining characteristics of post-lesbianism are femininity and sexual flexibility. The post-lesbian – a.k.a. the designer dyke or lipstick lesbian –

is sexy, glamorous, in control and doesn't necessarily define herself by her sexuality. As Julie Burchill observed in *Elle*: 'A designer dyke isn't any old muff diver ... to be in with the invert crowd you must be beautiful, powerful, rich or famous. Being all four won't hurt you.'[1] Put like this it is no surprise that post-lesbianism can count Sandra Bernhard, Martina Navratilova and kd lang among its 'cliterati' because they are lesbians, but not as we know them.

Add to this leather 'n' lipstick veneer an ideological underpinning taken from the new Queer politics, and the post-lesbian cocktail becomes even more potent. By rejecting the traditional definition of sexuality as built around a simple hetero/homosexual divide for more accurate reflections of the cross-over complexities and diversities of desire, Queer has given lesbianism a new lease of life. It has allowed women to call themselves lesbians while recognizing that their desire may not always be as straightforward as simply fancying other women.

In its turn, this to-die-for combination of gorgeous-chicks-who-don't-mind-pricks has allowed the flagging media a new angle on a old, old story. As Louise Guinness asserts in an article for the *Evening Standard*: 'The traditional lad's view that lesbians all wear boiler suits, bovver boots and Number One haircuts – and that they only hang out with women because they're so ugly no right-thinking man would look at them – must now be laid to rest for ever.'[2] And she is not alone in this view. A string of headlines over the last couple of years, including the *Guardian's* 'Want to get ahead? Get a girlfriend',[3] *Harpers and Queen's* 'Sappho so good',[4] and the *Standard's* 'Are we ready for a lesbian take-over?'[5] show that not since the bra-burning 1970s or Greenham Common in the 1980s has lesbianism enjoyed the same level of exposure. The only difference is that this time lesbianism has been given the blessing of the mainstream.

Gay commentators might also reason that this shift in mainstream mentality has occurred because lesbianism provides an antidote to a sex-led consumer culture which has become at the same time terrified of AIDS and bored by heterosexuality. When straight sex is used to sell everything from cars to Kleenex, the media have turned their attention to cunt culture in their unceasing hunt for eminently marketable titillation.

As the ad men see it, the equation is obvious: if women and sex sell, then two women having sex will sell more. And they're right. As Joanna Briscoe comments in her article 'Lesbian hard sell': 'From Dolce & Gabbana to *Brookside*, the new chic media-friendly lesbians are experiencing the commercial clout of being "out".'[6] The proof? Penguin's anthology of lesbian fiction[7] walked off the shelves, as did the August 1993 edition of

Vanity Fair which featured kd lang getting in a lather with supermodel Cindy Crawford, not to mention countless boxes of Tampax promoted by an all-girl basketball team and Banana Republic jeans sealed with a lesbian kiss. All these and more were sold by using explicit all-girls-together imagery to create that important oxymoron of belonging and taboo. Add to these the sympathetic Beth Jordache character in Channel 4's *Brookside*, Binnie and Della from *EastEnders*, supermodel Claudia Schiffer's 'marriage' to Nadja Auermann on the catwalk, films like *Go Fish!* (1994) and *Even Cowgirls Get the Blues* (1993), and it would seem that the new-style lesbian has been marketed very effectively indeed.

GIRLS ON TOP: WOMEN EXPLORE THE BOUNDARIES OF SEXUALITY

Of course, any newsagent will confirm that femme-on-femme pornography has always been a bestseller. What's new is that now it is women reaching up to the top shelves, only they don't have to reach that far any more. When even *Cosmopolitan* devotes pages to sexual diversity, as they did in their October 1994 survey on attitudes to bisexuality, you just know the issue really has become mainstream. Certainly, it seems that the boundaries of female sexuality are starting to blur. A trip to the Wow Bar, London's trendy dyke club, where more women queue at wash-room mirrors than at the bar, shows that dykes are certainly getting straighter. On the other hand, even a cursory flick through any of Nancy Friday's fantasize-and-tell books, such as *My Secret Garden*, or *Women on Top*,[8] will confirm that straight women are increasingly willing to voice their Sapphic desires and experiences.

How far should we really bow down, to celebrate consumerism as the great leveller, as a force for sexual democracy in a world writhing against the rigours of PC backlash? While consumerism and the media are powerful institutions, the proliferation of lesbo-friendly imagery can only really be seen as a symptom and not a cause. As Joanna Briscoe points out: 'As with fashion, it's hard to see where the street and spin doctor meet. The new lesbian visibility is mainly due to grassroots gay and feminist politics.'[9]

FUCKING WITH THE PHALLUS: LESBIANS GRASP THE PENIS

The root of this transformation – from reviled die-hard dykes to post-lesbian gorgeous media dollies – actually comes from lesbians themselves. Away from the media spotlight, there has been a fundamental shift in lesbian theory and practice in relation to men and heterosexuality. Quite simply lesbians, collectively and individually, literally and metaphorically, are starting to fuck with that totem of masculine power – the phallus. While in the past this was the stuff of 1970s radical lesbian feminists' guilty secrets, it is now argued that such 'closet heterosexuality' is essential to lesbian advancement.

To explain this, we need to go back to the equation of the penis/phallus with masculine superiority and power, as propounded in Freud's psycho-analytical theories of 'penis envy'. Put simply, for Freud all human psycho-sexual development stems from the penis – boys have one, girls want one. As he describes it in an essay written in 1925: 'She makes her judgement in a flash. She has seen it [the penis] and knows that she is without it and wants to have it.'[10] By making the penis the linchpin of human sexuality in this way Freud created men as 'normal' and women as 'other', thereby relegating femininity to an eternal second best in relation to the supremacy of masculinity as symbolized by the phallus.

But the tables are turning. In a 1994 edition of Channel 4's polemical arts programme *Without Walls*, lesbian academic Camille Paglia argued that in order for lesbians to harness any real social or economic power they must begin to engage with the male power base as symbolized by the phallus. Lesbians argues Paglia, are inherently scared of men and male sexuality, and it is this failing that has led to the mentality and practice of separatism, ultimately emasculating the lesbian movement. In short, Paglia maintains that if lesbians begin to fuck with men, they begin to fuck with the world.

Alison, a thirty-year-old self-confessed post-lesbian, who has had relationships with both men and women, thinks that dykes have exaggerated the importance of the penis, and would agree with Paglia's theory:

> I think the problem with a lot of lesbians is that because they haven't ever really slept with men they take the penis far too seriously, they confuse it with the phallus. In my experience penises are not the big, permanently rock-hard, thrusting manifestations of male potency that your boyfriend would have you believe, but instead are rather unreliable little creatures that usually don't last long enough! The truth is that willies are actually nothing to do with the phallus in a literal sense.

The phallus is about power, being out there in the world. It is about masculinity, in the sense of being in control. It's nothing to do with whether you are a man or a woman. I think lesbians have overemphasized masculine power and take men on the level of myth, not reality. I also think that men are kidding themselves a lot of the time – they want the phallus as much as women. All that stuff about cars as phallic symbols is true. The good thing about defining yourself as a post-lesbian is that you can go out and explode the myth. You can fuck a few guys and realize that there's a lot of fuss about nothing. Dicks can be nice and everything, but they're definitely not the phallus. Once lesbians realize that, they can go out and really get hold of the phallus. Get hold of some real power.

CLOSET HETEROSEXUALITY DEFINED

Of course common sense might dictate that this strategy – taken together with the feminizing of lesbianism – ultimately undermines the meaning of lesbianism. A lesbian who sleeps with men simply becomes straight – doesn't she? Certainly, it was this definition of 'closet heterosexuality' that caused many rifts in the lesbian/feminist movement of the 1970s and early 1980s where 'lesbian' was a single, set identity.

But in the lesbian landscape of the 1990s, where it is possible to occupy a multiplicity of sexual identities – as the lesbian Lothario character of Daria in the film *Go Fish!* demonstrated when she defended herself in a hostile dyke court martial for sleeping with a man – *being a closet heterosexual now simply means a lesbian who sleeps with men*. And it is this definition that is central to an evolving discourse of post-lesbianism, because it allows lesbians to engage with the power base on the most fundamental level – lying down!

Going back to her roots: postmodernism as the parent of post-lesbianism

While it can be argued that post-lesbianism is the product of a grassroots response in the gay community to the complexities of 1990s consumer culture, it may also have its roots in a circular relationship to postmodernism – the postwar movement which dismantled the accepted notion that all words have a set single meaning. To the extent that postmodernism made lesbianism, lesbianism – with its rejection of previously accepted dichotomies – also created postmodernism. And like any other product of postmodernism, 'post-lesbian' is a term that has become separated from its meaning. By divorcing the identity of 'lesbian' from its previous set historical meaning of 'a woman who only has sex with other women', any meaning becomes possible.

In historical terms the impact of postmodernism on lesbianism could be described as 'Madonna meets Radclyffe Hall'. For the gloomy biological inverts of Hall's pre-postmodern essentialism, lesbians were simply born, not made. The wretched character of Stephen Gordon in Hall's seminal lesbian novel *The Well of Loneliness* embodied the tone of the time (as propounded by sexologist Havelock Ellis) as a lesbian born into the inescapable hell of involuntary sexual deviance. Over sixty years later when Madonna hit the stage, following the impact of postmodernism and the assertion that sexuality is socially not biologically constructed, it was possible to depict lesbians as being made, not born. Lesbianism became an identity like any other: flexible and fluid but, most importantly, removable. By wearing lesbianism like a Gaultier corset, Madonna urged a whole generation of women to consider their sexual practices as a 'pick 'n' mix' parade of pussies and pricks. Suddenly lesbianism wasn't so bad any more – if you didn't like it today, you could always be somebody different tomorrow. As drag queen Ru Paul says: 'We're born naked; the rest is drag!'

Following the impact of postmodernism and its burying of the biological lesbian, the battleground has shifted to the arena of iconography and aesthetics. To shed the old identity, lesbians have had to shed the old image. Gone is the traditional butch aesthetic; and in its place has come a whole generation of women for whom 'lesbian' is a tag that can be put on or taken off – it's incidental, not essential.

So it is no accident that post-lesbianism has chosen make-up as its warpaint. The defining characteristic of any backlash is its dance of difference to all that went before: just as lesbian feminists in the 1970s rejected the oppression of patriarchy through a refusal to accept male definitions of femininity, such as shaved legs and long hair, so post-lesbians have adopted traditional signifiers of femininity to distance themselves from the time-honoured butch look. With big hair, short skirts, lipstick and lycra, post-lesbians are holding up a mirror to the mainstream and reclaiming the components of 'passing' as totems of transgression. Or, put another way, as overheard at a chic London dyke club: 'This is the Revlon revolution, Sister!'

In so doing, post-lesbians are once and for all rejecting identity,

ideology and aesthetic. Most importantly, they are challenging the definition of a 'real' lesbian as a woman who is a lesbian to the exclusion of any
other identity, possessing a single unproblematic sexuality, underpinned
by a total rejection of the trappings of patriarchal power. And it is
ultimately this rejection, this feminized redefinition of lesbianism, that
has up-graded the movement's ticket from a going-nowhere third class to
a one-way, they-mean-business class. The following section looks at the
route this journey took.

Growing pains: lesbianism and feminism grow up and fall out

While lesbian activity has been visible in art and history for centuries, it
wasn't until the development of identity politics in the 1960s and 1970s
that 'lesbian' became generally recognized as a self-conscious sexual
identity, a choice rather than a biological perversion.

Initially, lesbianism was inextricably linked with a new wave of feminism
which, unlike the feminism of the suffragettes, sought to create a power-
base *separate* from that of men and patriarchy through such communities
as women-only households and collectives. From there it became the
ultimate weapon in the sex wars, in a sort of 'if I can't run the country I'm
taking my vagina home' mentality.

Ironically, during the 1960s and 1970s, as the full impact of identity
politics, the civil rights movement and various 'otherness' debates manifested themselves in a burgeoning range of subjectivities, from gay to
black to female, it seems lesbianism itself was allowed no such flexibility.
For as much as lesbianism had been fundamental in creating the plurality
of identity so central to postmodernism, now it wasn't joining in. In 1970s
lesbian-feminism, identity politics meant one identity – dyed-in-the-wool
dyke.

As gay commentator Simon Watney comments in the cultural theory
journal *Critical Quarterly*:

> The implication . . . is that there is indeed some available uniform 'truth' about
> all gay people, a 'truth' which in practice has an unfortunate tendency to
> censor out the whole question of our actual diversity as a social constituency,
> in favour of a 'politically correct' line which does not look very favourably on
> drag queens for example, or SM dykes. Thus, while gay political theory was
> trying to take on board the wider question of the overall organization of
> sexual identities and power relations, gay culture tended to lapse back into a

'minoritist' approach which had (and has) strong continuities with the older homosexual culture and its problematic notion of 'gay sensibility'.[11]

Ellen, a forty-seven-year-old lesbian who was active in the lesbian-feminist movement in the 1970s supports this:

> I wouldn't say I had an unhappy marriage, but I did get married quite young and very soon realized that it wasn't what I wanted. I did love my husband and kids, but I'd always been quite bright and I think I just got bored by it all. It was about that time that feminism started to take hold in this country and a consciousness-raising group was set up in my area. I went along not really knowing what to expect. You see, I came from a very working-class background and this sort of thing seemed very ... well, middle class.
>
> At first there was a huge feeling of relief going there week after week and talking about things, about my frustrations with life, which I didn't realise so many women shared. It sounds corny now, but I really was finding myself. I got more and more involved with the group and, yes you guessed it, eventually my marriage broke up. My finding feminism was a part, but not all of it by any means.
>
> Quite soon after that I got involved with a woman at the group. She was a very high-profile lesbian in the feminist movement in my area at the time and there was lot of pressure on me to 'come out' in a big way. Looking back I think I let her pressurize me into it, because I didn't want to lose what I had. Not just her. The group, feminism. It was my life now. What she or anybody else in the group never knew was that I did continue to sleep with men. I couldn't tell them. I just couldn't. It would have been taken as treachery. But you see what I wanted was to be able to do what I wanted, sleep with who I wanted and not feel guilty. Experiment and make my own choices. It seemed ironic that my marriage had split up because I felt tied down and now lesbianism was making me feel the same.
>
> I'm glad I did what I did. I stopped feeling guilty eventually and realized that it's nobody else's business really. In the end I just got on with it. I've been with my partner now for twelve years and I call myself a lesbian, though I do still occasionally sleep with men.

THE SISTERS GO THEIR SEPARATE WAYS

This failure of lesbian feminism to side-step didacticism and address the plurality of women's being and desire made an impact in two distinct but interconnected ways. On the one hand, it allowed the attractions of the less didactic mainstream to come between the former bed-mates of lesbianism and feminism. On the other, it created the casualties of the sex wars, those women who identified as lesbians but continued to desire men, the sidelined lesbians who were to become the vanguard party of the new post-lesbianism.

In many ways post-lesbianism, with its own resistance to the 'necessary fiction' of a single, manifest lesbian identity, has more in common with post-feminism and its rejection of a single dominant ideology of feminism than with 'real' lesbianism. Certainly both post-feminism and post-lesbianism are the products of the lesbian/feminist internal struggle, which ultimately allows the mainstream to barter extremism for access simply by offering – ironically – greater freedom of sexual expression outside of the lesbian/feminist communities. This still has resonance with today's young lesbians. Jessica is a twenty-four-year-old lesbian who first became aware of her sexuality when she was fifteen:

> I remember being at school and having a really massive crush on my best friend. I didn't really click at first, but then one day, after we'd been on holiday together and I'd spent the whole of the last night in a strop because she'd got off with this boy, I thought, 'Oh my God! I'm a lesbian.' But it was about the time that Greenham Common was in the news, and I used to look at all these women on telly and think, I can't be a lesbian. I'm not like them. I wasn't bothered about saving the world or going on marches or any of that. And I definitely didn't want to cut my hair off or stop wearing make-up. No way! I did go to a couple of clubs – not real clubs – in my area, but they were the same. Too much arguing about men and not enough enjoying yourself.
>
> So after that I went out with boys for a long time, even though I knew I preferred girls really. I decided to start with girls again a couple of years ago after I met a woman at a party. She was really feminine. Really gorgeous. All the men were trying to chat her up, but she came home with me! I really liked her because she wasn't into all that feminist stuff like a lot of them. We had lots in common. We'd go out shopping together and go out to clubs. I don't think that feminism means anything really to young dykes now. I know it was probably important then, but I don't think it is so much now. I mean, I don't let anybody push me around or anything, or get on my case about being gay, but that's because I don't think it's any of their business. I've got my girlfriend, so I'm happy.

FALLING 'OUT': THE SPLITTING OF LESBIANISM AND FEMINISM

Feminism was separated from its initial association with lesbianism in order to create and negotiate the acceptable face of post-feminism into the mainstream. This throws up an interesting paradigm for what's currently happening with post-lesbianism. In both cases, what has been left behind is the unacceptable face of female autonomy, be it social, political, sexual or simply aesthetic. Put another way, it was a simple case of 'let's-keep-the-pretty-ones-and-dump-the-dogs'.

By the late 1970s the feminist movement had made such an impact, socially, politically and legislatively, it was clear that a broad-based philosophy of women's equality was here to stay. Women had fought for equal access to the power base and it was beginning to pay off, for example, in the passing of legislation such as the Equal Pay Act 1970, the Sex Discrimination Act 1975 and the Sexual Offences (Amendment) Act 1976. The problem now was how to bring 'them' – women – back into the mainstream from the extremes of feminism and lesbianism.

As the Italian Marxist Antonio Gramsci (1891–1937) sought to prove in his work *The Prison Notebooks* (published from 1948), in modern society, no single dominant ideology is forced into place by the ruling class: instead the hegemonic or dominant group negotiates power by consent and persuasion. In other words, the hegemonic group remains dominant by forming consenting alliances with other groups, after taking into account their interests and compromising on certain shifts in power: for example, bosses who allow their workers to set up unions to negotiate better pay or working conditions.

Applied to feminism, this means that the hegemonic group – men – in order to remain broadly dominant against the threat of lesbian/feminist revolution, had to find a way of forming an alliance with women by compromising on certain of their demands for equality. Put simply, how could men draw women into a persuasive new alliance with the mainstream?

As with the creation of post-lesbianism, the media had their part to play in setting out and defining what was on the negotiating table – just where concessions could and couldn't be made. This influence manifested itself in the traditionally female-readership, middle-market tabloids of the 1980s, where a discourse around a new kind of feminism began to emerge: a 'something old, something new, something borrowed, something blue' feminism.

The 'old' was the political underpinning of 1970s feminism, the basic demands for equality of pay and access. The 'new' was that this should not be achieved at the cost of femininity or heterosexuality – an implicit recognition that women, after all, can and do like cocks (as writer Naomi Wolf maintained at a feminism seminar organized by the *Sunday Times* in 1993, in the old days women used to say the penis was the enemy; these days they go home at night and the penis is clearly their friend). The 'borrowed' involved a growing concept of phallic women, that women can have 'cocks' too – as Madonna asserted memorably in her controversial book, *Sex*: 'I don't need a dick between my legs because I have one in my brain.' And the 'blue' manifested itself in the burgeoning backlash of 1980s Conservatism, where Margaret and Madonna performed a duet to prove that it was Material Girls, not the radical feminists, who got the real power.

LOOKING GOOD: THE FEMINIZING OF FEMINISM

Post-feminist woman had arrived and she looked great. Powerful, strong, ambitious, achieving, successful and highly feminine. While Selina Scott, the Princess of Wales and Margaret Thatcher, to name but a few, appeared on the pages of the *Daily Mail* as fine examples of the new-found feminism, another feminist fairy story was being told on different pages: the sad Sapphic sisters left behind to stoke the fires at Greenham.

Week after week pages were devoted to pictures of crop-haired, crazed women living in benders, while accompanying text written from the moral high ground told tales of lesbians living in mud with children begat with the aid of turkey-basters. Worse still, there were stories of women who had been persuaded by the extremes of feminism to leave their homes and husbands for a life of lesbian agitation at the Berkshire airbase. To the mass-market middle ground this was feminism gone mad, and one *Daily Mail* headline summed up popular opinion: 'The non-women of Greenham Common'.

Effectively, what had gone on between the pages of the middle-market tabloid press was a Gramsci-type negotiation between the male power base and women, which, while making concessions to women's demands, still allowed men to keep the upper hand. Under this 'deal' women got to keep the 'good' parts of feminism, like women's *equality*, which could still operate in the mainstream supported by traditional notions of femininity. Against this, the male hegemony could throw away the 'bad' parts, such as the sexual and social *autonomy* that was represented by the women of Greenham.

The juxtaposition of these 'good' and 'bad' faces of feminism was potent and persuasive, and the war of attrition escalated. No longer was the fight just between radical feminists and 'real' lesbians. It involved all women, as brought together in a new coalition of 'good' post-feminism, in a struggle against lesbians. The following passage taken from American *Cosmopolitan*'s twenty-page special on 'Feminism now' demonstrates the divide as only *Cosmo* can:

> If you never thought of yourself as a feminist, it's time you thought again. It's not about dungarees and hating men. Feminism is ... Relevant. Positive. Powerful. Sexy. Strong. ... Cosmo has always represented a specific kind of feminism: while eager and willing to work our tails off for every facet of equality for women, we also love men. (What else can we do – they're the only other sex we have!) Yes, some men – even those we are crazy about – can have simply awful attitudes about women and have to be made to understand and comply with our feminist needs. If they can't/won't we may have to find another man. The challenge then is to make sure, while adoring him, that he participates in our feminist views. Repeat: Loving sex and certain worthy men doesn't mean you can't be a feminist.[12]

The fact that this was written in May 1994 and not May 1982 shows how the spectre of that evil lesbian-feminist separatism looms large – even today.

PENILE DEMENTIA SETS IN: SM BECOMES CENTRAL TO THE CREATION OF POST-LESBIANISM

So, while the post-feminists settled into the 1980s with some serious power-dressing, great jobs in the City, a New Man and two adorable children, lesbianism was left out in the cold, detached from the power base of feminism and the bedrock support of 'ordinary' women. A victim of its own didacticism, which would not countenance the proliferation of 'otherness' debates, lesbians spent an unhappy decade bickering amongst themselves about what was 'allowed' and what was not. The argument went something like this: vanilla was, SM wasn't; monogamy was, promiscuity wasn't; sex with 'wimmin' was, sex with men wasn't; Crazy Colour was, lippy wasn't. As lesbianism began less and less to describe women's actual lives, prescribing instead a 'thou shalt not' litany of inverted sexual repression, the seeds of a more flexible, more sympathetic, more plural post-lesbianism began to grow, just as post-feminism had grown before it.

Central to this in-fighting was the SM debate, rejected wholesale by essentialist lesbians as based in phallocentric codes of misogyny, dominance, submission and violence. Being an SM dyke was definitely not being a 'real' lesbian, and for a time in the mid-1980s the vanilla lesbian community buzzed with excited stories of projectors being overturned at butch/femme sex seminars, the boycotting of cinemas that dared to show clips from so-called SM films, and heated demos outside the London Lesbian and Gay Centre protesting against SM nights.

Resist SM as it might, the vanilla lesbian movement could not stop its ideological penetrations into the ranks. For the first time lesbians were being offered plurality of desire and identification within the framework of lesbianism itself: something gay men and post-feminists had enjoyed for a long time.

TAKING IT LYING DOWN: SM GIVES WOMEN WILLIES

Dildos, strap-ons, butt-plugs, pornography and vibrators. These were a few of their favourite things. Through the reclaiming of the phallus and, by implication, fucking, SM broke the spell of vanilla lesbian essentialism just by giving women willies – literally and metaphorically – and in so doing offering them the plurality of identification missing from other previous manifestations of lesbianism. As Queer has taken in and expanded on this, the plurality of those identifications has become even greater. To quote Simon Watney again:

> It [Queer culture] points to the continuities of pleasure and identity *across* the barriers of both gender and sexual object choice. This is, for example, the 'queerness' of dykes who fist-fuck gay men and vice versa, or of the heterosexual woman who shares with some gay men a primary sexual identity as a 'bottom', or a gay man and a straight man who share a primary interest in football.[13]

In real terms this meant that lesbians were at last able to experience themselves as a multiplicity of identities capable of encompassing and enjoying the desire associated with both homosexual and heterosexual sex. Whether it was fact or fantasy didn't matter; dykes had got hold of the phallus and they could do what they wanted with it, as Joan Nestle describes in her story 'The Three' taken from her book, *Restricted Country*:

The butch rose above the other two women and fastened on her leather harness, the black straps fitting smoothly over her taut belly and cheeks. She kneeled there with her cock jutting out, and the older woman rose to her, taking the cock between her nipple-hardened breasts. Then, with a smile, she pushed the butch back on the pillows and took her cock into her mouth. She licked it, swallowed it, and told the butch what a wonderful cock she had and how much she wanted it.[14]

Postmodernism had finally met lesbianism, and the key to a discourse of post-lesbianism had been turned. Inevitably, more recently, as Queer and SM have fed off each other, the boundaries of what it is to be a lesbian have stretched further still. In these post-lesbian days it is possible to be a phallic lesbian, a lesbian boy, a dyke daddy, a lipstick lesbian, designer dyke or any other kind of lesbian, just so long as you say you are. Practice and gender don't mean a thing any more. It's what you identify with that's important, not what you are.

Catherine is a thirty-two-year-old lesbian who feels that relaxed ideas about sex and sexual identity have allowed her to experiment within her own relationships:

I think that, like a lot of women who grew up informed by the lesbian feminism of the late 1980s, that I resisted things like sex toys for a long time because I had been taught to think of them as being bad. They had become associated with SM and fucking, and the prevailing ethos in the movement at the time was that real lesbians had no desire for fucking in any way, shape or form. I suppose I knew that didn't describe me really, as I had fantasized about fucking, being fucked, watching fucking – you name it – from being pretty young. I knew that it was possible to have those desires and still be a lesbian. It wasn't problematic for me.

Having said that, it took me a long time to actually get around to doing it with a strap-on. Partly I think that was because I was hesitant about raising it with partners in case they didn't think I was a real lesbian either. But when I did get round to it – it was amazing. Totally mind-blowing. First off, my girlfriend fucked me. I did the whole bit, sexy underwear, rolling on the Durex, guiding it into my cunt for her, generally giving myself up in the most operatic Victorian way possible! I felt like the biggest het fem out. The next time we did it I fucked her – doggie style. Whereas with being fucked I half knew what I'd feel because I have slept with men, this time around I didn't have a clue what it would feel like. It was totally different. An absolute shift of position of power. Also I didn't let her do anything. I put on the condom again.

I put it into her, and I dictated the speed and depth of the fucking. I felt totally in control, like I was taking her.

It's crass I know, but I suppose I felt like a man must feel when he fucks someone. I don't know, how can you know without actually being a man? But I do know it felt really powerful in a way that I'd never felt before. I don't feel that using a strap-on tells any 'truth' about you. I don't think I always secretly wanted to be man. Or a heterosexual woman for that matter. I just like being able to experience sex from lots of different viewpoints. I think that even if I went out with a man next, I'd still want to use it to fuck him. I'd be really interested to know what that feels like! But for the time being with my girlfriend, it goes through phases. Sometimes we don't use it for ages. It's just nice to know it's there when you want it.

Pandora opens her box: the high price of post-lesbianism

Post-lesbianism as featured in newspapers, books, on TV and in the cinema in this all-new, all-singing, all-dancing, all-fucking, all-phallic leather 'n' lipstick form has given lesbianism an unprecedentedly positive profile in the mainstream. But ultimately, when she has stepped out of her heels, washed off her make-up and packed up her sex toys, even the most ardent post-lesbian must find herself asking if it will endure as an identity, and if so, at what price?

The component parts of post-lesbianism have undoubtedly given lesbians a new freedom of movement and expression. A reclaimed closet heterosexuality has allowed lesbians to experiment with politically incorrect sex practices, including penetration, while developing an aesthetic that is not afraid to connote the feminine flip-side of the traditional butch in a parody of 'passing', the problem with holding a mirror up to the mainstream in this way is that usually the mainstream fails to appreciate the irony. It simply sees itself – its own codes, its own concepts, its own kind.

The reason for post-lesbianism's current popularity with the mainstream media lies in the fact that it doesn't *look* or *act* any differently from other forms of accepted femininity. For as long as men can look at post-lesbians and see sexy women they want to fuck, and who indeed might even fuck them back, they will not consider that they have been forced to concede any ground. Very possibly this is because they *haven't* been forced to concede any ground. This is a situation acknowledged by Joanna Briscoe in her *Sunday Times* article 'Lipstick on her collar':

> In part, of course, lesbians have been let out of the closet by men. Men are sexually intrigued by the idea of women together, and nothing is too naughty if it can be translated into ads, pop stars or blockbusters.[15]

Some commentators reason this is no bad thing: that any acceptance is better than no acceptance; that it is better to be today's media babes than yesterday's weirdos; that a 'diluted' identity manifest in the mainstream is more valuable than a 'pure' identity agitating from the fringes.

There's no question that as a notion this is seductive, that the concept of a boundary that has been pushed never to regain its former shape is tempting. The 'problem' with post-lesbianism is that now it goes beyond seduction, temptation and concept into the realms of fact. The reality of post-lesbianism is now manifest, in both its history and the here and now. As I have described in this chapter, its existence is not the point at issue; more crucially, what is questionable is the validity of post-lesbianism as a representation and a way forward for lesbianism. For a movement which fewer than twenty years ago drew its lifeblood from difference, from its active politics of separatism, is what we are witnessing now a coming of age or is post-lesbianism simply an appropriated after-image of a lesbianism that is everywhere but nowhere, dominant but dead?

The obvious question to ask, of course, is just how dominant this notion of post-lesbianism is anyway; how much have the boundaries been moved for good? Sure, it's prominent in the media right now, but does it reflect the real world? This is not to say that post-lesbianism shouldn't exist or is a bad ideal. It's not. It certainly represents more accurately than separatism ever did the complexities of desire and identification as experienced by lesbians in the 1990s, even if they are not allowed to voice them publicly. But perhaps it is a case of too much post-lesbianism too soon. It's fine to aspire to a majority of minorities within a movement, as long as some of the minorities – the less media-friendly ones – don't get left behind in the dash to the next photo-shoot.

There is much to be said for a strategy – any strategy – that gains ground for lesbians in the mainstream. We just have to be careful that, as post-lesbians, we don't start believing our own press and think we've arrived when some of us haven't even set off.

NOTES

1. Julie Burchill, 'Some girls do ... ', *Elle*, August 1987.
2. Louise Guinness, 'The love that has learned to laugh', *Evening Standard*, 6 July 1993.
3. *Guardian*, 8 July 1993.
4. *Harpers and Queen*, June 1994.
5. *Evening Standard*, 24 February 1993.
6. Joanna Briscoe, 'Lesbian hard sell', *Elle*, May 1994.
7. Margaret Reynolds (ed.), *Penguin Book of Lesbian Short Stories*. Penguin, Harmondsworth, 1993.
8. Nancy Friday, *My Secret Garden*. Virago, London, 1975; *Women on Top*. Hutchinson, London, 1991.
9. Briscoe, *Elle*.
10. Sigmund Freud, 'Some physical consequences of the anatomical distinction between the sexes', 1925.
11. Simon Watney, quoted in Isaac Julien and Jon Savage, 'Critically queer'. *Critical Quarterly*, vol. 36, no. 1, March 1994.
12. 'Feminism now', *Cosmopolitan* (New York), May 1994.
13. Julien and Savage, 'Critically queer'.
14. Joan Nestle, *A Restricted Country*. Sheba, London, 1987, p. 46.
15. Joanna Briscoe, 'Lipstick on her collar', *Sunday Times*, 5 June 1994.

References

Nancy Friday, *My Secret Garden*. Virago, London, 1975.
Nancy Friday, *Women on Top*. Hutchinson, London, 1991.
Isaac Julien and Jon Savage, 'Critically queer', *Critical Quarterly*, vol. 36, no. 1.
Joan Nestle, *A Restricted Country*. Sheba, London, 1987.
Margaret Reynolds (ed.), *Penguin Book of Lesbian Short Stories*. Penguin, Harmondsworth, 1993.
Jeffrey Weeks, *Sex, Politics and Society*. Longman, Harlow, 1981.

no man's land

11

no man's land

lesbian separatism revisited

gerry doyle

Sappho was a right-on woman, so they say. Or was she? The popular lesbian imagination conjures up a sixth-century Mediterranean idyll in which Sappho recites her poetry surrounded by infatuated female scholars. Scantily clad in silken robes and seated under a brilliant azure sky among the olive groves, her admirers gaze lovingly at their heroine. All is bathed in a rosy Sapphic glow. When the muse takes her, Sappho calls on the goddess of love, Aphrodite, to intercede to help her win a new beloved.

In every way this is the perfect female community. All things male seem superfluous. Sappho, lauded for centuries as the world's greatest woman poet, did, after all, give her name to the love that dare not speak its name – Sapphism – and Lesbos, her Greek island home, gave us the name lesbian. But even the Sapphic ideal leaves a lot to be desired, and it is perhaps harder than we think to create alternative lifestyles. Sappho herself was exiled from her beloved Lesbos, and all but a few of her poems have been lost or burned over the centuries by fanatical Christians. And the plot ends with a final twist: legend has it that Sappho finally jumped off a cliff because of unrequited love for a man!

It is politics rather than romance, however, that has inspired attempts by lesbian feminists to set up women-only communities. Separatism blossomed in the exciting early years of the women's liberation movement. Conference after conference saw women taking the platform to expound the latest separatist theories. Revolutionary feminists and radical feminists hammered home their opposing points of view at plenary after plenary around the country. Many women – particularly in the 1970s and 1980s – were keen to experiment with alternative communities in a bid to bond more powerfully with other women and to expurgate 'maleness' from their minds and patterns of behaviour. By closing the door to men they opened up a world of new possibilities for themselves. Family ties were cut as women shunned brothers and fathers. Gay male friends were dropped. Anything written or produced by men was boycotted. In the 1990s small pockets of lesbian feminists are still flying the separatist flag, and living in hope of a revival of the movement.

But lesbian-feminist separatists of all persuasions have found the dominant male culture harder to shake off than they first anticipated. Even as a new breed of feminist sci-fi writers penned volumes of idealistic Utopian fiction, such as *The Wanderground*[1] and *The Female Man*[2], depicting women-only worlds, the first real-life experiments were already beginning to fail. The optimistic notion that collective living with women would always be a positive, life-enhancing experience took a battering as the personal became intensely political. Hard-liners laid down the law, and clashes between warring factions led to the disintegration of communities and relationships. Divisions opened up between black and white women over the need to retain ties with their brothers in the fight against racism.

It was not all bad, of course; and in reminiscing about their experiences many separatists and ex-separatists remember the thrill of women setting their own lifestyle agendas for the first time, and the opportunities to develop skills and relationships they might otherwise not have had.

The trivialization of the lesbian separatist lifestyle by outside forces also undermined its status as a serious political choice. In the media, lesbian separatists were caricatured as man-hating, aggressive women with no sense of humour – the very antithesis of 'lesbian chic', which was to follow years later with the blessing of the voyeuristic press. But lesbian separatists did have their own special brand of humour, which at times confirmed some of the stereotypes. Question: 'How many men does it take to tile a bathroom?' Answer: 'Depends how thinly you slice them.' Question: 'What's good about six men lying on the sea bed.' Answer: 'It's a start'. Behind the perceived hostility to men was a response to male violence in all its forms – sexploitation, murder and rape. Women's horror at the crimes of the Yorkshire Ripper, and the thousands of other instances of male brutality towards women, makes it easier to understand why women might opt for a life completely apart from men.

In this chapter, women share painful and impassioned memories for the first time. The debate over boy babies that split the lesbian-feminist community in Britain is tackled again by both current and former separatists. Life in long-forgotten but surviving women's communities is also discussed. I shall also consider the new, thriving, women-only communities, or women's lands, that have sprung up around the world, in particular, the USA, such as Pagoda in Florida, which boasts signs that prohibit the entry of men.

What caused separatism to ignite the passions of a whole community of lesbian feminists, and how did it become such a strong force to be reckoned with, only to fade into the background?

To answer these questions we must first appreciate the political, anti-establishment atmosphere that was prevalent in the late 1960s and early 1970s. The status quo was being challenged in almost every conceivable way. The fight was on for both women's and gay rights. It was an intoxicating climate in which almost anything could happen. Women were having a love affair with feminist politics. Pam Isherwood, from Hackney in London, found the whole experience exhilarating as well as liberating: 'It was completely seductive – that sense that what you put in was important. That sense of tons and tons of women being everywhere was so affirming. There wasn't the level of trashing there is now. There was a sense of community.' Jackie Forster, co-founder of the lesbian-feminist magazine, *Sappho*, recalls the atmosphere at women's conferences and political meetings: 'Someone said once it was like being in love. There was a wonderful electricity about it. You were not shy about going up to a woman you did not know. It was terrific!' Angela, now forty-four, remembers similar feelings of excitement after her first taste of new feminist politics:

> I loved the passion but I hated the tension and the arguments. Women talked ideas and theory and politics. I wanted to know what they were talking about. There was quite a feminist explosion. I was very involved in Earlham Street London Women's Centre, reading books and discussing lots of things. There was also the weekly women's newsletter.

The real 'big bang' occurred when women left the Gay Liberation Front and the Campaign for Homosexual Equality (CHE) *en masse*, dissatisfied with the men they had tried to work with. Jackie Forster recalls the bitterness surrounding the split:

> I was with the Gay Liberation Front and I was part of the women's breakaway group. We got fed up. A lot of us were feminists and learning about feminism, and the guys were not listening to what we were saying. It was always their problems that mattered, not ours.

The women were saying cottaging and cruising are issues for you men, but we have a hard time in discrimination in jobs and custody cases. The poison at one CHE conference was something else. The women were asking why we were all sitting in rows like a classroom. Why weren't we in a circle? What are all these points of order at meetings? Why weren't we all talking about our life experiences?

On the other side, the men were saying things like: 'You shouldn't be at this conference, you are not gay, you are women.' Some were totally misogynous. But I have never seen so many men crying as when we left CHE. We said, 'Sorry but you caused it'.

A leading figure in the initial stages of the women's movement, Jackie did not, however, opt for the separatist lifestyle herself. Instead, she campaigned extensively with men – though always with a feminist perspective – and she helped organize the women's liberation marches in 1971 and 1972:

I am a lesbian working within the system to overthrow it rather than waving banners outside it. I will use straight men and legislators. When the lesbian archive started off there was a big row about having no SM stuff and no pornography. I will never forget the verbal screaming! When I actually met lesbian separatists they scared me to death.

Other lesbian feminists became involved in the whole debate about male violence and, after the Yorkshire Ripper case, there was a huge explosion of women's activity in the North-East. At the time Dusty Rhodes was living in Leeds. A member of the organization Women Against Violence Against Women, she campaigned actively against male aggression. She still defines herself as a separatist:

Half a million signatures on petitions in a month was not unusual. You could do that then. Women had been terrorized, and women everywhere generally sympathized a lot with the feminist campaign against male violence. We held Reclaim the Night marches and supported direct action. There was three or four million pounds' worth of damage done to sex shops partially destroyed in fire-bomb arson attacks. We gave our support to one woman who was arrested on suspicion of being involved.

Politically it was very active. We supported many campaigns around women who had been murdered, calling for changes in the importuning law, and there was a lot of campaigning round the licensing of sex shops.

Dusty embraced the separatist principle of women's ability to live together and look after each other:

> It's important to visualize a world without male violence. I have a dream! Let's split the world in two halves. A couple of continents could be given to all these women who want to live on their own. I don't have any expectation that men can change their behaviour because of the way they are in the world. Looking to education to achieve this is a pile of shite. What I am talking about is that men are violent and oppressive.

Separatist living experiments

Women were getting angrier and angrier with men as the years progressed. Feminism was obviously about changing the world, but many women were beginning to realize that drastic measures might be needed to bring about such a brave new world, a world without men, male violence and oppression. Patriarchy, they believed, would have to be systematically dismantled in much the same way as apartheid. Creating as much women-only space as possible became a priority. All sorts of separatist experiments were set up, some of which survive into the 1990s.

Housing was a crucial issue. Shared housing was often a necessity for women who had rejected employment in the 'male' world, and whose income was consequently low. In taking control of their living space, lesbians took a large physical step away from male influences on their lives, a move that for many would lead ultimately to the idea to deny men access completely. In theory, separatist households were models of small communities in which preferred living processes could be practised.

PATRICIA

Patricia lived in a women-only housing co-op in West London, which is still operating today. Looking back, she views it as both a positive and negative experience:

> Although I never defined myself as a separatist, I liked women-only spaces. I felt excited about it all the time. It did feel important to show that women

could do things without men. I'm sure that I said some quite separatist things, but then I'd be sneaking off to Rolling Stones concerts, or whatever.

The first meeting of the co-op happened in 1976. The idea was that it was for local women only, and that we would have different houses for different women. So, we would have childless houses; men-free houses; houses for women with children; houses for heterosexual women who wanted to live with other women, and so on. There were always more lesbians in the co-op than heterosexual women.

Before we could get started, the housing corporation wanted to know what would happen when a woman wanted to get married. So, we made an arrangement with a mixed co-op that if a woman wanted to live with a man, she could go there. It would not have been easy for her to stay; I guess the honourable thing to do then would have been to move out.

I suppose that I now see the whole separatist debate as irrelevant to me. At the time, I think that many women thought that it was the only way to survive. Despite all the rhetoric, it wasn't very loving. There was a lot of 'women-hating women'. I found it very upsetting.

FRANKIE GREEN

Frankie, who was a drummer in the Women's Liberation Collective Band and Jam Today in the 1970s, describes how women lived separatist lives with the help of the squatting movement:

Call me old-fashioned, but our separatism was not just about lifestyles! I lived very near Radnor Terrace, where there was a very big lesbian community living in two streets of squatted houses. It was a very creative and challenging time. It was good feeling the energy between women, going to meetings and t'ai chi classes and things. There was music going on, and loads of discussion groups. It was wonderful, because women were taking control of their housing, lives and sexuality. In terms of personal living it was probably a bit too intense to be sustained.

Then I went to squat in Hackney and stayed there till the early 1980s. It was called Lansdown Road Co-op. There were lots and lots of women, mostly lesbian. It was a recipe for disaster really. There was anti-lesbianism and opposition to women-only housing from straights in the co-op. I felt quite bitter about a lot of things that happened there. In the end the women formed a separate co-op.

Some households didn't allow men in. Some would allow your brother to visit and some wouldn't. The key thing was to respect each other's views. For a lot of women, women-only space was a vital place where they were free from threats or violence. Another aspect of separatist households was that we were trying to develop skills for ourselves, like doing our own plumbing, roofing and electrical work. It wasn't about living together as jolly lesbians, it was a serious political choice as well as a personal one.

I was much more dogmatic then – I was really passionate about women-only issues, and a lot of women were. We generated women-only events and conferences and we needed to do it. I wanted to play only women-written music, but I would not put the same emphasis on that sort of thing now.

Critics missed the point, which was that it was not so important to be anti-men as it was to be pro-women.

DUSTY RHODES

Dusty rhodes, a lifetime separatist, also had contact with the women at Radnor Terrace, though she actually lived in a one-bedroomed flat in south London:

As much as I can, I have no men in the flat. It's a bit like a no-smoking policy. I don't have any involvement with men on a personal level. I live my life without being economically or emotionally dependent on men.

I knew the women at Radnor Terrace, Stockwell. I used to socialize with them, drink and play football. Women's music was a big thing there. Many would not have defined me as separatist because I was working in a petty bourgeois set-up, a school. I got quite a lot of disapproval. They were social policemen.

Having spent sixteen years in the country, to come and see 'out' dykes was phenomenal. I admired it all. I don't feel I have anything in common with that alien race – men. Men don't interest me, that's all. I don't like listening to men singing. I do watch athletics, but when I run I don't like running in mixed races. I did participate in the Gay Games in New York, though. I would stand up to people who are homophobic to gay men, as well as lesbians. In those terms I also have politics around racism which don't exclude black men.

I have learned from other women, from black women, disabled women, older women in a different way. I have also been told – 'Shut up and listen' – which taught me a lot.

SANDY

We really believed we were doing something that had not been done before, except possibly by mythical Amazons. We thought something extraordinary would come from it. It was all very Utopian, and I think I believed we would change the world, if we had the courage to experiment. We spent hours practising how to feel colours with our finger tips and waking each other up in the night to record our dreams!

There was a strong group of women who were separatist theorists and were fairly influential in my circle. Other women allowed them to be so powerful, there was a lot of girls' playground dynamics. We were all scared. They would tell us that this or that male thing about our lives was wrong. I am amazed now that I gave away my power to it, but there was a kind of romance in their extremism. They were always developing new theories, which they tried to impose on the people around them. I got a lot of stick for 'still being influenced by the male left'.

Sometimes their ideas were even racist or anti-working class. When I got involved with a working-class woman, one woman belonging to this radical group maintained she had developed the working-class accent deliberately to make middle-class women feel guilty! Then we heard they did a seance and the spirits told them she was a police informer. She and I became completely alienated, and we decided to go and live with some women getting a rural community together in Wales. We were still fairly separatist then. Something I still regret is that I didn't have my brother round to visit when he was in Wales, because I think he really needed my help then.

I have lots of mixed feelings and many regrets about the past, mainly because I know lesbians with boy children who were profoundly hurt by separatist women. Now I am sad and ashamed that I contributed to this in any way.

I think there is something about dedication to an ideal that can become dangerous. People who were originally inspired, but were quite ignorant on many issues to do with race and class, became evangelical and tried to impose it all on others, telling us we were not being separatist enough. That is when it can became oppressive. I was disappointed in women. Women were just not perfect once they got rid of men, it seemed. When separatism started to be horrifying to me was when it stopped being a crazy, wonderful experiment and became a dogma.

On the other hand, if we had not been separatists, it is hard to know if feminism and lesbians would have some of the gains we now have. We stopped looking for approval from the male-dominated left. It needed some women to be separatists and to create women-only spaces, which are so hard to achieve and maintain.

ALICE

We felt we were creating a better world for women, especially lesbians, to live in. Women-only houses were at the centre of our lives. They were our chosen 'family', and they were also a means of being independent with very little money.

I left my marriage in 1976 and moved into a women-only house almost straight away. We paid the rent, the bills and bought all our food for just £4 a week each! I had called myself a feminist before, but having moved away from the men in my life, I could appreciate the separatist ideas that were in circulation. I could really appreciate having a safe space in which to get ready for being a lesbian in the outside world.

When my brother visited from the USA I booked him into a hotel. I had been living in the house longer when my parents came, and the other women said it was OK as long as they were not involved. They didn't want to interact with my male relatives, and I wouldn't have chosen to interact with theirs. I wasn't a separatist in the strictest sense, but I did allow my relations with all my family to become strained.

There was a great desire to dance and play and celebrate. Women running their own bands was a novelty then. Bands like Jam Today and Ova wrote their own music with strong feminist lyrics. Olivia Records in the USA produced songs like 'Leaping Lesbians' and 'Ode To A Gym Teacher'. Gay Sweatshop women sang 'Any Woman Can Be A Lesbian'.

Women shared their skills generously. There were courses in things like T'ai Chi and African drumming. Sisterhood of Spit grew out of a brass workshop. There was a lot to laugh about and be proud of.

EMMA HINDLEY

Emma is a documentary film-maker and ex-separatist, who has mixed feelings about living in a short-life house in Brixton with other separatists:

I was involved in separatism for three years. At the time it felt like the only way to be a lesbian. I think a lot of it was based around being cool dykes. Cool dykes at the time hung out and shouted a lot about killing men.

I don't want to give the impression it was all holding hands under the sheets. We fucked a lot of women, we had fucking great parties and took a lot of drugs. It wasn't so much that there were no men allowed in the house and that we did not go to mixed events, only all-women's events. It was more about being progressive dykes round Brixton rather than high-brow dykes discussing theory. Yes, we went to the women's centre, read the newsletter and went to groups, but most of the time it was about going out to parties, hanging round our motorbikes and going on lesbian-strength marches and pickets.

I was brought up in a house run mainly by men because my mum died when I was eleven. I was very close to my brothers and my dad. I used to have real problems reconciling all that with separatism. There were various embarrassing times: when my brothers helped to fix my motorbike, I had to keep going in and out to them with cups of tea because they weren't allowed in the house.

A lot of women fell out and stopped talking to each other. It was more the Stalinist element I did not like. Basically, the trouble started with some women who I hung out with. I started going out with this woman who my friends said was masquerading as a working-class woman. We got frozen out. To some degree I felt scared to confront them.

I used to think really negatively about the time I was a separatist. We spent the 1980s beating the shit out of each other in the name of hating men and loving women. On the other hand, I did gain things from it because it did make me think about issues like class and race. What happened to all that political energy and commitment that was the cutting edge of the dyke community when the gay men were getting on with going to Heaven? We have become more cynical about it, but for many gay men politics is quite a new concept.

New separatists

There has been a resurgence of interest in separatism among young women in recent years. Living separately from men, these lesbians are struggling with some of the same issues and practical problems that their predecessors faced in the 1970s and 1980s. Indeed, their stories display an anger reminiscent of those women who were inspired to live as separatists two decades earlier.

JULIETTE DYKE

Juliette is twenty-seven and lives in Hackney, London:

I think there's a difference between now and ten or fifteen years ago. I think there is a general lack of politics. There's a much more commercial scene for one thing, and there's much more acceptance. It is easy to plod along with your life. The fewer women there are around being political, the easier it is not to be political. I can't imagine falling in love with anyone who is not political.

I don't think there are many separatists. I think there are a lot of lesbians whose lives are very much separate from men who are not defining themselves as separatists. It would be good if more women recognized how separatist they were already. But there still is a stigma attached to it. You know the stuff about all separatists being raving nutters, humourless and serious, and more worried about letting the meter man in than anything realistic.

When women join our houses we ask things like 'Do you know any men?' I don't want any men coming in the house at all. Living in a co-op we have some control over builders – I try and get them to employ women, anyway. We had to have a man to come and do our roof. I don't think it's that much of a big deal. It would be much more difficult to walk in and find a man eating his dinner. I just don't want them in my house. In some situations I do feel fearful of men. There is no such thing as a nice man. I have never met a nice man. It's an issue of trust.

TINA

Tina is thirty-three and comes from Essex:

There are always separatists and always will be. There's always enough to keep it going, but not enough to make a big impact. The community is very hedonistic and content with having a good time. It is ultimately quite self-destructive. There's no substance to it. It's very difficult for women to come out as separatists, and it's become so exhausting to be in the minority, to always be the one to set up groups and run things. It has become very hard to be politically active.

As far as possible I don't read books by men, I don't go to concerts and I don't get involved with men socially or politically. I lived in Oxford in a separatist household where men weren't allowed in, and we tried to get women whenever maintenance was needed. We were disliked by other lesbians who had male friends. I would like the world to be more receptive to the notion of quite large areas of women-only space – acres and acres of space. I would be quite happy if there weren't any men, though I don't see how practically that can be achieved. I have never met any men who earned my respect.

I was involved in the lesbian separatist network and in a group in London. We organized a conference in Wesley House and about thirty-five or forty attended. There's a new separatist group getting together now in Manchester, and they've just produced a magazine. The separatist network kind of fell apart over political differences.

KATHERINE KATS

Katherine is twenty-nine and comes from Bradford. She has lived in a separatist house run by a housing co-op for three years:

It is very hard for young people or new lesbians or gays who do get inspired to know what to do. Most people around them are pooh-poohing politics.

Christmas 1992 was the first known gathering of British separatists for a long time. There were about fifteen of us over three days. I got dead excited about it. It was about the same time I was trying to set up the London separatist group. It was nice but not particularly inspiring. There were no new ideas. Out of that came a magazine. There were three or four issues and then it folded. It all ended in arguments and rows.

I think there is something inherently wrong with men, and I have a problem with their sexual violence. I would never have social contact with men and boys. I don't put straight women in the same category, but I would not make a friend of one. I really find it very stressful being pleasant to men. I hate nice men even more. It is mostly nice men who are raping their girlfriends. I knew a friend's father who was saying all the right things and raping her as a child.

There are a lot of lesbians who would like to live in a house with no men, but many have one man they make an exception about in their lives. I think that each of their exceptional men is my rapist.

It is very difficult to maintain it as a separatist house within the co-op. There's no overt hostility, but there's likely to be talk going on behind my back. It's an awful pressure getting rooms let. We advertise all over the place looking for separatists.

FOREST GREEN

Forest is twenty-five. She identifies as separatist and lives on her own:

> Before I joined the separatist network I had one separatist friend in London. We've had a lot of contact with other separatists, visiting them up and down the country and writing to them, discussing politics all the time.
>
> I've learned that separatists are a volatile bunch and are each others' worst enemies. We share the basic politics; it is the details of everyday life that cause the splits. I am a lot more liberal than even eighteen months ago. I've become a little disillusioned. I feel you've got to have ideals, but the way I see it is those lesbians didn't treat each other any better. They were leading exclusive and enclosed lives.
>
> About two years ago a meeting was set up in Todmorden in the North. There were dykes from Scotland and England and Wales, probably about fifteen or twenty in all. At first it all seemed OK, but our differences came out. Personal stuff got mixed up with political differences. Some of us became separatists through socialist and anarchist political groups, and still want to be committed. They told me: 'You are still out there in the patriarchy', and 'You are scared to discover your separatist self'. I have been involved in a lot of rape cases, supporting heterosexual women. I couldn't turn away completely.
>
> I think there are a lot of radical dykes. I think there are a lot who have got burned out and gone underground. I think a lot would come out of the woodwork if certain things were to happen.
>
> Separatism is primarily about lifestyle for me. It's a decision to stay away from men. I don't deny there are nice men, but what about them? I don't want to waste my time with men. I don't hate all men, but I guess I see most of the evil of the world coming from patriarchy. Ideally, I would like to live in a world where men didn't exist, but that is pie-in-the-sky stuff. Perhaps I could create a world with other dykes where we are trying to come away from male ways of relating, such as objectifying women and seeing them as sexual objects.

Women's Lands

One long-term separatist-living experiment that has stood the test of time is Women's Land, near Lampeter, in Wales. This is a smallholding that is open to any woman who wants to stay there. Despite a chequered history, it still attracts women visitors from all over the world.

ALICE

Alice met her first lover at Women's Land in 1976:

It was high summer, just around solstice time. I arrived in the afternoon and drove my way through chickens and ducks. I found three women in the living-room in deep discussion. One of the two women who were a couple had got involved with the third and they were working things out. Nobody had had any sleep because they'd been talking all night. I bought a bottle of Chianti and we all talked. I was very impressed by the openness.

I used to visit a lot that summer. There was a small community of six or eight lesbians in the area. Some of these women went to Femo, the Danish women's camp, and brought back a trail of women from France, Sweden and Germany. More and more kept arriving; it was the place to be.

It was basically one very small house and one barn at that time. Women slept all over the place. There were lots of good ideas – sharing everything: property, lovers – which no one was handling very well. We were trying to break down patriarchal structures in our own lives, and I don't say I'm sorry for having tried and partly failed. The issues are still burning somewhere. Many of us were tired of battling with men. We wanted to put our energies into women.

The Welsh Women's Land was an experiment in separatism which demonstrated all the difficulties of separatist and communal living. People used to think they could live without money. In Wales there was never enough money to go round. I can remember trying to have breakfast and someone had taken all the nuts and raisins out of the muesli. That was far too spartan for me!

I was more and more uncomfortable, and the place wasn't going anywhere. It bored me. It was simply a lot of women hanging out talking to the trees. I liked it better living in London. The numbers of women's lands seemed to me to be a political thing. I travelled from women's land to women's land in America in 1977. There were a lot of women's lands in Oregon, California and New Mexico.

The biggest women's space was Owl Farm in Oregon. It impressed me because it seemed to be economically viable but still anarchic. Some of the original residents lived there for years.

Womanshare was run by four women in the same state. There were very big meadows and there was a lot of agriculture going on there. You could do workshops, and they believed in charging women reasonable amounts to stay there. I did a 'Country Skills' workshop. I really loved going to Womanshare.

Later, I lived with four women for six months in a winter let in Ditchling in Sussex. It was an attempt to recreate a women's land in a form we could cope with – but we started in a farm cottage with no land! It worked badly for a lot of reasons – isolation from our political roots, money worries, relationships. The local shopkeeper and landlord must have thought we were strange – one woman was growing her beard and we all wore second-hand clothes. We would have been happier had we been more political.

SANDY

What was good about Owl Farm was that they had decision-making by consensus. There was a lot of sitting around in a circle and talking. I liked the way they listened to each other.

But I was sad for a woman I was living with at Owl Farm at the time. She'd had her daughter adopted and she wanted her to come and stay on the land. The daughter wanted her fourteen-year-old brother to come as well, but this was impossible. I understood the separatist position of the women at the farm who had vetoed the boy coming, but although it was a huge place our separatist dream could not accommodate real-life situations. I saw my friend's distress; she felt let down by lesbians. She had given her daughter up for adoption because of homophobia. By the time I came back from the States I was no longer a separatist at all in theory.

Male animals and boy babies

Most separatists lay the blame for male violence and oppression fairly and squarely at the feet of male members of the human species. But there are even stricter separatists who believe that all male animals should be excluded from women-only space. At one time this was fiercely debated at Women's Land in Wales, and there is one particular tom cat who lost at least one of his nine lives over the controversy.

I do know separatists who draw the same lines with animals. A lot of research is being done that shows that males are a genetic mistake. Some species don't have males. I have a male cat. (Katherine)

There are different sorts of separatists. I'm not that strict about animals because I really like animals and think it's different. I would only have female animals myself.

There was a male cat on the women's land in Wales. He got taken off by one woman when the other women who looked after him were away for a while. He arrived back in a complete state, he was half-starved and completely bedraggled, having crawled back cross-country from his new home in the city. He very nearly didn't survive it and was very ill for a long time. Everyone decided he'd earned the right to live there.

Women do bring male dogs there, and there was a time when this would not have been allowed. The rule has been relaxed. They were just very hard-line separatists. You can't do much about wildlife, but they said no to male animals as far as it was controllable. (Tina)

The thinking is that the male of every species rapes and demands from the female of every species. Other separatists feel that male domination is particular to human beings, and male animals should not be persecuted. Personally there is a difference for me. (Forest Green)

Arguments also raged between separatists and other feminists about the pros and cons of allowing male children into women-only spaces, and whether lesbians should keep and raise their own boy children. The acrimonious arguments scarred many women's lives. It was a deeply serious debate, because women were making difficult choices about whether or not to give boy children up for adoption. Other lesbian mothers of boy children were bitterly angry about not being able to bring their offspring to crèches in women-only spaces.

I always knew the boy baby thing was ridiculous. I used to sit on many buses back from Greenham singing 'Kill Men' songs like we all did. But if you decide to have a child you should decide to have a child whatever the sex is. (Emma)

I find the boy babies issue a really difficult debate. I wouldn't want to have a boy baby. I wouldn't feel happy about dealing with the responsibility of bringing up a small man. I think if you are going to have a baby it is fifty-fifty which sex you have. People who aren't prepared to have a boy baby shouldn't have a baby. (Julie)

ANGELA

Angela and her partner both gave birth to boys.

I never would have called myself a lesbian separatist, but I haven't had any men friends for twenty years. I saw no men socially except for my father.

After the horror of a two-year custody battle in which my lover 'lost' her son, we each decided in 1979 to have a child. I got pregnant six months after Julie. Darren was Julie's baby, Peter was mine.

In the lesbian-feminist world there were loads of things to go to like the Women's Arts Alliance. That is where we really did encounter separatists and a great deal of hostility. There was one lesbian mother in our group who had a relationship with a woman who was very hostile to anything that was male at all. It was a big issue for the woman. She was very distressed. Later they split up over it. It was a terrible thing to live through. There was another woman in a housing co-op that didn't want male children, and so when she had a boy child there was a meeting and it was decided they would have to move out. Why is a male child of three weeks such a threat to a whole community?

There was a policy at WAA that 'no male children' included babies. We decided not to go there, even without the children. I said: 'I'm not entering a place that has these sorts of policies that are so hostile to people I care about so deeply.'

Our experience was that you would be surrounded by women saying that 'no boy children' is a reasonable policy. Everything around you was telling you that you were completely unwelcome there. It was supposed to be an amazon nation where only women existed.

I had no place in this crazy world they were creating. I have been hurt and angry about the way I have been treated. I read things in the newsletter that horrified me. One entry in particular stood out, about how boy children should be locked in a cupboard to teach them a lesson.

Each time there was an incident in a crèche, the power of boy children would be written about. A little boy would thump a little girl. Women would say this proves boys were aggressive. The fact that the little girl might have stolen his toy or hit him first wasn't considered. In any group of kids you get this behaviour. But it was all seen as being the evil of males. Everywhere there was a real hostility, and we were asked what were we doing nurturing the aggressor.

I understand why some women are drawn to separatism. I understand what a pain men can be – I know it's men who rule the world. But I feel it's possible to have that commitment to women without the need to be so harsh and proscriptive.

DUSTY

I would have thought it was fairly obvious that if a dyke has a baby and identifies as being a separatist then it is not surprising that the whole lesbian community isn't running out to support them.

I was friends of a lover of another woman who had a boy baby who left her – it was terrible. She did make it clear what her politics were beforehand. What lesbian mothers could not understand was what was going on in the heads of lovers and friends who didn't want anything to do with them if they had a boy. If they had not known the politics of these women beforehand we would have some understanding of it, but they did.

It's not a matter of right or wrong. You must try and understand what their politics are.

Separatists in the 1990s are aware that the boy-baby debate has never been resolved, which means that it is still going on! Nothing much seems to have changed. The animosity towards boy children appears to be as fierce as ever:

Separatists years ago had all the arguments about women-only space and boy children. Do we really have to have them all again? I don't have much optimism that anything new will be said.

My dream is that one day there will be a wonderful purge and there will be no male babies. Incest is so massive. Men are incredibly warped. People say they will bring their sons up differently, but it's not like they're doing something wrong and they'll stop. We're talking about men enjoying hurting people.

There is only one lesbian I have known who was prepared to give up a boy child. I don't think she sees him. She wasn't planning it. Even if the child is a girl there is no reason to think it is any more likely to be a lesbian.

The girl children, when do they experience women-only space? They're always stuck in mixed children's crèches with boys. Young boys do rape girls. We never consider our girl children. (Katherine)

I know a dyke who decided to have a kid. She made arrangements she would have it adopted if it was a boy. She was a separatist – it is a very difficult choice. I'm of the strong view that lesbians shouldn't have children full stop. As lesbians who are trying to create a better community for ourselves, we need to put energies into each other. (Forest Green)

If a woman I was involved with wanted a child, that would be difficult. I would not want to have a relationship with that child. Boy babies grow up! I don't think you can raise a child differently. Maybe if you went off to a desert island it could be different. I think boy children are dangerous to girl children. I don't think it's unreasonable to exclude boy babies from women-only spaces. (Juliette Dyke)

A new wave of political activism may well be on its way after a lengthy period of hedonism and apathy within the lesbian and gay community. Certainly, there is a renewed interest in lobbying and direct action. Politics goes in cycles. In the same way that lesbian feminists left the Gay Liberation Front in the early 1970s because of men's failure to put lesbian issues on the agenda, so, too, women have left Outrage collectively and formed a new separate organization called Lesbian Avengers.

JULIE

Julie joined Lesbian Avengers soon after it was formed in London in the early summer of 1994. She talked to me about her own personal view on the organization:

> The Lesbian Avengers aim to challenge and avenge anti-lesbian acts by non-violent direct action with humour and as much visibility as possible. We are very media-aware. It's inspired by things like the direct action taken during the Miss World contest in the 1970s, when feminists had flour bombs and went on stage wearing 'Lavender Menace' T-shirts.
>
> Also there was inspiration from groups like OutRage!, though OutRage! had a very male agenda. Apart from a couple of token efforts most of the actions were very male. A lot of women had gone to OutRage! and then left. Women asked about planning lesbian actions and we were told to set up our own group. OutRage! didn't seem prepared to incorporate lesbian issues.
>
> The time is very right now for the Lesbian Avengers. We have had enquiries from around the country to start up groups. There's much talk now about how young lesbians are not politicized any more, and don't need to be, but the issues around now are not just about having lesbians mentioned on television or ensuring every soap has a lesbian in it.
>
> We don't wish to have men involved, but we do obviously welcome gay men's financial and other support. It's a matter of showing we can do it for ourselves.

It is tempting to think that the time has come for a lesbian political revival. With women's organizations growing in number again, perhaps a new separatist movement is a real possibility for the end of the century.

NOTES

1. Sally Miller Gearhart, *The Wanderground*. The Women's Press, London, 1985.
2. Joanna Russ, *The Female Man*. The Women's Press, London, 1985.

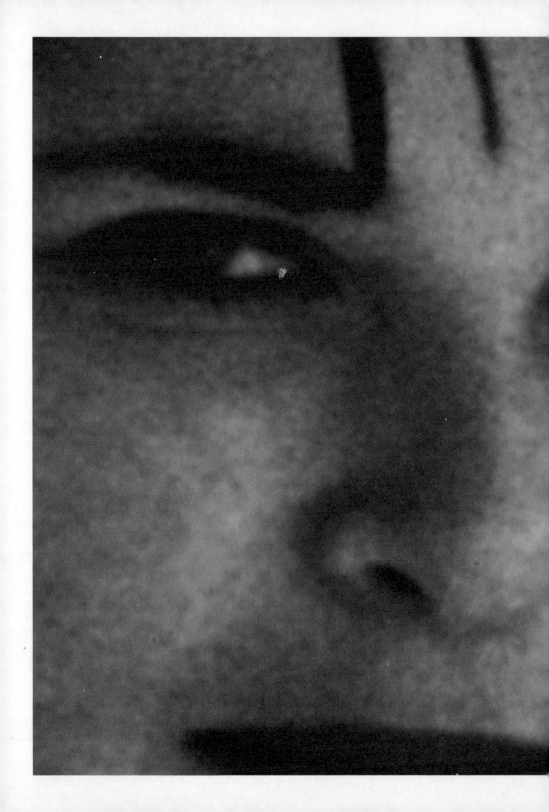

reclaim
the rite

reclaim the rite

women on the verge of a spiritual breakthrough

sharon whittington

Nine women hold hands around a fire. Nine naked women in a Welsh field preparing to enter a sweat lodge. We've fasted all day, built and burned a fire to heat rocks, built our lodge – a Greenham-style bender weighed down by blankets and a tarpaulin to keep the heat in and the light out. Now at the summer dusk we ritually cleanse ourselves with sage smoke and take our heated rocks inside the lodge, sit, sweat, breathe, give thanks and requests, sweat, meditate and sweat. Nine women – teacher, lawyer, ambulance driver, social worker ... three lesbians and six straight. Afterwards we rinse in shockingly cold water, commune silently round the fire and then feast, sharing our experiences, our feelings and our insights into the altered states we reached.

At moments during the preparations I wonder what I'm doing here. Part of me stands back when we are circled round the fire. It sits in the tree behind us and laughs at the absurdity of it all. I dread the heat – I hate saunas and it turns out to be even hotter – so why am I here? Peer pressure.

I was part of a small group of women who would meet once a month for a year to explore our spiritual lives and selves, each looking for meaning, direction and sometimes healing. Between us we brought knowledge of various belief systems and techniques, which we shared: over the year we meditated and chanted, rebirthed and visualized creatively, carried out symbolic rituals, cleansed, regressed, burned candles and incense, and now we sweated. This was part of our venture into native American practices, and, once it was over, I wouldn't have missed it for the world.

What set me on this path might just as well have sent me into therapy – at the age of twenty-nine I was feeling depressed and directionless. Initially, it was a book on rebirthing that attracted me. It offered a breathing technique for releasing all those blocks in my energy that had accumulated from past problems, when I had 'closed down' as a defence against feeling bad about myself. More than that, rebirthing offered a very practical philosophy for understanding what the events in my life were about, and even how to change them – powerfully attractive material for someone who worried about inheriting her mother's cycle of numbing depression.

When I finally found London's only (at that time) lesbian rebirther, I began to discover answers to questions I hadn't thought to ask, answers which did indeed make sense of life around me as well as inside. Finding a lesbian to work with at the beginning was important. Already feeling a little raw emotionally, I didn't want to risk homophobia when I was opening up to something so new and unknown. Of course, it would have been good to have contacts to check it out – just in case it really was some sort of cult, as several of my friends feared – but everyone I knew was into clubs, motorbikes, football and fashion. So was I, but I needed something more.

That was in 1987, when interest in all kinds of New Age activities had been growing for a few years. Although the noticeboards in women's centres and the classifieds in the gay press offered co-counselling, homeopaths and astrologers, there seemed to be a lack of alternative spirituality within our community. A few years before, I could have expected consciousness-raising groups or meetings on gender politics to be on offer, but now these were less apparent and community activity for the London lesbian focused mainly on the endless debate over SM and the struggle to establish the validity of different types of erotic expression. If your personal issues were not about your sex life, there were very few options for self-exploration available.

Fortunately, four or five lesbians did turn up during the first few years I was exploring, but no more, and this at a time when I would go to groups or weekend seminars attended by anything from fifteen to a hundred people. To be fair, I never encountered a moment's homophobia, but it was also true that until I learned to include my lesbianism in my introduction (when others felt no need to mention their sexuality) I did not feel fully present – the silent presumptions of heterosexuality were too evident for me to believe that these universal teachings also applied to me.

In 1994, my path is more individual and personal. Having adapted the natural laws and spiritual practices, I have learned to make them my own. Although I sometimes felt isolated, the value of what I was learning always outweighed the risk that people might think me odd. As I tested each new principle, I discovered an intelligent universe run by natural forces as powerful and pervasive as gravity. I could plug into this energy by consciously using the creative power of thought, accepting the responsibility and the opportunity of guiding my own life. Then there was no one to blame for anything, and no option for me to assume the role of depressed victim waiting passively for better luck. My self-knowledge grew in parallel with an increasing sense that I was secure in myself; able to trust, I was in the right place at the right time for the experiences I needed for my development. And my depression has not returned.

Since then, my friends have got over their fears about cults, and so have I, but the opportunities for support from like-minded lesbians are still rare. The impetus of AIDS has led gay men to form healing circles, run meditation classes and rebirthing groups, and the New Age mainstream is still popular. But if the patriarchal and/or homophobic teachings of most established religions make them inaccessible for many lesbians as avenues of spiritual growth, then why hasn't lesbian culture given space to the alternatives? Is lesbian spirituality an underground movement, or are we missing out? Is it more private than our sex lives, for one consenting adult alone, or yet another area where lesbians cannot agree? The rest of this chapter tries to address some of these questions with the help of personal accounts from four women, each of whom has discovered a profound spiritual centre in her life.

Michele: spiritual growth and sexual healing

Michele's spirituality at first seems a more traditional alternative. A hereditary clairvoyante through her Italian mother, she has accepted as normal her abilities to know the unknown and to heal since she was three years old. She didn't consider that it marked her out as special; it was just another talent, like being good at football. Her mother is a Catholic and a witch, not such an unusual combination in the northern Italian village where her female ancestors were traditionally the village wise women. Michele grew up among books of spells and pictures of Jesus.

Now twenty-eight, she practises her clairvoyance and healing at her attic office in Covent Garden. Her clients are lesbian, gay, straight and sometimes famous, and she is about to present a new show on cable television, mixing conversation and clairvoyance. Not every clairvoyant healer's career takes off like this, but Michele's work is characterized by a very powerful presence born of enormous energy, humour and above all an unusual directness. She's the most honest person I've ever met in her willingness to talk about her feelings and experiences of, for example, working through early sexual abuse, and is equally blunt in telling her clients and friends what she 'gets' about them. Michele is used to the mixed reactions these insights cause. She understands that they can be both fascinating and frightening.

While Michele's unorthodox career seems set to introduce her to a wider public, there is another side to her which probably won't make it onto TV: Michele draws her spiritual strength from the ancient goddess religion and she is a priestess of Ishtar. This is not exactly a secret, but she draws a line between the personal and the professional:

> I was a clairvoyante before I had any spiritual beliefs and I do keep them separate. I don't mention the goddess because everybody's symbolism is different and a personal choice. It's a very misunderstood religion – in the mere 2,000 years that Christianity has had a hold, people consider it evil. The term 'witch' evokes such a negative response. Different symbols come through me as appropriate for clients. I was healing once and Christ came through, another time it was a man with wings – I suppose you could call it an angel – which was weird for me but must have been right for them. So I don't project my symbolism onto other people.

How did she become a priestess? Apparently, not easily – Michele resisted at first, but recognizes now that she was being called to her destiny:

> When I was fifteen, by accident I walked into the first initiation in England of Dianic witches in a women's centre. About six months later I ran into one of the women from there again at a festival. She had realized I might be a hereditary witch from a very rare north Italian group called *stregas*, who have practically died out, but were involved with the goddess Diana going back centuries. I didn't really pay much attention, I was just using my gifts, I took it for granted. I was working-class, down-to-earth, end of story.

But it wasn't the end. Over the next few years several more chance meetings kept the possibility of this strange claim of her witch blood at the back of her mind, until one day she was ready to listen when her new mentor again confirmed that Diana was calling her:

> I just thought the goddess was some sort of feminist invention; I never believed it had any roots in reality. And now I was totally shocked, because it

was like coming home. I couldn't believe it. She blessed our food and I felt so different eating it when we had thanked the life energy in it. After that I learned everything I could about women's ancient magical knowledge.

Michele joined a women's group to complete 'A Year and a Day', the traditional preparation for initiation into the religion as a witch, dedicated to honouring the goddess. The Dianic group is the only women-only and goddess-centred craft:

'A Year and a Day' is about exploring the festivals of the year and marking the phases of the moon. In this religion you follow the seasons to attune yourself with the earth's energy. You have winter. It does lead to spring, and we've forgotten all about that and it's causing a lot of problems. Some other religions have made the earth negative. For them it's all about looking upwards, ignoring the earth, and that's one of the reasons we're destroying it now. I'm not a hippy, I'm a meat-eater. I drink, I'm your average working-class lesbian – well, maybe not average. I could be doing a lot more for the earth, but at least I'm aware of it. And it's so life-affirming. It's grounding and it's wonderful to actually feel that you are connected to the earth, and that we're all part of the whole.

At the end of the 'Year and a Day' Michele was initiated, and it was during the ceremony that Ishtar came into her life:

She chose me. When I was initiated I didn't have any goddess in mind and her name came to me – she claimed me as her daughter. I didn't know much about her at the time, but she's a very sexual goddess.

This seems only appropriate, as an important theme for Michele is the sacred healing power of sex:

I'm a very sexual person – I have a lot of sex all the time, I'm well into it. But from a spiritual point of view, the goddess religion brings it all together for me, because sex is a sacred act. Sex is an energy, a love energy and a very positive healing energy, and it's an expression of life. So it's sacred and an act of joy. Being a lesbian means that when I have sex it can be like making love to the goddess, and it's like being a goddess too. To me it's not a coincidence that this goddess should come to me – I have a deep affinity with sexuality and sex after struggling through my own abuse. I was sexually abused from the age of two and my religion has re-empowered me to heal myself. That was part of my learning process and I've got a lot from it.

> Discovering the goddess has been brilliant, like the icing on the cake. It makes me feel whole that I can be wildly sexual as an expression of my spirituality, or not – sometimes I just plain make love – and it's a wonderful sacred act, condoned and applauded within my religion. To me it's my life's lesson and I'm very happy, let me tell you.

Although Michele will answer any need for healing put to her, relationship problems are one of the main reasons why people consult clairvoyant healers, so every day presents an opportunity to put her most heartfelt mission into practice – often going unerringly to the core of her clients' hang-ups. She may respond with a healing transfer of energy you can sometimes feel as a warm tingling pouring from her hands. The passionate enthusiasm in her advice and encouragement amplifies the impact of her insight, and it's no surprise that many clients call her at home, day and night, for help. Michele's generosity with her time and energy matches her forthright honesty, but she would have it no other way. Anything less would be to fail in the duty of her vocation as a priestess. But what impact do her beliefs have on her own relationships?

> I'm involved with a woman who's very strongly into the same things. We do things like go to stone circles and get in touch with their energy – I think they are energy sources for the world and have always been used that way. We balance the energies there and we drum together, or she can do a massage that beats the rhythm of the earth on my body. And we've done rituals for world peace, making love to orgasm and sending the sexual energy out to heal the planet. But we can do it just as well here at home.

Goddess worship benefits the world in other ways too. Michele has just completed a degree studying its origins and history, and has come to the conclusion that it's all a question of balance: a balance which is thrown off by the emphasis of more orthodox religions on a single male deity:

> You need a whole – women's energy is important. From the ancient beginnings of time, when goddess worship was the norm, there has been this changeover in symbolism, emphasizing one male god. Since then, we've had technological advances which have come away from honouring the earth, so now we've got a hole in the ozone layer. The values of the goddess are making a revival now because they have to; it's just common sense. Otherwise, we're going to totally wipe out the planet.
> I'm not just into the goddess because I'm a lesbian either, although it helps on a sexual, spiritual and emotional level. I don't invalidate the god. We need

male energy to make a whole, but there is an imbalance and my practice and beliefs are important because they counterbalance it. I am representing the part that would be missing, just in my little self and whoever else believes it.

Although she has not yet been formally ordained, for Michele her lifetime commitment to the goddess's work and its transformation of her own life can only mean she is a priestess:

I'm not ordained as such. I'm only initiated, but I consider myself ordained – in the sense of chosen – and I will be, because of the work I've done. You can't just do 'A Year and a Day' and become a priestess. It means you dedicate your whole life to healing people, and once you've become one you're always on call. You're either prepared to make that commitment or you're not, and it's not right for everybody. It's not like saying: 'I'm a priestess. I'm more powerful than you'. It means I have to do all this hard work and help zillions of people who happen to cross my path. It's not a five-year contract, it's with me for ever. Anybody who is prepared to say the same is quite welcome to the title.

Lorraine: change from within

Lorraine woke up to her spiritual side quite recently. Prompted by those end-of-year, end-of-relationship blues, she said 'yes' when a friend suggested doing something different for the New Year. That something was a sweat lodge at a New Age centre of the edge of Dartmoor in a mixed group of thirty to forty people:

I had an amazing experience there of just letting go – I could actually see energy coming out of me and into the earth, and I was thinking: 'Wow, this is incredible!'. It was a really clear night, there was just one cloud in the sky, and when I came out of the sweat lodge it rained, and it was like the final cleansing. Knockout stuff!

Inspired by her New Year experience, Lorraine was keen for more and tried various groups oriented to spiritual development back in London. But she found, as I had done, that she was often the only lesbian in the group:

Actually I did feel able to express what I felt in mixed groups, because I didn't care what they thought, but I felt quite isolated. Nine times out of ten I would be the only lesbian in the group, and I wouldn't speak about my sexuality at all. I feel very strongly about my lesbianism and what kind of things you share with men, so I decided to go on a women's camp. And to my complete shock-horror there was a real split between the lesbians and the straight women. It was not what I thought was going to happen at all. I think I had some kind of idea we were all women together – sisterhood and all of that crap. The straight women were saying: 'I just really miss being around men', and I was thinking: 'What are they doing on a women's camp then?'

Despite the schism, Lorraine found the camp a transforming and empowering experience, taking part in rebirthing and another sweat lodge. But she began to feel that her personal spiritual quest lay in a different direction:

Native American stuff didn't feel very real to me – I'd come into spirituality through it, but it just didn't feel like my culture. I really wanted to get into Celtic and goddess ways – I felt it would fit me much more. What I wanted to do was to develop my intuition and my relationship with nature, here in this culture. I think we have to remember our own spiritual heritage, how it got wiped out with the rise of Christianity and the killing of thousands of women as witches. We have to get back in touch with all that again in order to feel real.

Deciding to develop her own practices gave Lorraine the chance to break down another barrier which often stands in the way of women wanting to learn the way of the shaman, the goddess or the witch – money. Many of the courses and workshops offered by established teachers are prohibitively expensive. On occasion, I've felt uneasy about treating my self to wonderful weekends of rebirthing and spiritual philosophy which I know many of my friends on low or no incomes couldn't afford. For Lorraine the issue was sharper still – she works as the head of the welfare rights unit for a London borough, dealing daily with people disempowered by poverty:

I was really pissed off with paying loads of money to go on workshops. I believe you don't need a guru or anything like that. I thought there must be a way that women can do things together without having to pay phenomenal amounts of money to facilitators.

What Lorraine decided on was a women-only sweat lodge in the countryside, to be run collectively by the participants. And it worked: the group of eleven organized everything from finding the land, transporting all their own water to it, and taking tools, food, candles and rocks to be heated up for the ceremony:

> The idea behind the sweat lodge was to feel closer to nature and have a purification ceremony. I said we should honour the trees before we cut them down to make the lodge and to burn – may be leave a bit of hair in them as thanks. And everybody really got into it, including all the city girls!

So who were these women?

> We were mostly lesbians, and we had all sorts of women with different beliefs and no beliefs. Some were close friends of mine who could see that I'd really transformed through getting in touch with this stuff. Others were their friends or lovers, and my sister.
>
> We did some drumming around the fire and an hour's silence before we went into the lodge. Inside I called in the goddess and we had a theme for each turn around the circle. One was to ask for something for yourself, another was what you wanted for other people, and then what you wanted for the planet.

Two of the group chose to stay outside the sweat lodge itself, taking the roles of Water Carrier and Fire Keeper. While the group inside communed in the heat through their invocations, the others prepared a surprise:

> We were inside for a good few hours – you do lose your sense of time in there. When we came out it was like a fairy tale. They had put branches all around and hung candles in jars from them and laid out a banquet of all our food. The stars were out, the fire was still burning, it was just fantastic.

And afterwards, what had they got out of the experience?

> We each had our own individual experiences, but there were women saying their lives felt completely different. One woman is building a lodge in her back garden in Bristol, and she'd never done anything like it before. Some people remembered past experiences – one woman remembered abuse from a long time ago, but it was OK because I think the right women had come together to support each other. And every single one of them wants to do it again.

These responses sound like the kind of breakthrough people seek from therapy – the transformation of my own depression is certainly the most dramatic change that I have ever experienced in my life. For me, the breathing technique of rebirthing released me from my mind's futile struggle to analyse blocks and patterns which it could not alter: the breathing process united mind, body, spirit and emotions in the moment of healing. Has Lorraine found that people are looking for similar benefits?

> Yes, I think people do want to change and get in tune with themselves. It's offering them an alternative way. The only other choice seems to be psychotherapy, and that only helps you to understand the situation, without helping you to change it. I already understand why I repeat patterns in relationships, and what helps me change them is getting in touch with 'me' and how I really feel. The whole spiritual thing has been very linked to personal growth for me.

Sarah: coming out as a witch

Sarah is an old friend. I met up with her in San Francisco, a year to the day after she had moved there from London. When I mentioned in passing that I was researching this article she surprised me, saying shyly: 'Well you'd better interview me then.'

What about? The Sarah I knew practised astrology and gave me herbal teas for my period pains and emotional upsets. She also kept cats, worked at a hostel for the homeless, supported the Revolutionary Communist Party, was into SM and played a mean game of Yahtzee. Now I learned she was also a witch, and maybe always had been.

Her shyness was another surprise. The more we talked, the more I understood that Sarah wasn't shy about doing an interview, it was the subject that prompted her hesitancy. Sarah had been drawn to the craft of Wicca for a long time, but her experiences in Britain had taught her that there were dangers in 'coming out' as a witch:

> My spiritual awakening has only become conscious in the last year. It's always been in me, but I was in denial. I only let myself get involved in more publicly acceptable aspects – like I've always been interested in astrology. I saw the reaction a friend got from our other friends when she started to practise witchcraft. It was really critical, almost fearful when they found out and saw her wearing a pentacle. I heard comments about not trusting her or that she was simply 'bad'.

Sarah's unease about following up her latent interest was rooted in her childhood experience:

> When I was at school I used to get paid in cigarettes for reading my friends' minds. It started out as a joke, but I gradually got scared by how often I was right about really deep thoughts. Then I started to get bad reactions because my friends got upset or scared too. I already stood out – the tall, athletic, smart one who wasn't into boys, and I was already being called a lesbian. And now I was being called a witch too. I wasn't sure what 'lesbian' meant, but I knew about witches – they got tortured and burned.
>
> I embraced my lesbianism when I was eighteen. Then three months later I came out again as being into SM. And that got me thrown back out from the lesbian community I'd just discovered. So I had about four years of struggling to be myself, a lesbian and belonging in that community. I spent some time at Greenham peace camp during that period – they knew I was into SM and it was just not discussed, but they were more open to my witchcraft. Even so, there were differences between my spiritual beliefs and those of the other lesbians, which showed up through our politics. Men were seen as the enemy and I couldn't agree with that. I see the 'enemy' rather as capitalism and the type of people it tends to put in power: people who have no respect for nature because it is not profitable; people who will dump waste in a river if it's the cheapest way to deal with it. But I think maleness has its place in nature.

Sarah left Greenham for London and gradually built up a network of lesbian friends who were supportive, or at least neutral, about her taste for SM. But it was these women who reacted badly when another witch was discovered among them, so, unsurprisingly, Sarah wasn't keen to face her third coming-out.

She turned instead to study herbalism and astrology, although even here the reticence learned from her youthful experiences coloured her activities. The turning point was her move to San Francisco. Sarah was not conscious of looking for a spiritual direction, but soon after her arrival she began to notice signs that things could be different for her:

> I immediately started to notice more open signs around me of witchcraft, paganism and occult activity – finding adverts and stores specially for buying supplies for rituals showed me the scale of local interest. And tolerance: I realized people here felt OK about it, enough to be more open than I had ever felt I could be. It was actually easier for me in London to be openly into SM than Wicca.

So moving here has really helped me to come out to myself as a witch, but even now it's hard to get used to the idea that I am saying this about myself – even to myself, after years of denial. I suppose it's something like women who learn to say 'I am a lesbian' only after they have been sleeping with women for quite a while.

Of the lesbians I have talked to, most emphasized that their beliefs had evolved as a very personal amalgam of what worked for them, much as mine have done. They might use labels like 'witch' or 'pagan', but they stressed that they might not mean quite the same thing for someone else. So what does Wicca mean to Sarah? How does she practise it?

For me it's on two levels – an everyday physical one, which is nature-based, and a spiritual level of worshipping the goddess and the god. The nature aspect involves respecting the earth as mother and both surrounding myself with nature and also harnessing the natural forces to use their energies towards creating things I want to achieve.

Sarah lives in a very small flat at the edge of the Lower Haight, where Sixties flower power bloomed. Now the area is a living sociological study of hippydom and every youth/alternative subculture that has passed through since. The murals and the psychedelic shops mingle with the anarchist bookstores, the latter-day punks, gay culture, homeless street people, fetish clothing stores and some of the cheapest places to eat in the city. Every faction has its devotees sitting in the coffee shops and bars, and the fledgling witch is well provided for, with shops selling candles and incense, crystals and amulets, feathers and animal bones.

Her home reflects Sarah's major interests, and two things dominate. There is the workbench at which she crafts the leather whips which generate her income (and an enviable reputation for taste and quality among practitioners of SM), and there is her altar. A low table draped in cloth, it is covered with burning candles in various symbolic colours, nature's produce – fruit and flowers – and pictures and artefacts representing things important to her. The altar is a focus, a reference point to affirm the things she seeks to empower with natural energy:

I renew it from time to time, whenever I feel like it. I change things around so it always reflects what's important to me and what I want to bring into my life.

There are celebrations which are about the seasons and nature changing. At the major festivals – Imbolc, Beltane, Samhain and Lughnasadh – I might go out into nature to observe them on my own or with friends. And there are other ways to mark them. I was once at an SM party on Samhain [Hallowe'en], the night of the year when we believe the separation between our world and the next is thinnest. It happened that a lot of the other people there were pagans or witches, so we started the party by calling in the elements to bless the space and then inviting our dead friends and family to enter. It happened here in San Francisco, so because of AIDS there were many more people to be invited in. And the room really began to feel much more full – the party took off with a great atmosphere!

Sarah clearly has no doubts about the value of owning Wicca in her life:

My head and body feel in tune for the first time. Suddenly I feel like I've got a life, like I've been reborn and I have more energy. Partly, it's from fitting into the whole lifestyle, but it's also about being able to be completely me instead of hiding important parts.

Anne: 'What you think is what you get'

Meeting Anne is like stepping into a Sara Paretsky novel. The sign on her office door in downtown San Francisco says 'Private Investigator'. She's had her licence for several years and runs her own business tracing people who don't usually want to be found, serving subpoenas and interviewing witnesses for cases ranging from sexual harassment in high places to child abuse or fraud. Isn't it dangerous?

Sometimes I have to go into dangerous situations, but I don't carry a gun. I have been in some very bad neighbourhoods where just walking around is very risky, but I have never felt I was in a life-threatening situation. I call upon my spirit guides to protect me, and I put a white light around myself and ask that I get the information – or whatever the job is – and people won't even see me.

Putting her safety on the line confirms the strength of Anne's spiritual beliefs. Like everyone I spoke to, she has taken the teachings that struck the deepest chords and blended them into her own belief system, one that is closer to paganism than anything else, but unique in its whole: 'I consider myself sort of a mutt – I'm a combination of so many things.'

At the core of Anne's beliefs lies a tenet that a traditional pagan would not recognize: she creates her own life through her conscious and unconscious thoughts. So when she imagines the white light and invokes her spirit guides it isn't a piece of wildly optimistic whimsy but a practical protective measure – she's deliberately using those symbols to focus her thoughts on a safe reality and to disempower the 'fear thoughts' that could otherwise run unchallenged and attract the very dangers she wants to avoid:

> We choose everything that happens to us in our life on some level; this enlightenment lets me be aware of the choices I am making. And to me this is a very empowering philosophy, because the alternative is to believe your life is controlled by what some would call fate, and then it doesn't matter what you do, fate could just give you an unlucky life.

A belief in the creative power of thought is not unique to Anne. It is found in many branches of New Age philosophy and, for me, it was the single most empowering discovery that I made when I started rebirthing – more valuable even than the healing power of the breath. Like most people, I was sceptical at first – it sounded too good to be true, too glib, too simple. But when I practised creative, conscious thinking my objectives were repeatedly realized. Rebirthing's contemplative techniques revealed my hidden patterns of unhelpful beliefs, beliefs that sabotaged my life and lay at the root of its more unhappy aspects. The principle of creative thought went against everything I took for granted about how the world works but, like Anne, I grew to trust it:

> I think that the violence in our world is about people feeling they have no personal power. Western civilization doesn't teach us the power of meditation and thought, that you can change things in your life and make it really good for yourself. It tells us that if you can't touch it, it doesn't exist. People need to understand that they are powerful and they can make things happen.

Anne studied other religions and cultures, looking for a spiritual tradition compatible with her belief in creative thinking:

> I came upon paganism. There are male pagans, but it's called 'the old women's religion' because it originated in a time when it was women who were looked upon as the shamans, the spiritual caretakers. And I have a real affinity with

their practices – the rituals around the phases of the moon and the earth's seasons. Part of pagan belief is that we are not separate from the earth and its elements, we are part of it.

Anne tries to project constructive beliefs into her world every day, but admits this takes time and energy, and sometimes she still finds herself struggling against her strict Catholic upbringing. So, to focus her thoughts, she also sets aside time for rituals. Taking the pagans' celebration of nature and their rituals for harnessing natural forces, she simply adds to this the energy of her own conscious thoughts. I asked her to describe a typical ritual:

> It would vary according to your particular purpose, but it would have these basic things. We usually call in the four corners of the earth in order. They each represent an element, so it's east for air, south is fire, west for water and then north is earth itself. You symbolically mark out a circle – maybe just having candles to mark the directions, burning some incense to cleanse it. For me the candles represent the light and help to focus your attention, and the incense makes it easier to go into a deeper state of consciousness. They help to define it as a sacred space.
>
> You might bring things you want to bless inside the space. I like to 'jump start' a ritual by taking things from my altar and using them. That way you get all the stored energy from your altar. Usually someone would also say a blessing or invocation to the effect of 'good come in – evil stay out'.
>
> A ritual is like theatre, and somebody has to direct it. That's really all the ritual leader is doing, it's not that they necessarily know more, or are more enlightened than anyone else. If I'm the leader I'll talk everyone through it before we start, so they can make some choices about what we do. For me a good ritual is one where every person participates and it empowers everybody in the circle. A ritual is really everybody's energy coming together through actions that have meaning for them. In one ritual that I led, everybody brought their own sacred object they wanted blessed and had a candle on which they wrote their own intention for the ritual and then anointed it with oil.

What are lesbians using rituals for?

> I use them when I want to manifest something specific, or to open myself up to healing or an answer to a problem by getting into an altered state. I do them for personal and business reasons.

But I've been in groups where we've done rituals for the wider good too. When Reagan was president there was a particular judge who was nominated for the Supreme Court. And there was no way you'd want Judge Bork on the Supreme Court – he was opposed to the Watergate investigation, was anti-abortion, anti-women and generally ultra-right. There was a tremendous amount of popular opposition to him. So, a group of us decided to hex him from getting the position. It was specifically to prevent that, not to kill him or harm him, but to keep him from power. Now a lot of people would say it didn't matter a bean whether we did this ritual or not, but my bottom line is the result: whether it was our ritual or the energy of all the people everywhere who didn't want him to get it – and he didn't.

Something I've learned is that women may have been raising personal and political consciousnesses, but we are losing a lot of our power if we don't come into our spirituality too. It doesn't matter how many protests we make against war or whatever, you need spiritual resources to achieve deep changes. If you don't have spiritual development your political power is more limited.

Not surprisingly, Anne feels her lovers need to share some degree of her awareness for their relationship to work.

For me a lover is potentially a very intimate spiritual experience. I need to feel that the potential is there to go deep together. It's not going to work if she is calling my philosophy 'psychobabble'! She doesn't have to have similar practices, but if she doesn't believe that life has a spiritual meaning to it I don't think it's going to go anywhere.

It's a personal choice and an interesting question. Do lesbians believe life has a spiritual meaning? For those of us who don't, how do we understand it at all? The 1980s and 1990s find us asserting our own culture and politics, our sexuality and style, making them large enough to encompass a plurality of lesbian individuals. Now some of us are putting down the dyke marker on the meaning of life itself, reforming what has been out there for millennia into not just a world that works for us, but a whole universe as well.

National Eating Disorders
  Association   67, 73, 79
Navratilova, Martina   12, 82, 97,
  159
Nestle, Joan   170
New Age activities   201, 202, 206,
  213
Newton, Leigh   92-5

Oates, Joyce Carol   44
oestrogen   90, 91
Options   89
Orbach, Susie   64, 66, 67, 88
OutRage!   196

Paglia, Camille   161
Pain and Strength   133, 137–9
Permission   27
pornography   181
post-feminism   166-9
post-lesbianism   158-72
postmodernism   146, 162–3, 171
postmodernists   9
Presley, Elvis   9
progesterone   91
Purgold, Joan   68

queer politics   158-9
Quinn, Anthony   43

radical feminism   178–9
Reagan, Ronald   215
Renzetti, Claire   129
Requiem for a Heavyweight   43
Roberts, Nicky   146
Robinson, Sugar Ray   46
Roth, Geneen   69

San Francisco Sex
  Information   25

Sappho   61, 178
Sappho   180
Schiffer, Claudia   160
Schwarzennegger, Arnold   85, 97
separatism   164, 173, 178-96
serial killers   116–21
SM   26, 86, 170–1, 181, 209, 210,
  211, 212
Sommers, Robbi   82
sport   84, 89, 94, 95-8
Stallone, Sylvester   97
Steinem, Gloria   96
steroids   84, 93, 94
Stevenson, Juliet   17–20
stregas   203

Tanner, John   107–10
Trimiar, Tyger   40, 45

Vanity Fair   160
Vines, Gail   91
Vogue   64

Watney, Simon   164, 170
Weightwatchers   67
Welbourne, Jill   68
Wicca   209, 211, 212
Wilson, Elizabeth   87, 90
Wolf, Naomi   88, 168
Woman's Land   180, 190–1
Women Against Violence Against
  Women   181
Women's Aid   129, 136, 137, 138
Women's Arts Alliance   194
women's movement   9
Wournos, Aileen   3, 104–22

Yorkshire Ripper   179, 181

Zemsky, Beth   139